Kenneth L. Pike: An Evangelical Mind

Kenneth L. Pike

An Evangelical Mind

BOONE ALDRIDGE

☙PICKWICK *Publications* • Eugene, Oregon

KENNETH L. PIKE
An Evangelical Mind

Copyright © 2021 Boone Aldridge. All rights reserved. Except for brief quotations in critical publications or reviews, no part of this book may be reproduced in any manner without prior written permission from the publisher. Write: Permissions, Wipf and Stock Publishers, 199 W. 8th Ave., Suite 3, Eugene, OR 97401.

Pickwick Publications
An Imprint of Wipf and Stock Publishers
199 W. 8th Ave., Suite 3
Eugene, OR 97401

www.wipfandstock.com

PAPERBACK ISBN: 978-1-7252-9375-5
HARDCOVER ISBN: 978-1-7252-9374-8
EBOOK ISBN: 978-1-7252-9376-2

Cataloguing-in-Publication data:

Names: Aldridge, Boone.

Title: Kenneth L. Pike : an evangelical mind / Boone Aldridge.

Description: Eugene, OR: Pickwick Publications, 2021 | Includes bibliographical references and index.

Identifiers: ISBN 978-1-7252-9375-5 (paperback) | ISBN 978-1-7252-9374-8 (hardcover) | ISBN 978-1-7252-9376-2 (ebook)

Subjects: LCSH: Pike, Kenneth L. (Kenneth Lee), 1912-2000. | Linguistics. | Evangelicalism. | Missions.

Classification: P26.P48 A43 2021 (print) | P26.P48 (ebook)

Copyright Notices

Kenneth L. Pike, "Pain Teaches Choice" and "Violin under Stress," used by permission, © SIL International, *On Pain, Beyond Suffering: Kenneth L. Pike Poetry,* vol. 1, edited by Sharon Heimbach, (1997), further redistribution prohibited without permission.

Kenneth L. Pike, "Heart with Mind" and "The End," used by permission, © SIL International, *On the Philosophy of Life, A Kaleidoscope: Kenneth L. Pike Poetry,* vol. 2, edited by Sharon Heimbach (1997), further redistribution prohibited without permission.

Kenneth L. Pike, "Crushed" and "My Blue Refrigerator," used by permission, © SIL International, *On Scholarship and Work, Service and Success: Kenneth L. Pike Poetry,* vol. 4, edited by Sharon Heimbach (1997), further redistribution prohibited without permission.

For Ted Bergman
(1938–2020)
who steered me into academia and the world of scholarship

Contents

Acknowledgments ix
Abbreviations xi
Note to the Reader xiii
Introduction xv

1. Beginnings 1
2. A Missionary Scholar in the Making 14
3. New Frontiers 47
4. Translator and Leader 68
5. Serving and Defending SIL 97
6. With Heart and Mind 132
7. The Obedience of a Christian Man 160
8. Philosophy and Peace in an Era of Conflict 190

Epilogue: A Life in Retrospect 209
Bibliography 215
Index 231

Acknowledgments

THIS SPACE PRESENTS THE happy occasion for thanking all those who have in one way or another made this book possible. First, my appreciation goes to David Bebbington, for it was upon his suggestion that I undertook to write this biography of Ken Pike. And, then, to SIL's Chip Sanders, who made it all possible by arranging for me to have the time and freedom to pursue this lengthy project. My heartfelt thanks goes out to SIL members Vurnell Cobbey, Karl Franklin, George Huttar, Gary Simons, and Mary Ruth Wise, each of whom read the entire manuscript and provided valuable input. I received additional help in various ways from SIL members Freddy Boswell, Tom Headland, and John Watters during my research for this volume. I found discussions of things Pikean with Doris Bartholomew, Tom Branks, Peter Fries, Larry Lyman, Vern Poythress, Jim Rupp, and Mary Ruth Wise both informative and enlightening.

I am indebted to Ken Pike's children, Judith (Pike) Schram, Barbara (Pike) Ibach, and Stephen Pike, and his son-in-law Terry Schram, for their generosity and candidness during interviews. I am also very grateful for their support and encouragement.

Much help at various times came from archivists. Cal Hibbard (who sadly passed during the writing of this book) at the Cameron Townsend Archives was always generous with his time. Vurnell Cobbey, curator of the Pike Special Collection, provided help on many occasions. Vurnell's extraordinary efforts in sorting, copying, and archiving Pike's voluminous papers has provided a veritable gold mine for historians interested in Pike and SIL.

A small grant from the Pike Center for Integrative Studies was very helpful in getting this project published. Moreover, an invitation to present a paper on Pike's approach to theoretical linguistics at a 2014 retreat, sponsored by the Pike Center, was very beneficial to me as I struggled to sort out the complexities of the Pikean mind.

And, last but not least, I want to express my appreciation to my wife Julie for her love, patience, and encouragement while I labored to complete this book. I am also grateful for her adroit editorial advice and help with the details of preparing the manuscript for publication.

Abbreviations

AAA	American Anthropological Association
ABS	American Bible Society
ABWE	Association of Baptists for World Evangelism
AV	Authorized Version
CAM	Central American Mission
CIM	China Inland Mission
EFMA	Evangelical Foreign Missions Association
GMU	Gospel Missionary Union
IFCA	Independent Fundamental Churches of America
IFMA	Interdenominational Foreign Mission Association
ILC	International Linguistics Center
IMIL	Instituto Mexicano de Investigationes Lingüísticas
JAARS	Jungle Aviation and Radio Service
MAF	Missionary Aviation Fellowship
MIT	Massachusetts Institute of Technology
NACLA	North American Congress on Latin America
NAE	National Association of Evangelicals
NCC	National Council of Churches
PMA	Pioneer Mission Agency
PSC	Kenneth L. Pike Special Collection
RSV	Revised Standard Version

SIL		Summer Institute of Linguistics
SPC		Seattle Pacific College
SPI		Serviço de Proteção aos Indios
TA		William Cameron Townsend Archives
UCLA		University of California at Los Angeles
UNESCO		United Nations Educational, Scientific and Cultural Organization
UTA		University of Texas at Arlington
WBT		Wycliffe Bible Translators

Note to the Reader

Much of the primary material for this biography comes from two archives, the Pike Special Collection and the William Cameron Townsend Archives. Rather than listing each individual item from these two archives in the bibliography, which would be cumbersome and unduly lengthen the bibliography, I have instead cited most letters and a few other items only in the footnotes. Hence, when the footnote lists the item as appearing in the Pike Special Collection ("PSC" for short) or the William Cameron Townsend Archives ("TA" for short), then the item is not listed in the bibliography. The information supplied in these short-form footnotes is completely adequate for locating the archived item in question.

When it was deemed useful to supply additional information for a piece of correspondence from one of these two archives, then the item is listed in the bibliography. Note that the short-form footnote in these cases do not point the reader to the PSC or TA, since this information is listed in the bibliographic entry. Likewise for all other footnoted items that do not specify one of these two collections; in these cases, all items are listed alphabetically in the bibliography.

Finally, it should be noted that chapter 6, which details the relationship between Pike's theism and his theory of language, is somewhat complex. For those who do not wish to delve into the intricacies of theology and linguistic theory, it is possible to skip this chapter. However, there are key aspects of Pike's thought on both religion and linguistics in this chapter, and it is central to the overall argument of the book. Each reader will have to decide whether this chapter serves their purposes.

Introduction

THIS BOOK IS ABOUT Kenneth Lee Pike (1912–2000), who was a missionary Bible translator, a world-class linguist, and an evangelical intellectual.[1] Pike's name is well known in the discipline of linguistics. Indeed, in the Oxford University Press volume, *Key Thinkers in Linguistics and the Philosophy of Language*, Pike is listed as one among eighty other notable figures ranging from Plato and Aristotle to René Descartes and Immanuel Kant to Noam Chomsky and Ludwig Wittgenstein.[2] On the other hand, his name does not appear in the *Biographical Dictionary of Evangelicals* and rarely appears in the historiography of the evangelical movement.[3] This is due, in part, to the fact that professional historians have only recently begun to study the history of the dually-structured Wycliffe Bible Translators (WBT) and the Summer Institute of Linguistics (SIL) combination, with which Pike was associated for most of his life.[4] Explaining how an anxious and awkward young man not only became a missionary Bible translator, but also a scholar of international repute, is one purpose of this book. Another is to illuminate one of the most unusual evangelical minds of the twentieth century. Pike possessed an extraordinary intellect, one that defies easy categorization and was far from typical within the evangelical movement of his time.

Within the pages of this volume, I mount the argument that Pike was an evangelical intellectual. Historian Mark Noll, in 1994, wrote that

---

1. Throughout most of this book Kenneth L. Pike will be referred to as "Ken Pike," after the fashion of how most of his colleagues knew him, save for his many students for whom he remained "Dr. Pike."

2. Chapman and Routledge, *Key Thinkers in Linguistics*, 206–7.

3. Larsen, *Biographical Dictionary of Evangelicals*.

4. Aldridge, *For the Gospel's Sake*; Hartch, *Missionaries of the State*; Svelmoe, *New Vision for Missions*.

"the thought has occurred to me regularly over the past two decades that, at least in the United States, it is simply impossible to be, with integrity, both evangelical and intellectual."[5] The life of Ken Pike is an exception to this supposition. He was more than a scholar and a Christian, he was an evangelical intellectual.

As a linguistic theorist Pike was also somewhat unusual. When he began to construct his theory of language in the 1950s, he did so with theistic presuppositions. In doing this, he set himself apart from the other leading linguistic theorists of the day, who were generally mechanists of one variety or another in theoretical perspective. Pike therefore distinguished himself by approaching linguistic theory from a specifically Christian point of view. The failure of evangelical scholars, as Noll put it, "to think within a specifically Christian framework," is not applicable to Ken Pike.[6] If one grants Noll's view on the state of the American evangelical mind in the twentieth century, that "there is not much of an evangelical mind," then Pike is an outstanding exception to this general failure of intellect.[7] He not only succeeded as a scholar, he also "exercised his mind for Christ," and thus cannot be implicated in what Noll contended was the "scandal of the evangelical mind."[8]

Ken Pike's influence on the development of Wycliffe and the Summer Institute of Linguistics was immense and indelible. Well before the leaders of the neo-evangelical movement sought to reform fundamentalism beginning in the late 1940s, the co-founders of the WBT-SIL combination, William Cameron Townsend and Leonard Livingstone Legters, had already formulated a strategy that parted ways with the fundamentalist movement. Whereas a majority of fundamentalists tended to downplay the social aspects of the gospel and were inclined toward anti-intellectualism, WBT-SIL displayed a deep sense of social concern for indigenous peoples and a strong commitment to linguistic scholarship. Although Townsend and Legters co-founded the organization, Pike was very influential in pushing the organization much further along this progressive path. The dual religious and scientific program, along with the WBT-SIL policy of "service to all," created an entirely new type of faith mission, one that defied the contemporary

---

5. Noll, *Scandal*, ix.
6. Noll, *Scandal*, 7.
7. Noll, *Scandal*, 3.
8. Noll, *Scandal*, 7.

status quo within American evangelicalism. As Pike himself would one day observe, the WBT-SIL religious and scientific combination afforded the opportunity to serve God and humanity with both the heart and mind equally.[9] And he, above most of his contemporaries, excelled in marrying the heart and mind as a scholar and translator, as a teacher and leader, and as a linguistic theorist and philosopher of language.

Since this biography attempts to situate Pike within the narrative of North American evangelicalism, a word is therefore in order on evangelicalism and fundamentalism. Historian David W. Bebbington's four-fold definition of the evangelical movement has become something of a standard. The chief characteristics of evangelicalism identified by Bebbington are conversionism, activism, biblicism, and crucicentrism. Preaching the gospel is a priority for evangelicals, since born-again conversion is the only hope for sinners. Once they have been converted, evangelicals actively seek to lead others to conversion. The Bible has held pride of place for evangelicals, for they believe that only within its pages can religious truth be found. Finally, the cross holds a special place for evangelicals, for upon it rests the doctrine of atonement.[10] While some might wish for a more nuanced definition of evangelicalism, Bebbington's "quadrilateral" defines the movement with sufficient precision while not becoming unwieldy.

The term "fundamentalist" first appeared in *The Watchman-Examiner*, a widely read Baptist paper, in 1920. The paper's editor, Curtis Lee Laws, defined "fundamentalists" as Christians prepared "to do battle royal for the Fundamentals."[11] Laws took the term from a series of publications, *The Fundamentals*, which appeared under the sponsorship of California oilman Lyman Stewart between 1910 and 1915. Written by well-known Bible teachers and published in twelve volumes, *The Fundamentals* comprised a large number of articles aimed at buttressing the "fundamentals" of the Christian faith at a time when modernist (liberal) theology was on the rise.[12] Perhaps the most suitable approach to describing fundamentalism is to borrow a convention employed by the well-known historian George Marsden, who made a practice of referring

---

9. Pike, *With Heart and Mind*.
10. Bebbington, *Evangelicalism in Modern Britain*, 2–17.
11. Marsden, *Fundamentalism and American Culture*, 159.
12. Marsden, *Fundamentalism and American Culture*, 118–23.

to "tendencies" that characterized the movement.[13] In the broadest sense fundamentalists were militant anti-modernists and ecclesiastical separatists. Most fundamentalists also exhibited a marked tendency to emphasize doctrinal orthodoxy, scriptural inerrancy, premillennial-dispensationalism, and creationism. This cluster of traits typified what might be loosely referred to as classical fundamentalism.

Fundamentalists were not given to pursuing the life of the mind. With a populist and pragmatic bent, most fundamentalists were oriented toward action. From their perspective, erudition, scholarship, and high thinking did not contribute to the spread of the gospel and the making of converts. Indeed, such activities seemed to hinder the gospel. These habits had a baleful effect not only within fundamentalism but also on the broader evangelical mind. But, it was this very state of affairs that makes the life of Ken Pike all the more fascinating and surprising, for he himself had been touched by the fundamentalist movement. Moreover, although WBT-SIL was closely associated with leaders and organizations within the fundamentalist movement, it was WBT-SIL that helped Pike to transcend the intellectual strictures of fundamentalism. As we shall see, Ken Pike owed much to Cameron Townsend, for it was he who first parted with tradition in order to create a new kind of evangelical mission. Although Pike never identified himself specifically as a neo-evangelical, he was always on the leading edge of that movement to reform fundamentalism into a more socially aware and intellectually credible form of evangelicalism.

This biography also situates Pike within the discipline of structural linguistics, since he was a major linguistic innovator and theorist. He was drawn into the study of linguistics through Bible translation, and spent the greater part of his life as a linguistic researcher and teacher. But we should not consider Pike the Christian and Pike the scholar as comprising separate stories. Perhaps the most difficult aspect of writing this biography was the challenge of presenting a life that was lived in two worlds at the same time. Yes, Pike was an evangelical missionary, but he was also deeply involved in secular academia. Thus, after a fashion, his life is a testament of how one Christian man successfully navigated the post-Enlightenment science and religion divide. With that said, it should be noted that the present volume serves as a corrective to my earlier characterization of Pike as having largely compartmentalized

---

13. Marsden, *Fundamentalism and American Culture*, 3–8.

his Christian faith and his theoretical linguistics.[14] After a thorough and sustained period of research, I have concluded that Christian theism deeply informed Pike's theory of language. Hence, not only was he motivated by faith to pursue linguistics as the handmaiden of Bible translation, the very foundation of his theoretical linguistics was thoroughly Christian. The Pikean mind was an integrated mind.

This book makes no claim of being a comprehensive account of Pike's life. It is more of an intellectual biography for two reasons. First, Pike was a scholar and intellectual, and thus the life of the mind was a central characteristic of the man. The second derives from the first. The archival record and Pike's writings are a testament of a mind at work. By and large, it is only in his diaries and letters to his family and wife Evelyn that we glimpse Pike's emotional side. He appears to have maintained a certain distance in most of his relationships, which was a function of his highly intellectual mind. He was not a man comfortable with small talk or at ease in social settings. He was at home in the world of theory and academic discourse. There is, in the archival record and through interviews, ample testimony of Pike's Christian faith and belief, and therefore his religious life is covered at some length in this volume. He had a profound sense of Christian duty. Obedience to what he saw as God's will was a significant force in his life. In many ways, Pike's life of faithful commitment echoes that of another Bible translator, William Tyndale, who wrote *The Obedience of a Christian Man* (1528). In this long essay, Tyndale argued that one must fulfill their social and religious obligations out of obedience to God. There is no evidence that Pike ever read this work, but he surely would have wholeheartedly endorsed it.

In summary, then, this book is an endeavor to elucidate the Pikean mind while giving us a sense of his Christian faith and belief. It is also an effort to set the man within both the evangelical movement and the discipline of structural linguistics, and to chart his considerable influence on WBT-SIL.

---

14. Aldridge, *For The Gospel's Sake*, 73–78.

1

Beginnings

KENNETH LEE PIKE WAS born in the small town of East Woodstock, Connecticut, on June 9, 1912. His father, Ernest R. Pike, was a dedicated and respected rural doctor who was prone to illness. After only a year of service as a medical missionary in Alaska, he was forced to return home due to poor health.[1] One East Woodstock resident described Doctor Pike as "a wisp of a man, almost frail in appearance. He wore black rimmed glasses and spoke very softly. I never heard that he possessed a sense of humor; certainly I never heard him utter anything that was considered humorous." This same villager did recollect that if Dr. Pike was not mirthful, he was nonetheless "a kindly man, a thoughtful caring person."[2] By all accounts, he was a good family man. Ken Pike certainly esteemed his father. Indeed, when Dr. Pike became gravely ill, his son promised God that he would enter the ministry if his father survived. From his father, Ken Pike seems to have inherited his profound sense of service and devotion.

May Granniss Pike was the mother of eight children, of which Ken was next to the youngest. Hers was a life of toil in a home with no electricity or central heat. She also had to act as the doctor's secretary, admitting patients, taking calls, and handling office finances. Yet, she found time to nurture her children. One of her favorite ways of doing this was to teach them hymns. Ken's favorite was "There Were Ninety and Nine that Safely Lay," a versified portrayal of the lost sheep, which he

---

1. Pike, "Hefley Interview," tape one, 15.
2. May, *Private Thoughts*, 55.

later connected with his deep concern for indigenous peoples who had often been neglected by missionaries. His mother also played a small but important role in his gaining acceptance to college. Pike was so socially insecure that she had to register him for classes at Gordon College of Theology and Missions in Boston.³ She also forced him to leave for college when his father once again took ill. It was from his mother that Ken Pike seems to have inherited his dogged perseverance.

The Pike family attended services at the local Congregational church. Pike's younger sister, Eunice, recollected that it was a church where "salvation and missions were not emphasized." Ken and Eunice both acknowledge it was their father who contributed most to their spiritual formation through daily family devotions and the telling of Bible stories on Sundays.⁴ And to this was added their mother's teaching of hymns. "I grew up," Pike wrote later in life, "in a godly home—with prayers, and worship, and Christian commitment by my parents."⁵ Raised in a Christian home and churched in a tradition that did not give prominence to born-again conversion, Pike could not recall how or when he came to faith. "When I came to the Lord I don't know," he wrote in 1938, "though it seems that it was when I was very young. I know that at six[,] I was looking to Jesus to watch over me."⁶ By most accounts, it was an irenic Christian home in which Pike came of age.

Yet, there was a strain of something less religiously pacific in his father's outlook. In a letter to his sister Sally, Pike gives evidence that his father had been affected by the fundamentalist movement. "Dad," he wrote in 1931, "used to rave about the modernists, I too had my dreams of denouncing them from the pulpit."⁷ Ernest Pike also seems to have taken up an interest in premillennial-dispensationalism, which was largely promulgated through the fundamentalist network.⁸ Hence, through the influence of his father, Pike was nudged toward the fundamentalist wing of evangelicalism. The fundamentalism to which Pike was attracted was the more refined and learned variety epitomized by the urbane J. Gresham Machen, the Presbyterian theologian who formed Westminster

---

3. Pike, "Journey With God," 1; Pike, "Chief Turning Points," 1.
4. Pike, *Ken Pike: Scholar and Christian*, 7.
5. Pike, "Journey With God," 1.
6. Pike to Griset, September 25, 1938, 1, Pike Special Collection (hereafter "PSC").
7. Pike to Roberts, February 16, 1931, 5, PSC.
8. Ernest Pike to Clarence and Hattie, December 14, 1935, 2, PSC.

Theological Seminary as a conservative alternative to Princeton. He also took a lead role in the formation of the Orthodox Presbyterian Church, a conservative rejoinder to the liberalizing Northern Presbyterian Church. Machen was the most prominent figure of the more moderate wing of fundamentalism. The Machenites were a small minority in the fundamentalist movement, which was otherwise largely led by populist leaders with mass appeal.[9] Although Pike would manifest signs of militancy in his early missionary career, the brand of fundamentalism he absorbed was more that of Machen than, for example, the militant separatist Bob Jones Sr. After reading some of Machen's works in college, Pike expressed his admiration for the theologian and, in many ways, his life and thought would come to resemble that of this scholarly theologian.[10]

As an adult Pike became a vigorous volleyball and water polo player, but in high school he did not participate in any organized sports. Study, not play, was his forte while attending public school, and he was twice advanced educationally in grade level. The only student of his second grade class to pass, he was forthwith promoted to fourth grade. He also skipped the eighth grade. He graduated in 1928 with a class of twelve.[11] Quoting from Pike's valedictory speech gives us a sense of the young man's perspective on life, an outlook that permeates the entirety of his life from beginning to end. "We are now on the threshold of our graduation, and as we look back over our four years' work we realize that it is not the facts themselves which we have learned which are important, but only their application to our present life. . . . In our sciences, too, we have learned how it makes no difference whether or not we have learned facts and rules, if we do not apply them to our needs in life."[12] Although shy and socially awkward, Pike relentlessly drove himself to action and service in the world.

As in high school, Pike proved an excellent student at Gordon College. One professor noted that he possessed a "logical mind and a retentive memory." His work in Greek and scriptural exegesis were outstanding, and he was asked to write a series of expositions on the book of Luke for *The Evangelical Student*, the periodical of the League of Evangelical

---

9. Hart, *Defending the Faith*.
10. Pike, "Hefley Interview," tape one, 18.
11. Pike, "Journey With God," 1.
12. Pike, "Valedictory Address."

Students, an early forerunner to later student organizations such as Inter-Varsity Christian Fellowship.[13] This request remained unfulfilled, since Pike had already made other commitments. His performance in college was marred only by a lazy streak, something he would continue to struggle with for many years. Merrill C. Tenney, a professor of New Testament and Greek who would later become well-known in evangelical circles, once commented on an assignment of Pike's, saying that it "would be good but its [sic] late."[14] "It haunts me," Pike confessed, "that in college I had pretty near everything late."[15] Evidently this habit included being tardy for classes. On one occasion he was late to a science class. Thus, he was unaware that the professor had opened his lecture with a bit of humor. Pointing to a brain suspended in a jar of formaldehyde, the teacher quipped, with tongue-in-cheek, that if anyone had lost their brain they could now come up and collect it. At this unpropitious moment, a sleepy-eyed Pike walked in with mussed hair and a lost look on his face. The professor regarded the sluggish student, gestured at the jar, and deadpanned: "There they are." Pike seemed more amused than insulted by this incident. "The class roared into a living volcanic spasm," he wrote his family. "How should I know what I was stepping into, . . . I was late enough already without taking time to tame my rebellious hair."[16] Late assignments and tardiness to classes aside, Pike was granted a Bachelor of Theology degree in 1933.

During his time at Gordon College, Pike became interested in the China Inland Mission (CIM). His first encounter with CIM came through reading a biography of the mission's founder, Hudson Taylor. After hearing Taylor's son Howard speak at Gordon, Pike sensed a call to missions and to China more specifically. He began praying for China and memorized the nation's provinces and the population of each. As the end of his four-year program neared, Pike posted an application to the mission on Christmas Day 1932. He was accepted as a candidate and invited to the mission's home in Philadelphia for the examination process that coming summer. Ken Pike believed that he was on the way to fulfilling his promise to enter the ministry if his father recovered from a

---

13. Ernest Pike, selections from letters, July 23, 1935, PSC.
14. Quoted in Pike, diary, December 29, 1937, 91–92, PSC.
15. Pike, diary, December 29, 1937, 91–92, PSC.
16. Pike to Sally, Dad, and Mom, April 11, 1935, PSC.

life-threatening illness. In matter of fact, he was headed for the first great failure of his life.

The Summer Institute of Linguistics

As Pike set his sights on a missionary career in 1933, William Cameron Townsend and Leonard Livingstone Legters were laying the groundwork for what would become the Wycliffe Bible Translators (WBT) and the Summer Institute of Linguistics (SIL). Legters, a former missionary to the Kiowa and Comanche Indians, was a Victorious Life (Keswick) preacher. Townsend was a former missionary who had, until recently, served with the Central American Mission (CAM) in Guatemala. Only a few days after Townsend's November 1933 resignation from CAM, the two men undertook an exploratory survey in Mexico, where they hoped to carry out Bible translation projects among the nation's indigenous Mayan and Nahuatl (Aztec) descendants. It was expected that once a foothold was established in Mexico, Legters would rally support for the venture in North America under the auspices of the Pioneer Mission Agency, a stateside organization closely associated with American Keswick. As for Townsend, he would direct the work in Mexico. The creation of a mission focused specifically on Bible translation was a first in the development of modern era missions.

The following year, the two men undertook another innovative project. In the summer of 1934, Townsend and Legters launched the first summer session of Camp Wycliffe, a rustic summer school held at an old farmhouse near Sulphur Springs, Arkansas, to train missionary translators in basic linguistics. In its first few years, the summer camp's course offerings were rather meager, but the object was to prepare missionary candidates for translating the Bible into previously unwritten languages. The rustic camp setting was also intended to toughen them for the rugged living conditions they would encounter in Mexico. As with the establishment of a translation-specific mission, the founding of a linguistic school for missionaries was unprecedented.

With the recent emergence of the science of structural linguistics (discussed below), it was a propitious moment to create a specialized school of linguistics for missionaries. On the other hand, it was an altogether unfavorable moment for missionaries expecting to enter Mexico. In 1933, as Townsend and Legters set off for the border, new missionaries of any stripe were unwelcome. The prevailing revolutionary climate in Mexico was decidedly anti-religious, since religion was regarded as an impediment to social progress and state modernization. Townsend, a missionary, and Legters, a preacher, could therefore expect to be turned away at the Mexico-US border. All this proved less an intractable problem for Cameron Townsend than an opportunity to exercise his outsized faith and ingenuity. Once he made up his mind that he was in the center of God's will, he indefatigably pursued the object of his faith against all odds.

In 1919, fourteen years before the Mexico venture, Townsend had joined the Central American Mission after itinerating for a year and a half as a colporteur in Guatemala with the Bible House of Los Angeles. Standard missionary practice typically called for evangelization in Spanish, even when trying to communicate the gospel to the non-Spanish-speaking indigenous population. Trying to sell Spanish Bibles to mostly indigenous-speaking monolingual and illiterate Indians was a frustrating exercise. Thus, the precocious and independent-minded Townsend came to the opposite verdict of his fellow missionaries on the desirability of indigenous language ministry and Bible translation. Having early on reached this conclusion, Cameron Townsend's tenure with the Central American Mission in Guatemala from 1919 to 1933 was oftentimes an uneasy one. On numerous occasions, he butted heads with the mission's leadership as he doggedly pursued indigenous-language ministry and Bible translation.

In Spanish-speaking Latin America, an unfavorable view of Indian languages functioned to dampen interest in indigenous Bible translation and language development. In her study of Protestantism in Guatemala, historian Virginia Garrard-Burnett found that missionaries in the early twentieth-century were generally of the opinion "that indigenous idioms were simple 'dialects' rather than true languages capable of conveying complex ideas and thought. From this perspective, to lend legitimacy to the unwritten indigenous vernacular through codification and use seemed . . . to border on the absurd."[17] Townsend was clearly swimming against the stream of contemporary opinion on indigenous languages in the 1930s.

In part, Townsend's argument for vernacular language development, literacy, and Bible translation rested on the belief that Guatemala's

---

17. Garrard-Burnett, *Protestantism in Guatemala*, 52.

indigenous inhabitants would never achieve religious, social, and economic equality with the dominant Spanish-speaking *ladinos* until such time as the Indians were instilled with some measure of respect for their own languages and cultures.[18] Toward this end, with little official mission support but ample assistance from several indigenous co-translators, he produced a Kaqchikel New Testament. When the translation was completed in 1932, Townsend set his sights on translating the Bible into another language. The leadership of CAM pressed him instead to settle down and consolidate the work he had begun amongst the Kaqchikel. Likewise, church and mission leaders in North America, such as the well-known pastor of the Moody Church in Chicago, Henry A. Ironside, discouraged the idea of translating the Bible into additional Indian languages.[19] Facing resistance at every turn, Townsend decided to leave the Central American Mission so that he could create his own organization, one that focused on Bible translation and linguistics.

A few days before venturing into Mexico in November 1933, Townsend resigned from CAM so that he could plausibly deny being a missionary. In an introductory letter sent to Mexican officials, he presented himself as an "ethnologist and educator" and Legters as a "lecturer, explorer and humanitarian."[20] Despite these measures, when the two men appeared at the border entry was denied. That is until Townsend proffered a 1931 letter from Moisés Sáenz, a Mexican educator, diplomat, and politician. Sáenz had met Townsend in Guatemala, and was sufficiently impressed with the American missionary's combination of social uplift and Bible-based moral instruction in the vernacular to extend an invitation to Mexico. Sáenz, as an educator, was acutely aware that the linguistic barriers to indigenous education were insurmountably high and that the chances for lifting the Indians out of the mire of social inequality slim.[21] Mexico needed all the help it could get, and Townsend's program looked promising. Sáenz held no official government post in late 1933, but the two-year-old letter nonetheless worked its magic. And the rest, as they say, is history.

18. *Ladinos* were the Hispanicized upwardly mobile class in Central America, especially in Guatemala.

19. Townsend, "Hefley Interview," c. 1970, 1, William Cameron Townsend Archives (hereafter "TA"), document number 43597.

20. Townsend to Soto.

21. Townsend to Legters, November 11, 1931, TA 1630; Townsend, "Hefley Interview," c. 1970 TA 43657; Townsend, "Mexico's Gift Airplane."

Legters cut his stay in Mexico short, but Townsend completed a five-thousand mile expedition during which he met a number of Mexican educators, businessmen, clergy, and military officials.[22] Upon his return to the United States in early 1934, he began publishing in American educational journals and newspapers glowing accounts of Mexico's educational efforts and social objectives. Publicizing his views in this manner bolstered Townsend's standing with Mexican officials. Having gained their ear, he explained that the linguists he intended to deploy in Mexico would undertake community development projects, formulate alphabets for unwritten indigenous languages, and conduct vernacular literacy campaigns. Townsend promised that his workers would confine themselves only to these tasks and Bible translation, and he gave assurances that they would not found churches under SIL's control, baptize converts, or preach. He also subtly couched the provision of vernacular scriptures in anti-Catholic terms by suggesting that the Bible would serve as "an antidote to fanaticism."[23] In other words, providing access to the scriptures would undercut Catholic dogma, something of which Mexican revolutionary elites were keen to effect. Townsend eventually gained the trust of a few important Mexican officials, who were convinced that his altruistic aims of creating alphabets, grammars, and dictionaries for indigenous peoples were in fact compatible with their goals of education, social amelioration, and state modernization.[24]

One of the early and most important figures backing Townsend's endeavor was Rafael Ramírez, Mexico's director of rural education. He was the official who authorized Townsend's initial tour of the country.[25] It was also Ramírez who introduced Townsend to Mariano Silva y Aceves, the director of the Mexican Institute of Linguistic Research, which had been established in 1933. Aceves, in 1936, arranged for some of Camp Wycliffe's budding linguist-translators to become official researchers attached to the National University.[26] Townsend's fledgling relationship with Mexican officialdom was cemented in January 1936, when President Lázaro Cárdenas turned up for a firsthand inspection of this intrepid

---

22. Townsend, "Record."
23. Townsend, "Is Religion Doomed," 8.
24. Hartch, *Missionaries of the State*, 1–61.
25. Townsend to Elvira Townsend, December 20, 1933, TA 1716.
26. Townsend to Pioneer Mission Agency (hereafter "PMA"), September 8, 1937, 3, TA 2102; Townsend, et al., *Wycliffe Sapphire*, 55–56; Pike, "Hefley Interview," c. 1970, 17–18, TA 43472.

American's work in the impoverished town of Tetelcingo, located in the state of Morelos (about 60 miles south of Mexico City). Residing with his wife Elvira and niece Evelyn Griset in a camper-trailer parked in the village square, Townsend carried out a number of community development projects in this Aztec-speaking village. Unobtrusive, low-key personal evangelism also figured among his activities. Cárdenas, a *mestizo* of Tarascan heritage, was a champion of the peasant. In Townsend, he discovered a kindred spirit. Cárdenas was less of an anti-religious zealot than his predecessors, and therefore Townsend's nonsectarian and undogmatic Christianity posed no great obstacle to cooperation in the president's mind. Indeed, Cárdenas even agreed to pay small salaries for a number of Camp Wycliffe graduates. Under a program called the "Inter-American Service Brigade," they engaged in literacy and rural education projects on behalf of the government.[27] From this initial meeting between Townsend and Cárdenas in the dusty little town of Tetelcingo, the two men went on to forge a lifelong friendship.[28] Unfettered access to Mexico was now assured.

Revolutionary Mexico proved no obstacle to the entrepreneurial and pragmatic Townsend. He simply adapted his project to the socio-political climate of 1930s Mexico. What would become the Summer Institute of Linguistics was crafted as a humanitarian and scientific enterprise, with Bible translation as one goal among several. Having sold linguistic expertise as a significant aspect of the work, Townsend would either have to produce scientific results or see his venture collapse. The odds of his backwater summer school turning young fundamentalist evangelicals into capable linguists were not in Townsend's favor. Evangelical missionary candidates of this period, as a general rule, were far more interested in evangelism and soul winning than science and community development. Townsend, never one to doubt if he believed that God was on his side, did not worry himself over such matters. And, as will be seen, he was either very lucky or providence truly was on his side.

27. Weathers, "Some Intimate Observations"; Townsend to PMA, September 8, 1937, 1–2, TA 2102.
28. Aldridge, *For the Gospel's Sake*, 44–46, 120.

Linguistics and Translation

The timing of Townsend's venture to translate the Bible into indigenous languages was ideal in at least one important way: a new approach to the study of languages was in the making. Down to the early twentieth century, the science of linguistics mainly consisted of comparing the relationships between Indo-European languages and researching the historical development of these languages. Under the impetus of such figures as Leonard Bloomfield and Edward Sapir in the 1920s, American linguists began to direct their research efforts toward Amerindian languages. In vogue now was research on the internal structure of these indigenous languages of the Americas. Hence, the emergence of "structural linguistics" as a new science. In 1927, Bloomfield, Sapir, and anthropologist Franz Boas established the Committee on Research in Native American Languages to support research in this burgeoning field.[29] At the very moment when SIL was faced with the complex task of creating alphabets and writing grammars for unwritten languages, structural linguists were beginning to develop the methods and theories with which to perform those very tasks more accurately and efficiently.

Small beginnings with SIL and Camp Wycliffe certainly did not portend things to come. Within a decade (by which time Camp Wycliffe had been folded into SIL) the institute would become a leading player in the discipline of structural linguistics in North America. By way of example, in the July-September 1948 issue of *Language*, the prestigious journal of the Linguistic Society of America, SIL was lauded as "one of the most promising developments in applied linguistics in the country."[30] Townsend's moves to forge links between SIL and American structural linguistics was destined to give rise to the largest organization in the world focused on indigenous languages. But all of that was in the future. In the mid-1930s, Camp Wycliffe was no more than an upstart summer school, and the Summer Institute of Linguistics (known as the Instituto Lingüístico de Verano in Mexico) was simply an informal designation for the "Townsend Group," a handful of neophyte linguist-translators.

Bible translation as mission proved attractive to young evangelicals. By 1942, SIL members in Mexico numbered nearly one hundred, straining the capacity of the Pioneer Mission Agency's Philadelphia

---

29. Leeds-Hurwitz, "Committee on Research," 129.
30. *Language* 24 (1948) 4.

office to handle SIL's administrative affairs.[31] Thus, the agency pressed Townsend to form his own stateside organization. SIL, with its quasi-scientific nature, was not well suited for relating to the organization's evangelical constituency in North America. Therefore, a separate but parallel organization was formed to engage the Christian public, recruit candidates, and handle finances at home. Adopting the English translator John Wycliffe's surname—as had Camp Wycliffe before it—Wycliffe Bible Translators was incorporated in 1942. At the same time the Summer Institute of Linguistics was also legally incorporated, although it had been semi-officially in existence since the mid-1930s. The two organizations shared identical membership, leadership, and boards of directors.[32] In effect, the two organizations comprised a single mission with a twofold character. WBT-SIL was a hybrid that combined the faith mission objective of spreading the gospel through Bible translation with the scientific aims of linguistics and language development. The organization also departed from traditional evangelical missionary practice by working in close cooperation with governments of all stripes. From the mid-1930s, Cameron Townsend was, in the words of historian William Svelmoe, advancing a "New Vision for Missions."[33] By pursuing indigenous-language Bible translation as a specific missionary strategy, and coupling it with the science of linguistics, Townsend expanded the frontiers of evangelical missionary thought and practice. WBT-SIL would certainly require some unusual missionary recruits: young evangelicals willing to carry out scientific research and scholarly publication, willing to curb their enthusiasm for overt evangelization, and willing to serve left-leaning governments. Ken Pike would present himself as one of the first, but his path to SIL hardly augured success.

Misfortune at the China Inland Mission

Ken Pike appeared for candidate examinations in June 1933 at the China Inland Mission's North American offices in Philadelphia. He was determined at all cost to succeed. Three years after the event, he wrote his brother describing his experience. "In the Mission course [of] the China Inland Mission I studied like a dog. In three weeks I did more

31. PMA to North American constituents, July 10, 1942, TA 41526.
32. SIL Articles of Incorporation; WBT Articles of Incorporation.
33. Svelmoe, *New Vision for Missions*.

than the other fellows had in five. But I paid for it. My nerves were shot and told heavily against me as they figured I could not stand the gaff. I could not keep them from seeing I was nervous. I have never studied like that anywhere else."[34] Anxiety and nervous tension were only part of his undoing. During language study, he struggled to distinguish the difference between aspirated and unaspirated consonants in Mandarin.[35] On the whole, it was not an impressive performance, but there was more.

Pike's woes were compounded when he wrongly accused CIM founder Hudson Taylor's daughter-in-law, Mrs. Howard Taylor, of plagiarism. It will be recalled that Pike had read her biography of Hudson Taylor while in college. But this was before she was married; hence, the author of the older edition was listed as Mary Geraldine Guinness. At the CIM candidate school, he read the new edition of her book giving the author as Mrs. Howard Taylor. Here it is perhaps best to let Pike tell the story: "After I got to the CIM home and was talking with one of their officials[,] I was quite upset because I'd by then read a book by Mrs. Howard Taylor about the founder of CIM. The book struck me as a bit of plagiarism because they were so alike. They just blankly stared at me when I told them what I thought[,] and I suddenly realized that they were the same woman. One was her maiden name and the other her married name."[36] This deeply embarrassing *faux pas*, coupled with his other problems, certainly did not help his case, but for the rest of his life Pike maintained publicly that a nervous disposition was the primary reason for the CIM's rejection of his candidacy.

One of the principle reasons for his rejection has never been made public. During an inspection of his dormitory room, a package of cigarettes was discovered in a desk drawer. This was an egregious infraction, after all CIM was a deeply conservative mission. But were the cigarettes Pike's? Almost certainly not; he was known never to have used tobacco in any form. How or why the package found its way into his desk drawer will likely remain a mystery. However it came about, he was mortified. Perhaps even more so because the offending item was not his. To be accused of smoking was sufficiently humiliating that he kept it hidden from everyone but his children, to whom he only disclosed this

---

34. Pike to Otto Pike, May 24, 1936, 8, PSC.
35. Pike, faculty seminar, October 18, 1976, 39.
36. Pike, "Hefley Interview," tape one, 19.

episode later in life.³⁷ His reaction to this affair is telling in that it reveals a very important aspect of his character. Ken Pike was a man with a very strong sense of moral rectitude. He aimed to live a life of integrity and, as we will see, he largely achieved this goal for which he strove so diligently.

The cigarette incident aside, Pike made a poor showing that summer of 1933. He was terribly shaken by this episode in his early life. After all, had he not been summoned by God for missionary work? Decades later he recalled that these events precipitated a "tremendous spiritual battle—I had been so committed to the belief that God had called me, that the rejection shook my whole understanding of [God's] leading." Robert Hall Glover, CIM's home director, suggested that Pike should perhaps try pastoring a small rural church.³⁸ Surly this advice stung. It was an awful letdown from his high aspirations for missionary service with the prestigious CIM. The wounded Pike followed Glover's counsel, but failed again when he unsuccessfully candidated for the pastorate of a small church. "I was the academic type, so I studied 50 hours to get that sermon ready. I couldn't get it cut down so I preached 50 minutes to a congregational audience in New England that didn't want to be preached at more than 25 mins. So I didn't get the call to be a preacher. I blew that one."³⁹ It appeared that any prospect for ministry was over. Nevertheless, and with no sense of what the future held, he returned to Gordon College in the fall of 1934 for graduate studies in New Testament Greek. On the whole it was an inauspicious beginning for one set on Christian ministry. At question was whether or not the young Ken Pike could pull himself together and find a vocation that comported with his apparent shortcomings.

---

37. Judith Schram, interview.
38. Pike, "Chief Turning Points," 1.
39. Pike, "Hefley Interview," tape one, 19–20.

2

A Missionary Scholar in the Making

KEN PIKE'S REJECTION BY the China Inland Mission left a question mark hanging over his future. After a year of forestry work with the Depression-era Civilian Conservation Corps, he returned to Gordon College for the 1934–1935 academic year, where he took a graduate course in New Testament Greek. During the spring semester he met Sam Fisk, a teacher at John Brown College in Arkansas who was pursuing a Master of Arts degree at Gordon to advance his academic career. In 1934, Fisk had helped Cameron Townsend publicize Camp Wycliffe by printing and distributing brochures at John Brown. While studying at Gordon, he observed Pike's aptitude for Greek, and thus suggested that he should consider attending Camp Wycliffe.[1]

Pike forthwith wrote Townsend and was invited to attend the summer 1935 session.[2] Since he "had troubles with being sociable," Pike chose to hitchhike most of the way to Camp Wycliffe, reasoning that the 1500-mile trip would provide opportunities for "social training."[3] Once at the camp, he characteristically failed to make a good first impression. When SIL's outspoken and hard-nosed co-founder, L. L. Legters, happened to see the new student perched in a tree collecting firewood, he muttered, "Oh Lord, why didn't you send us something decent."[4] A failed missionary candidate, nervous, and self-conscious, there was

---

1. Pike to Fisk, May 28, 1935, PSC: Fisk to Hibbard, July 11, 1987, TA 39624.
2. Pike to Townsend, May 2, 1935, PSC.
3. Pike to Hibbard, December 19, 1986, TA 39527.
4. Pike "Hefley Interview," c. 1970, 5, TA 43472.

certainly little to suggest that Pike was suitable material for the kind of demanding pioneering missionary work envisaged by Townsend and Legters. Yet, with only five students appearing for the second summer session of the camp, Townsend was not inclined to be overly fussy about candidates. He queried Pike about his future plans. When the young man replied that he had none, Townsend invited him to come to Mexico. "And that," Pike later recalled, "was my total investigation by the Wycliffe Bible Translators, which wasn't invented yet, and by the Summer Institute of Linguistics, that was almost invented by that fall. And so I went to Mexico with him."[5] And with that, the course of his life was settled.

Pike's encounter with the science of linguistics at Camp Wycliffe was a momentous event in his intellectual development. Elbert McCreery, a former Presbyterian missionary to Sudan, taught the phonetics courses at Camp Wycliffe between 1934 and 1936. McCreery's lectures fired Pike's interest in the subject.[6] In part, his new found fascination for phonetics was piqued by discovering the difference between aspirated and unaspirated consonants. Here at last was the key to the irksome difficulty that had plagued him during his study of Mandarin while undergoing CIM candidate evaluation.[7] He was also captivated by a pedagogical device Townsend had invented for demonstrating the thousands of possible permutations of Kaqchikel verbal morphology. Constructed of cardboard with sliding vertical panels and window cut outs, Townsend's apparatus displayed endless permutations of the complex system of prefixes and suffixes that modified a root verb for tense, voice, mode, person, and number. Pike later credited Townsend's lectures and his demonstration of this device with furnishing some of the foundational concepts underlying the linguistic theory that he eventually developed.[8] Adding to all the excitement was a trip to Lawton, Oklahoma, where the camp's students practiced their newly acquired phonetics skills with Cherokees, Comanches, and Apaches.[9] Both his eagerness and aptitude for linguistics were duly noted, and Townsend invited him to teach phonetics at the following year's camp session.[10] Legters remained skeptical, believing it

    5. Pike, interview by Ron Gluck, 5.
    6. Wilt, "Biographical Data."
    7. Pike to McCreery, c. September 1936, PSC.
    8. Pike, "Reminiscences," 32; Pike to May Granniss Pike, June 19, 1935, 5, PSC.
    9. Pike to May Granniss Pike, July 9, 1935, 6, PSC; Pike, diary, August 25, 1935, 12, PSC.
    10. Pike to May Granniss Pike, August 1, 1935, 6, PSC.

was foolhardy to turn teaching duties over to this untested and anxious young man.[11] Townsend proved to be the better judge of Pike's potential.

During the 1935 session of Camp Wycliffe an event took place that has since passed into organizational folklore. In the 1920s, President Plutarco Elías Calles ruthlessly harassed the Catholic Church, eventually inciting the Cristeros War. Ruling with an iron fist, Calles suppressed the rebellion. In the same vein, he did little to fulfill the promises of the Mexican Revolution, initiating few reforms aimed at ameliorating the conditions of landless peasants. Calles left office in 1928, but continued to exert a powerful influence over his successors. General Lázaro Cárdenas was elected president in 1934. A truly committed progressive reformer, he took a more conciliatory approach on the question of religion. Calles was incensed by these moves. In barely disguised phrasing, he essentially called for Cárdenas to resign. Rather than concede, Cárdenas instead dismissed cabinet ministers loyal to Calles, along with a number of lower level political administrators. For Townsend and his protégés this was nothing less than an answer to their prayer that the political winds in Mexico would shift in their favor. When the news of events in Mexico reached Camp Wycliffe it was cause for celebration. Pike enthusiastically reported to his mother that it was "a great day" at the camp.[12] Having prayed and yearned for permanent access to Mexico, in the eyes of Townsend and his group this event was an obvious manifestation of God at work in human affairs.

Into Mexico

At long last the opportunity for missionary work was a reality for Ken Pike. In a letter to his mother, he enthused that "I am going to jump hard at this door." But with his CIM experience fresh on his mind, he added: "If I bump my head again, pick up the pieces."[13] It would seem that Pike was caught up in Townsend's infectious enthusiasm for Bible translation, as would hundreds and eventually thousands of others after him. That Townsend had confidence in him, especially when his prospects seemed at low ebb, no doubt boosted Pike's zeal too.[14]

11. Townsend, "Hefley Interview," c. 1970, 2, TA 43598.
12. Pike to May Granniss Pike, June 19, 1935, PSC.
13. Pike to May Granniss Pike, July 9, 1935, 2, PSC.
14. Pike, "Hefley Interview," tape one, 17.

On the evening of August 20, 1935, Pike, along with fellow Camp Wycliffe graduates Max Lathrop and William Sedat, crossed the border into Mexico. Brainerd Legters (L. L. Legters' son) and Richmond McKinney had crossed earlier in the day. Cameron Townsend, his wife Elvira, and his niece Evelyn Griset followed several hours behind Pike's troupe. With one hundred and sixty dollars to his name—thirty-five from his brother and the rest, ironically, procured by Legters—Pike was granted a two-month tourist visa, renewable upon proof of sufficient funds. Flush with excitement, the novelty of the experience intensified his perceptions. He filled his diary with travel details and lush descriptions of the landscape. Sleeping outdoors on the desert floor, he marveled that the "satellites of God's throne sparked in brilliance over the moonlit 'desert.'" Rough roads, infrequent gasoline stations, and a vintage Buick prone to mechanical failure turned the trip to Mexico City into an arduous three-day journey. Failed brakes, inoperable lights, a locked starter, an empty gas tank, and a damaged bumper from being towed by a passenger bus all figured in his running account. Food too was a topic of interest. "Their chillis [sic] are hot," is how he succinctly summarized Mexican food. "The best insurance for Mexico," Pike quipped, "is a heavy rope, a complete set of mud hooks and a two gallon can of gasoline," to which one of his colleagues added, "a brass stomach."[15] At no point did he complain. For one presumably given to nervousness and social anxiety, his diary account is striking in that it reveals a young man delighting in the adventure of harsh travel and enjoying the camaraderie of his companions.

Although Aztec had been mentioned for his research and translation efforts, he eventually chose to focus on a variety of Mixtec, a language spoken by an indigenous Mesoamerican people of Oaxaca, in west-central Mexico. In September, Pike called on Eulogio Martinez, an elderly Mixtec man willing to help him begin learning the language. At their first meeting, he discovered that Martinez was blind, toothless, and bedridden. Communication was exceedingly difficult, but he still managed to discover that Mixtec was a tonal language, where varying levels of pitch accents on syllables changed the meaning of otherwise identical words.[16] Pike would therefore need to develop a method whereby he could discover the linguistic significance and patterning of the tones. Since SIL translators were destined to encounter these difficult-to-analyze tone

15. Pike, diary, August 20, 1935, 1–15, PSC.

16. Pike, diary, September 5 to 18, 1935, 51–57, PSC; Pike, *Stir, Change, Create*, 137; Pike, "Autobiographical Note on My Experience with Tone."

languages on a regular basis, it was just as well that he cut his teeth on one, for it would serve him and his colleagues well in the future.

Pike not only applied his mind to the task at hand, but he also felt his way forward through concerted prayer and reflection. After discussing his newly developed linguistic ideas with Brainerd Legters, the latter suggested a time of prayer and, in Pike's words, they "had a glorious time asking the Lord to have His will." In early October, he initiated a week-and-a-half season of intense spiritual reflection, during which he prayed at the top of each hour for three specific concerns: "To see God's bigness;" "To keep Devil from my Mixteco place;" and, "To make me 'Think Indian' before summer."[17] In these early days, he laid down a pattern of spiritual habits that remained throughout his life.

Pike soon found himself mixing with Mexican educators, scholars, and government officials. At the Instituto Mexicano de Investigaciones Lingüísticas (IMIL) he developed a professional relationship with Mariano Silva y Aceves, the director of the institute and rector of the University of Mexico. It was at the offices of the IMIL that he first discovered Edward Sapir's *Language: An Introduction to the Study of Speech*, one of the early and most important books on structural linguistics.[18] Pike returned several times to peruse the volume.[19] In late October, he presented a draft of his preliminary research on Mixtec phonetics to Aceves, who suggested that the completed research should be submitted for publication in the IMIL journal.[20] It was during this period too that Pike interacted on a number of occasions with other key government figures, such as Rafael Ramírez, the Director of Rural Education, and Javier Uranga, secretary to the Minister of Labor.[21] Pike was certainly moving in very unusual circles for an evangelical missionary in the 1930s, and, as will be seen, keeping such company made him acutely aware of the necessity for producing credible linguistic scholarship.

In November and December of 1935, Pike undertook his first extended research expedition. This excursion would be a true test of both his physical and mental fortitude. Would worries over his nervousness

---

17. Pike, diary, October 6, 1935, 65, PSC. Note: "Mixteco" is an older variant of the now preferred "Mixtec."

18. Sapir, *Language*.

19. Pike, diary, October 16, 1935, 28, PSC.

20. Pike, diary, October 25, 1935, 74, PSC.

21. Pike, diary, November 3 and 4, 1935, 78–81, PSC.

and frailty prove accurate? If he were prone to breakdown under stress, this venture would certainly uncover any weakness.

During the first week of November, Pike gathered supplies for his trek to Oaxaca and called on Ramírez and Uranga, both of whom supplied him with official letters of introduction. To fortify himself spiritually, he devoted the morning before his leave-taking to prayer and fasting. Since he had not yet acquired Spanish, Pike was accompanied by a young bilingual Mexican, Antonio Guellano Garza. After the first long day of trekking over the grueling mountainous terrain, he jotted in his diary that he was feeling "tired," "dopy," and "headsick."[22] Reinvigorated by a night's rest, he set off early the next morning without complaint. When they arrived in Chalcatongo de Hidalgo on December 5, news of a death in Garza's family suddenly took the interpreter away. Pike was now on his own until mid-January 1936, when he would set out for Mexico City to rejoin Townsend.[23] Up to this point, he certainly demonstrated that he possessed physical stamina. But now that he was in strange surroundings and without a Spanish interpreter, the stakes were upped in his bid to prove his mettle.

In the mountains around Chalcatongo, temperatures plunged with the setting sun. And with his bedroll somewhere in transit along the trail, Pike passed several uncomfortable nights shivering in the cold.[24] By this time too he was suffering from leg abscesses. Several days later backaches and chronic pharyngitis were added to the list. He applied salt to the leg lesions, underwent several treatments by a local nurse, and later saw a doctor, but all to no avail. When the sores appeared on his feet in early January, he was confined to bed. But, after repeated treatments with "wet salt packs," he was finally "up & at'em" four days later.[25] The tenor of his diary and correspondence during this period is remarkably upbeat. Writing of his return trip to Mexico City, he even engaged in some humor. Traveling in an over-packed bus, Pike and several other passengers experienced motion sickness with bouts of vomiting. He sardonically exclaimed that while retching out the bus window, he had at least "missed the man on the running board!"[26] More than merely standing up to the

22. Pike, diary, November 14, 1935, 87, PSC.
23. Pike, diary, December 5 to 7, 1935, 106–7, PSC.
24. Pike, diary, December 5, 1935, 105, PSC.
25. Pike, diary, December 15, 1935 to January 6, 1936, 116, 120, 125, PSC.
26. Pike, diary, January 18, 1936, 129, PSC.

hardship, Pike took pride in acclimating to the demanding situations in which he found himself. "You see I have turned Mexican," he wrote home in December, "because when I wanted to walk the 32 kilometers from Yukuañe to Tlaxiaco, I carried only a blanket. It works quite well, since it is easily folded and carried on the shoulder when walking, and serves as a bed as well as a coat."[27] From the standpoint of bearing up under at least some degree of physical punishment, Pike proved equal to the situation. He also demonstrated that he could manage without an interpreter. Perhaps he was a little tougher than his appearance and demeanor suggested.

It was also becoming evident that Townsend's confidence in the young man's linguistic aptitude was not misplaced. Pike visited a number of towns in which he collected sufficient linguistic data to determine that there was a range of phonetic variation in Mixtec from one geographical location to another.[28] An examination of his correspondence with Thomas E. F. Cummings, a professor of linguistics at the Biblical Seminary in New York, exhibits a remarkable degree of analytical insight coming from one with only minimal training and a cursory reading in linguistics. The exchanges between the two men reveals that Pike possessed an understanding of phonetics and the operations of the human vocal apparatus that belied his elementary education on the subject. Moreover, he was already grappling with the underdeveloped state of phonetic representation, where as yet no uniform descriptive terminology existed for graphically representing the multitude of various sounds produced in the world's languages.[29] This particular aspect of linguistics would continue to occupy him for much of his early linguistic career. Indeed, he would later produce a near-comprehensive inventory of phonetic occurrences found in the world's languages.

Pike also demonstrated remarkable linguistic insight when he cautioned against attempts to elicit grammatical data directly from Indian informants, insisting instead that vocabulary and linguistic structure should be derived from the collection and analysis of naturally occurring language—such as stories, which were "couched in the Indian thought processes."[30] In light of these initial accomplishments, it is not too surprising that his colleagues were already calling on him for

---

27. Pike to May Granniss Pike, December 8, 1935, 1, PSC.

28. Pike to Friend in the Lord, December 18, 1935, 1–2, PSC.

29. Cummings to Pike, February 23, 1936, PSC; Pike to Cummings, March 5, 1936, PSC; Cummings to Pike, April 25, 1936, PSC; Cummings to Pike, June 10, 1936, PSC.

30. Pike to Brainerd and Elva Legters, February 10, 1936, 3, PSC.

assistance with linguistic analysis. This had the effect of heightening Pike's already keen awareness of his linguistic accomplishments. "Whenever [Townsend] has been able to use any evidence that the kids he wants to bring to Mexico will be able to produce the goods, I have been handy evidence," he crowed to Richmond McKinney. "A bunch of them here who know absolutely nothing about Mixteco are hanging by their eyelashes to see the stuff I am getting ready."[31] His earlier sense of failure was quickly giving way to a youthful conceit.

Observing at close hand how Townsend promoted his venture in Mexico as a scientific enterprise, Pike, much more than most of his fellow Camp Wycliffe graduates, was deeply concerned that their linguistic research should live up to the founder's rhetoric. Keeping company with Mexican officials on a regular basis also served to impress upon his mind the importance of demonstrating scientific credibility. During a sleepless night in late September 1935, he conceived of a paper that "would give us scientific standing in the country and possibly help get permanent scientific passports."[32] Likewise, with the express intention of demonstrating scholarly competence, he sent transcriptions of legends and stories that he had collected to Silva y Aceves, Ramírez, and Uranga.[33] Perhaps the most concise expression of his concern that there should be little or no gap between the rhetoric of scientific competency and reality is found in a 1937 letter to his mother. "Townsend has his plan of action here in Mexico upon the basis of scientific research," he wrote. "In the bargain we will of course plan to do the translating which is our goal. But we do not want to masquerade as linguists and be anything else but that. The only answer is to become linguists, in fact, not theory, and deliver the real goods."[34] As will become evident in succeeding chapters, Ken Pike's sense of personal responsibility for producing real scientific results, along with his sincere belief that SIL should live up to its billing as a scientific institute, served as catalysts inspiring him to push Camp Wycliffe and SIL to academic heights beyond what even the imaginative Townsend could have envisaged, and at times beyond what he even considered expedient.

31. Pike to McKinney, April 7, 1936, 2, PSC.
32. Pike, diary, September 21, 1935, 58, PSC.
33. Pike to Townsend, May 18, 1936, 4, TA 2040.
34. Pike to May Granniss Pike, January 14, 1937, 1, PSC.

Early Translation Efforts

Bible translation was at the forefront of every SIL linguist-translator's mind. Few of them were able to curb the impulse to translate at the earliest possible moment. If this tendency went unchecked, there was the danger of translation usurping the obligation to produce technical linguistic materials as required by SIL's commitment to the government. This was something Townsend fretted over. If SIL members turned into conventional missionaries bent on translation and evangelization, then his program would collapse. In the race to turn out a New Testament, Pike was in this respect no different than his colleagues. Working from a Greek text in early December 1935, he translated a small portion of the Gospel of Luke. After typing the translated passage, he sent what he claimed was the "first copy of the Mixteco Scriptures in this century" to his father. The ink was barely dry on this initial bit of translation when a letter arrived from Townsend advising "caution about evangelism." Pike was chastened, if only for a moment. The very next day he was again attempting more translation, but Townsend's cautionary note troubled his conscience. He therefore avowed to focus more on Mixtec linguistics.[35] It was a short-lived oath. By early January, Pike had translated the entire book of 1 John, and he hoped to draft four more books before he returned to Mexico City.[36] Bible translation was the clarion call for Pike and his colleagues, otherwise they would not have taken up with Townsend in the first place. Hence, the urge to translate competed with linguistic research, even for Pike, who more than most worried about the scientific aspect of their work. Achieving the proper balance between the religious and scientific aspects of the task would sometimes turn into a genuine tug-of-war in SIL.

Pike's assertion to have produced the century's first portion of a biblical text in Mixtec was almost certainly accurate. In 1546, the Council of Trent decreed that the Latin Vulgate was the sole authorized version of the Judeo-Christian scriptures. This declaration, made in response to the Protestant Reformation, all but ended the publication of vernacular translations of scripture in Catholic dominated Latin America for over three hundred years.[37] Bible translation was revived by Protestants in the

---

35. Pike, diary, December 11 to 12, 1935, 109–10, PSC.
36. Pike, diary, January 8, 1935, 125, PSC.
37. Soesilo, "Bible Translation," 172–73; Coke, "Ethnohistory of Bible Translation," 2–3.

nineteenth century, but little attention was given to indigenous language communities.

Townsend's incursion into Mexico with his band of linguist-translators in the 1930s was about to resurrect indigenous Bible translation in a major way. But these initial translation efforts, such as Pike was experimenting with, while useful as a practical exercise in the language learning process, proved mostly defective. Moreover, even after achieving some mastery in the vernacular language, the translations produced in the first few decades of WBT-SIL's existence varied in quality. Translators could hardly be faulted though, since there was as yet little or nothing in the way of developed theory or practice to guide their efforts. At this stage of the game their ignorance was probably a blessing in disguise. Had Pike and his colleagues realized the full magnitude of what they were attempting, it might well have overwhelmed them to the point of irresolution.

Townsend, who had produced a translation in Guatemala, understood what his linguist-translators faced. He therefore pressured his recruits to learn the indigenous language before tackling Spanish, fearing that if they initially acquired Spanish they would then come to rely upon it and never master the local idiom. Such advice suited Pike just fine. "As for Spanish vs. Indian," he wrote McKinney, "I am just as glad that I started Indian first, . . . I have studied Mixteco only, and can carry on some conversation, get all that is necessary to eat, wear, or what have you. I can have a good time, and after an hour of talking the stuff . . . I get a thrill out of it. I really like the language."[38] As with Townsend, whose early missionary activity plunged him into the non-Spanish speaking world of Central America's indigenous peoples, Pike too was immersed in the cultural milieu of the Mixtec Indians, and this imbued him with a profound appreciation for indigenous languages.

Deep and sustained contact with the indigenous language and culture also produced in Pike an earnest empathy for the social injustices endured by Mexico's native inhabitants. He described the dominant culture as parasitic upon the Indian peoples, who "were robbed years ago by a grasping race." This outlook disposed him to look with favor on the revolutionary impulses of the Mexican government, which he observed "only now realized its folly and is working out a very beneficial program for the depressed." Although efforts were being made in Mexico to right past wrongs, the situation remained dire in Pike's view. "But even yet,"

---

38. Pike to McKinney, April 7, 1936, 2, PSC.

he went on to explain, "little children run about with only a brief shirt to keep them warm and one-third covered, tummies bloated twice the normal size by hookworm and other disease. Men shiver at night huddled together like jackstraws to keep from the cold. . . . No, it is not pretty, this business, but the decedents [sic] of a mighty race await the healing touch of One Who would not break a bruised reed."[39] As the narrative of Pike's life unfolds, it will become evident that this perspective on the plight of all socially and culturally disadvantaged peoples remained not only a chief concern of his but also of SIL itself. It is nearly impossible to understand Pike's mind and SIL organizationally unless one recognizes just how deeply affected Pike and other linguist-translators were by their sustained and intimate contact with indigenous peoples. The very roots of their determination to overcome the linguistic isolation and social marginalization of Latin America's native peoples can be traced to their coming to see the world from the indigenous point of view.

Proving himself capable of elementary field linguistics, adaptable to the cultural context, and up to the physical and emotional demands of pioneering missionary work, Pike was also showing himself ready to live out the "faith" component of missionary life. By October 1935, his family had become somewhat perplexed as to how he was funding his extended stay in Mexico, since he had made no mention of his financial needs. In response to a question on this very matter, his father Ernest replied that "it is obvious that the work they are doing cannot go on without money, [but] Ken has no promise expressed or implied of a salary that I have heard of."[40] In keeping with a central tenet of the faith mission creed of "full information, no solicitation," he never mentioned his financial needs explicitly. Yet, he was readily supplied through those acting on his behalf. His brother Galen had handed him thirty-five dollars after hearing that he would need funds to remain in Mexico upon the completion of summer studies. L. L. Legters later drummed up a steady thirty-five dollars a month for his ongoing support from a Bible conference attendee. Townsend also arranged for a teacher's salary of twelve dollars a month from the Mexican government.[41] By exercising his faith in matters financial, he settled in his mind that the path of faith was the only acceptable one. "Never," he declared to his family in May 1936,

---

39. Pike to Friend in the Lord, December 18, 1935, 2, PSC.
40. Pike to Sister Martha, October 9, 1935, PSC.
41. Pike to Hibbard, December 19, 1986, 1–2, TA 39527.

"would I blame man for failing me in funds or money, no matter what the cause or his previous promises." Even if this entailed going hungry—something which he expected to suffer in his missionary vocation—he insisted that God would not test him until he was spiritually prepared for such occasion. "No doubt," he went on to say, "someday it will come when I am man enough to take the punishment without running out on God."[42] Whether or not the young man possessed the mettle to match the bravado of these declarations remained to be seen. In any case, at this point, he was sold on the faith mission approach.

He was also an enthusiastic missionary. Pike's father was of the impression that his son was "almost hilariously happy with his work."[43] After a little over seven months in Mexico, Pike conveyed his feelings to a college friend. It is worth quoting from this letter at length, since it offers a window into his heart and mind (and his eccentric sense of humor) at this important juncture in his life. In April 1936, he wrote:

> Would you object if I put in one or two serious words? I really enjoy the work. The devil has had me sick two or three times, with malaria, leg ulcers, diaroehoa (you spell it), and what not. Boy, am I glad that I know that God [is] God and not a compound hyeropea astimatism[44] of the philosophical cerebralism with which this world is afflicted at present. . . . I have been happier than for ages, have seen miracles working here . . . , have been spanked many times by the Lord because I have not come up to standard, have not known two days ahead of time where I would be, but have rarely had a time when I have been less free from worry. The Lord is boss, and I am happy to work for him.[45]

If there were any doubts about his chosen vocation, they were laid to rest during his first foray into Mexico.

As Pike made his way to Arkansas for teaching duties at Camp Wycliffe in June 1936, he could look back over the past year with a sense of accomplishment. He had managed to hold his own while interacting with Mexican officials and academics, and had carried out some field research. He had also withstood the mental and physical rigors of backcountry

---

42. Pike to Folks, May 24, 1936, 2, PSC.
43. Pike to Sister Martha, October 9, 1935, PSC.
44. Pike misspelled "hyperopic astigmatism," a form of farsightedness referred to as "compound hyperopic astigmatism." To correct this condition one would need a pair of complex corrective lenses.
45. Pike to Dan, April 1, 1936, 2, PSC.

living and travel. Townsend had seen something in this young man that others had failed to notice, and thus gathered the first of what would prove to be a long string of exceptionally gifted missionary candidates. On the other hand, this first season in Mexico was what missionaries have sometimes referred to as the honeymoon phase, when newness of culture, language, and surroundings are tinged with excitement. What would happen when isolation from his own culture and language became burdensome, when the novelty of his surroundings turned wearisome? Moreover, he had yet to realize the true complexity of the Mixtec language, not to mention the myriad difficulties attending Bible translation. In a word, bigger challenges lay just over the horizon. But, for the moment, Pike could bask in the glow of success.

A Divided Mind

The summer of 1936 found Ken Pike at the third session of Camp Wycliffe in Siloam Springs, Arkansas. Once again, the Bible Institute of Los Angeles professor Elbert McCreery taught the ten-day course in phonetics. Pike assisted McCreery by introducing real-world examples of phones (sounds) found in Mexico's indigenous languages. He also provided one-on-one coaching to students struggling with the nuances of unfamiliar speech sounds. Pike had come a long way over the previous year. When he departed for Mexico in 1935, McCreery's ten-day course was the extent of his training in phonetics, but it was enough for a start. With a little training under his belt he made rapid progress, and discovered that he actually possessed a finely-tuned ear and an aptitude for taking down transcriptions. He proved this by transcribing entire stories phonetically. This was no mean feat. Anyone who has ever endeavored to transcribe extended segments of speech can vouch for the difficulty of this exercise. Cameron Townsend noted the young man's flair for phonetics and pressed him to write a practical phonetics textbook. He told Pike that he wanted something "very simple and clear to be used by missionaries," since literature of this variety was unavailable.[46] Pike was "aghast" at the idea, judging that his knowledge of the topic was too meager.[47] Although he had plenty of spare time while in Mexico City during the months of September and October 1936, he only managed to scratch out four or five

46. Pike to Edith, October 24, 1936, PSC.
47. Pike, "Hefley Interview," c. 1970, 1, TA 43473.

pages.⁴⁸ Above all else, the spiritual aspect of the work was foremost in his mind, and he therefore dodged any entanglements that might hinder his primary objective of translating the New Testament into Mixtec.

In early 1936, Pike selected the village of San Miguel el Grande, Oaxaca, as the place where he would live and carry out his translation work. Located in southwestern Mexico, San Miguel was situated on a rolling plateau at about six thousand feet above sea level and surrounded by mountains. This small town was accessible only by foot or mule. Log cabins served as the principle mode of habitation, and Pike would eventually design and supervise the building of one for his own dwelling. Few of the inhabitants resided permanently in San Miguel, since most of them were dispersed on farms and scattered settlements, only coming to town for short periods of time. While on his way from Camp Wycliffe to San Miguel at the end of October 1936, Pike experienced a life-changing event, one that would mark another milestone in his journey toward becoming a scholar. Waiting on a load of supplies to catch up with him before resuming his journey, he observed some men unloading two-hundred-pound sacks of grain and carrying them into a warehouse. He decided to join in for exercise. He also took a hand in the work for the simple reason of cultural amity. Seeing that the two-hundred-pound bags were beyond his strength, the men suggested that he attempt a smaller one-hundred-pound sack. What happened next is best related by Pike: "But as we started, two things happened which I hadn't calculated on. First the weight increased by the square root of the distance. It got heavy awful fast. Secondly, they didn't just stumble and walk along, they went into a little trot. I couldn't go that fast. Now I was completely ashamed and humiliated. I'd obviously bitten off more than I could chew even with this small sack. It was more than my ego could stand if I would just drop it in the middle of the street and admit it was too much for me. So I tried to hurry."⁴⁹ This proved unwise. He slipped on a railroad track, fell, and broke a leg. With the help of some of the town's residents he boarded a train for Puebla, where at the Hospital Latino Americano he was treated.⁵⁰ This was not the first occasion Pike joined in on such activities. He once hauled wood with some Indians, and overslept the next day from fatigue. In another instance he helped clear stones from a field. "I have a

---

48. Pike to Edith, October 24, 1936, PSC.
49. Pike, "Hefley Interview," tape two, 2.
50. Pike to May Granniss Pike, November 7, 1936, 14, PSC.

lot of fun," he wrote his family, "in trying to do the things these Indians do."[51] He was not having fun now. Expecting to be well on his way to San Miguel, he now faced a six-week stay at or near the hospital until his leg healed and the cast removed.

With nothing to occupy his time, Townsend's book idea intruded upon on his mind. Pike saw providence at work. "I started on phonetics," he informed his sister Eunice, "because that was the only reason I could actually figure out why the Lord busted my leg. Since I did not want Him to bust my neck too, I got busy right away."[52] Once set in motion, the manuscript took on a life of its own. Page after page describing the phones found in various languages piled up at his bedside. By December he had written a hundred pages.[53] His retentive mind held more phonetic data than he perhaps realized. Committing his knowledge to paper served to lubricate the flow of ideas. It is clear from his correspondence that he relished the challenge. Any worries over his confinement and broken leg faded as he labored at "Pike's Phonetic Manual for Beginners."[54] "A greater blessing has rarely come to me," he later recorded in his diary, "than in the hospital starting my book."[55] As will be seen, the involuntary delay in reaching San Miguel and beginning the book would mark an important turning point in Ken Pike's early career as a missionary and scholar.

As Pike toiled over his manuscript in the latter part of 1936, Cameron Townsend's other linguistic prodigy, twenty-one-year-old Eugene Nida, was in the rugged Sierra Madre Occidental of northwestern Mexico, where he was cutting his teeth as a pioneer missionary among the Tarahumara. Earlier in the year, Nida had graduated *summa cum laude* from the University of California at Los Angeles (UCLA), with a major in Greek and a minor in Latin. While at UCLA, he learned of Camp Wycliffe from Townsend's niece, Evelyn Griset, who was a fellow student.[56] Fascinated by languages, he leapt at the opportunity to attend the camp. Having already undertaken some studies in linguistics, he brought this knowledge to Camp Wycliffe. His academic prowess was conspicuous,

51. Pike to Folks, April 24, 1936, 3–4, PSC.
52. Pike to Eunice Pike, November 21, 1936, 1, PSC.
53. Pike to Folks, December 1, 1936, 4, PSC.
54. Pike to Eunice Pike, November 25, 1936, 1, PSC.
55. Pike, diary, November 12, 1937, 72, PSC.
56. Stine, *Let the Words Be Written,* 27.

and Townsend at once placed him on the teaching staff.[57] Nida's brilliance certainly impressed Pike. Writing to Griset (in whom he was beginning to take more than a passing interest), he exclaimed, "I had a swell time at camp last summer. I sure did appreciate Gene, too. Boy what a man he is! . . . And does he know his stuff!" The two men at once became friends. "We click like two peas in a pod," he told Griset.[58] They also complemented one another as instructors, with Pike teaching phonetics and Nida morphology (the most basic units of grammar). Townsend's summer camp was turning out to be a magnet of sorts for more academically inclined missionary candidates. Within the span of one year, the school had attracted two outstanding students, both of whom would become notable scholars. This was a great boon to Townsend. If he had any hope of convincing Mexican educators and officials that his young recruits were truly linguists, and if he were to turn them into competent Bible translators, he was going to need all the brainpower that he could lay his hands on.

Eugene Nida's linguistic abilities continued to shine in Mexico. In late October, a week after arriving in the municipality of Tónachi, Chihuahua, he reported to Townsend that "I have two men helping me with the Language and though it does seem a little slow I have found the tenses of verbs, the pronouns, most of the cases, and have charted a good many of the dialectical variations."[59] The apologetic tone alongside what amounted to a dazzling linguistic performance is almost comical. While his colleagues struggled with linguistic analysis, Nida made it look simple. "Actually," he wrote two weeks later, "it amazes me how easily the language goes together." His correspondence from October to December 1936 reveals astonishing acuity in parsing the language.

Yet, all was not well. These same letters bear witness to an equally swift descent into despair over the primitive living conditions. In a letter dated November 5, Nida informed Townsend that the Lord was leading him to depart Tónachi for more comfortable surroundings, and someplace with better prospects for linguistic research. He complained of cold weather and poor food, and found the Tarahumara of the area "particularly dull and unintelligent."[60] Subsequent missives from Nida followed

57. Stine, *Let the Words be Written*, 8, 28.
58. Pike to Evelyn Griset, October 24, 1936, 1, PSC.
59. Nida to Townsend, October 22, 1936, TA 2017.
60. Nida to Townsend, November 5, 1936, 2, TA 2012.

a pattern of describing advances in linguistic research coupled with increasingly gloomy remarks on the conditions he was forced to endure. By mid-December, an utterly discouraged Nida reached the breaking point. Suffering with a broken tooth, a stomach malady, and an irregular heartbeat, he pulled up stakes and, without prior warning, returned to the home of his parents in California.[61] By February 1937, he felt rejuvenated enough for a second effort. Linking up with Pike in Mexico City, they set out for San Miguel. This time he lasted less than a month. He was back in California by early March, and once more without giving advance notice to Townsend.[62] This would prove to be Nida's last attempt at pioneering missionary work and, by all appearances, his keen mind appeared lost to missionary Bible translation.

As Nida made his way back to California, Pike was in the midst of his own trial by fire. Failure to take his quinine resulted in a case of malaria, and this was followed by a head cold. When he arrived in San Miguel, he found his language helper intoxicated and the man remained so for several weeks. The cabin in which he was residing was not well chinked, allowing free access to the chill wind. Adding to the misery, he was plagued by fleas when trying to sleep.[63] He also reported to his sister that he had a tooth extracted and, for an unknown reason, was suffering unusual fatigue.[64] Undaunted, he soldiered on.

Suffering his own ills, Pike had nothing but compassion for his beleaguered friend, who had abandoned him on the way to San Miguel. Soon after they parted ways, he wrote Nida: "You may be sure that you have my sympathy. A broken tooth or leg is bad enough. This is worse. The Lord surely knows what the score is. Somehow you are going to get [a] great blessing from it and come back much stronger and better equipped for your service. . . . Keep a stiff upper lip. It is not a pretty silver lining you are hunting, nor hoping nor wishing for. Simply claim God's promise. That includes courage, joy, contentment and peace for the present and service far beyond your dreams for the future."[65] Pike certainly empathized with Nida, but we see here too a somewhat lofty display of spiritual ardor. He pitted himself against adversity as a way

---

61. Nida to Townsend, December 19, 1936, TA 1997.
62. Townsend to Pike, March 6, 1937, 1, PSC.
63. Pike to Townsend, February 22, 1937, PSC.
64. Pike to Eunice Pike, February 25, 1937, PSC.
65. Pike to Nida, February 27, 1937, PSC.

to test his spiritual and physical mettle. It is important to understand this aspect of Pike's character, for he continually drove himself in this fashion throughout his life. He thus assumed that Nida was working at the limits of endurance too. And this goes a long way toward explaining Pike's sudden reversal of attitude when he discovered that Nida might have given up too easily.

Nida's second departure from Mexico worried Townsend considerably, and he shared his apprehension with Pike. "The doctors in Puebla must have ordered him home in a hurry for he didn't take time to get in touch with me after he decided to go. His father wrote me a long, perplexed letter, saying that he can't imagine what has happened to Gene. It's a serious call to prayer, for we can't afford to let Satan get that boy sidetracked."[66] Two weeks later word came from Nida's parents confessing that their son might well be suffering more from hypochondria than any genuine infirmity.[67] Pike's sympathy for his colleague evaporated upon hearing this news. He lashed out in a strongly-worded communiqué to Townsend, accusing Nida of cowardice in the face of sickness and death. He insisted that Nida should "forget his health, and come to live or die, sink or swim, live or perish."[68] Pike then waxed heroic. "I am ready to meet the Lord to-morrow and would be only happy to give my life with my boots on."[69] All this was far from unusual. In fact it was entirely characteristic. On a previous occasion, for example, he jotted in his diary that the townspeople of San Miguel warned him against going to town on Sunday "because it was dangerous." "Well," he remarked, "I am trusting in God, . . . [and] if trouble is coming to me as part of the plan I just ask to take it singing."[70] This kind of bravado was very much in keeping with the faith missionary ethos of the day. Indeed, the young Pike was flush with idealistic missionary enthusiasm. He was by nature much better fitted to the spirited faith mission culture than was his more circumspect colleague. This, at least in some measure, explains why Pike remained throughout his missionary career in SIL, whereas Nida would eventually resign in 1953 to take up full-time work with the American Bible Society, where the organizational culture was rather more reserved.

66. Townsend to Pike, March 6, 1937, 1, PSC.
67. Townsend to Pike, March 19, 1937, PSC.
68. Pike to Townsend, March 29, 1937, 10, PSC.
69. Pike to Townsend, March 29, 1937, 6, PSC.
70. Pike, diary, December 18, 1936, 119, PSC.

Pike's own ardent desire to live out his faith by surmounting difficulties imbued him with a strong sense of duty, and this left him impatient with Nida, whom he now believed was retreating in fear. As the previous chapter indicates, and as the occasion of breaking his leg recounted above reinforces, Pike exercised a remarkable degree of self-discipline when it came to facing hardship. In his mind, then, simply walking away from the field of spiritual battle without real cause was an act of cowardice.

Pike also scolded Nida for putting science before religion. He was troubled that Nida appeared more interested in solving an esoteric historical aspect of Uto-Aztecan linguistics than laying a practical foundation for translation. Pike admitted that he too was interested in these matters, "but," he declared to Townsend, "I would rather find out how to say 'the fullness of God' in something like correct Mixteco grammar." Hence, he concluded that Nida was more interested in trying to put a "Scientific feather" in his cap than anything else.[71] In light of the fact that Pike later became a scholar of no mean accomplishment, all this is somewhat ironic. But it does demonstrate that there remained a measure of anti-intellectualism in his thinking.

Pike's worries that Nida was overemphasizing science were groundless. Indeed, in an odd twist of fate, it was Nida who would go on to focus most of his scholarly energies on the more specifically religious domains of translation theory and the practice of Bible translation, whereas it was Pike who would concentrate much more on the science of structural linguistics. The future aside, this early event reveals a young man elevating heartfelt faith above matters of scientific interest. All this was in keeping with the faith-mission evangelistic impulse. He certainly enjoyed linguistic research, but his academic aspirations were subordinated to the presumably more important task of Bible translation. Therefore, when it appeared that Nida was reversing these priorities, Pike responded with vehement condemnation.

There remains the simple fact too that Pike was capable of mounting a broadside when the mood struck him. He admitted, in a 1970s interview, to being "a fire-eater" in his younger days. And he still struggled, lamenting that "unless the Holy Spirit tames me, I am still a Son of Thunder that bungles, boggles and blows everything and stamps on everybody

---

71. Pike to Townsend, March 29, 1937, 7, PSC.

without mercy."⁷² Put concisely, sharp reflexes were part of Pike's personality, and this was something he long struggled to overcome.

With all that said, Pike's excoriation of Nida was episodic. Any conjecture over lasting enmity between the two men must be ruled out based on the extant record. They continued to work well together each summer while teaching at Camp Wycliffe. As charter board members of WBT and SIL (the organizations were formally incorporated in 1942), they nearly always took the same position on issues. Pike had fired his salvo in a burst of heated ardor that soon cooled. This was a singular outburst against Nida that was never repeated. Nor is there any evidence that Pike ever confronted Nida personally. The letter in question, then, tells us more about Pike's temperament and beliefs at the time than it does about the two men's relationship in these early years.

Before moving on, a brief word should be said in defense of Nida and his ill-fated venture with the Tarahumara. It would have been difficult to find a less hospitable situation for the young man to initiate his Bible translation career. The widely dispersed Tarahumara, inhabiting the remote mountains of northwestern Mexico, remained both geographically and culturally isolated.⁷³ Moreover, the tribe had a history of fending off efforts to evangelize them as far back as the seventeenth century, and were thus not inclined to cooperate with SIL translation efforts. After years of struggle by a number of SIL translators, a New Testament translation was eventually completed in 1972, but there was only a single convert to Christianity.⁷⁴ After a fashion, then, it was a fool's errand for Nida. The cold, high altitude, and poor food, along with the cultural isolation and the indifference of the Tarahumaras—not to mention the fact that he was working alone—would have defeated all but the hardiest of missionaries. Of course, this does not explain his second failure to stay the course in the company of Pike. Perhaps all that can be said is that he was probably not cut out for the rigors of pioneering missionary work. On the other hand, there is no doubt that he was perfectly suited for sustained intellectual effort. Whatever Nida lacked in physical stamina, he more than made up for in raw brainpower.

Pike's impatience was not limited to others, he flogged himself with equal or greater lashes of self-criticism. His diary and letters are littered

---

72. Pike, "Hefley Interview," c. 1970, 6, TA 43472.
73. Marak, "Failed Assimilation of the Tarahumara," 411–35.
74. Hartch, *Missionaries of the State,* 100–104.

with self-reproach when he believed himself to have underperformed or made insufficient progress. He certainly considered himself less capable of extended study than Nida, whom he once referred to as a "human dynamo."[75] "Often I wish I could drive like that," he confided to Evelyn Griset, "but it is too much. I have to content myself with loafing at least three-quarters of the day. I just cannot take it, poor delicate me."[76] "To study nothing but Mixteco," he explained to his family, "is just like strumming a banjo on one string for two hours without changing your finger. My mind needs something else badly."[77] He could clear his head only by breaking off from research to peruse less demanding reading or by engaging in physical activity. During his first year in Mexico, he begged his father to send him magazines, and, at various times, he could be found reading books such as Mark Twain's *Life on the Mississippi* or James Fenimore Cooper's *The Pathfinders*.[78] (By way of contrast, Nida's recreational reading included classical Greek poetry and the Church Fathers, and all in the original languages).[79] Pike, in his own judgment, better tolerated manual labor, claiming that he could "hold a pace of eight hours of work with a gang of men, as I proved two years ago in Woodstock with the Civilian Works Administration."[80] Yet it was study that satisfied his soul. He seemed perplexed by the paradox arising from the sense of contentment brought on by intense intellectual effort and the difficulty of overcoming mental torpor that would result in such gratification. "The studying is the thing which makes me happy," he wrote to a missionary colleague. "Some reason," he added, "seems to be needed to explain why I hate to get down to work." This question begged for an answer that he struggled to supply. In characteristically colorful language, he explained the conundrum. "When things begin to roll out from under the presses and drives of energy it somehow grabs hold of my cheek muscles and bursts them wide open into a smile, but when nothing is done, when all is stagnant and I am loafing . . . the smile fades and old man blues comes to call."[81] Achieving the precarious balance between study, research,

75. Pike to Edith, October 24, 1936, PSC.
76. Pike to Evelyn Griset, October 24, 1936, 1, PSC.
77. Pike to Folks, May 24, 1936, 1, PSC.
78. Pike to Folks, May 24, 1936, 1, PSC; Pike to Mrs. Hull, April 4, 1937, PSC; Pike, diary, February 14, 1938, 12, PSC.
79. North, "Eugene A. Nida," viii.
80. Pike to Otto Pike, May 24, 1936, 7–8, PSC.
81. Pike to Mrs. Hull, December 7, 1936, PSC.

and writing—all of which afforded fulfillment and kept feelings of guilt in abeyance—and the potential for overwork that brought on nervous fatigue and even collapse, was never an easy one for him.

Pike's pangs of guilt over his periods of lassitude were only partly assuaged after Townsend cautioned him against overwork. With Nida out of action, their leader was on the verge of losing one of his star linguists, and he now feared the possible forfeiture of another if Pike pushed himself too hard.[82] "Both you [and] he," Townsend cautioned in March 1937, "must learn to take things easy—yes—be lazy!"[83] This advice was only partly effective in easing Pike's mind, since he continued to be plagued by worries over his inability to sustain longer hours of concentrated effort. "The way days go [by] with no work done," he complained in his diary later that year, "is a pain and at times makes me feel wicked."[84] Pike was acutely aware of his limitations, but a strong sense of moral obligation served as a spur to action.

On June 9, 1937, Ken Pike turned twenty-five. He was on the trail making his way to Tetelcingo for a visit with the Townsend's before returning to Camp Wycliffe. "Twenty-five years old today," he jotted in his diary. "Somehow it seems momentous. Past ones incidents, this one an event. . . . The date I have looked forward to for a long time. Now or never seems the time to really work. If ten years from now something is not actually accomplished of good hard work, well done, the future will not be so bright." Good intentions aside, he seemed to entertain some doubts. "[I] am just as lazy as ever," he confessed in a postscript, "fortunately Townsend said to be or it would weigh heavily on my conscience. Trouble is it does anyhow."[85] As he boarded a north-bound train later in June, he was on the cusp of a new venture that could, if he held up under the strain, launch him on the path to achieving his ten-year goal.

The Linguistic Institute

In the summer of 1936, Eugene Nida brought Leonard Bloomfield's recently published *Language* (1933) to Pike's attention. It was arguably the most important work of the period on structural linguistics. This led

82. Pike to Eunice Pike, March 28, 1937, PSC.
83. Townsend to Pike, March 6, 1937, 1, PSC.
84. Pike, diary, December 2, 1937, 77, PSC.
85. Pike, diary, June 9, 1937, 60, PSC.

to the ironic situation where Pike, at the very moment he was reproving Nida for an overdeveloped interest in purely scientific matters, was himself being sidetracked by repeated readings of Bloomfield's book. Although he struggled with the subject matter of *Language*, it had become a "lovely companion."[86] He had also developed a book-buying habit, ordering linguistic volumes through a Mexico City bookstore and others from America with the help of the Pioneer Mission Agency.[87] He certainly wished to extend his knowledge of linguistics in general, but research related to the phonetics manual that he was writing was the primary impulse behind the book-buying spree.

That he viewed the phonetics book primarily as a contribution to the missionary community, and only secondarily to science, seems to have kept his conscience clear on the proper relationship between science and religion. But other worries kept this matter at the forefront of his mind. Mariano Silva y Aceves, the director of the Mexican Institute of Linguistic Research, was especially keen to have Pike produce linguistic analyses based on folk stories. Here Pike was on the horns of a dilemma, since his only capable storyteller was habitually intoxicated. By paying the informant, he feared complicity in the man's alcoholism. "The thing Silva is nuts about," Pike wrote Townsend, "and [the] thing which Sapir and Bloomfield published to prove their work is a collection of texts. I very much want those stories, but not enough to sacrifice the Lord's work for them."[88] The necessity of linguistic scholarship notwithstanding, Pike hesitated to prioritize it over the religious or spiritual aspects of his project.

As he struggled with the ethical issues of the relationship between science and religion in early 1937, the daunting task of writing the phonetics book also began to weigh on him. "What a work it is to write," Pike confessed to Professor Thomas F. Cummings at the Biblical Seminary in New York. "I never realized," he added, "why it should take so much time."[89] That he made any progress at all is remarkable. Whether in the hospital, in the village of Tetelcingo with the Townsends, or in San Miguel, the conditions under which he labored were far from ideal. With no access to a research library, he was compelled to purchase what

86. Pike to Eunice Pike, April 12, 1937, 2, PSC.

87. Pike to Townsend, March 29, 1937, 5, PSC; Pike, "Autobiographical Note on Phonetics," 182.

88. Pike to Townsend, March 29, 1937, 2–3, PSC.

89. Pike to Cummings, April 5, 1937, PSC.

few linguistic books his meager finances allowed. At times, the paucity of available scholarly sources produced the worrisome effect of having written material only later to find the same matter in a published source. There was a very real danger of unintentionally committing plagiarism.[90] Pike was in desperate need of academic resources that were simply unavailable in rural Mexico.

It was in this period too that Pike began to analyze the tonal features of Mixtec. He soon discovered that tones not only changed the meaning of words but also affected grammar.[91] The Mixtec tonal system was, in Pike's words, "miserably complex."[92] Here, working on tone analysis, he was operating on the frontier of linguistic research, since there was little in the way of formalized methodology to guide his efforts. The enormity of the task he faced should not be underestimated.

Cameron Townsend recognized both the handicaps under which Pike was laboring and the need for professional linguistic training. Therefore, when the two men were together in December 1936 and January 1937, a prominent topic of discussion was where and how Pike might pursue linguistic studies.[93] Their deliberations prompted a burst of correspondence from Pike sounding out the possibilities of studying at Yale, Harvard, or the University of Michigan.[94] Townsend was aware that if his linguist-translators failed to produce quality scholarship, his organization would surely be ejected from Mexico. He was therefore eager to draw upon linguistic expertise wherever he could find it. And, as he had already demonstrated, he had no scruples over engaging with secular academia. With two prodigies in his possession, Townsend sensed it was an opportune moment to knock on doors in the highest reaches of academia.

Townsend was nothing if not ambitious. "In fifteen years," he boasted in the late 1930s, "we will make the [linguistic] scientists sit up and take notice."[95] Although he was angling to get Pike and Nida into academia, it is doubtful that he truly understood what fulfilling this assertion would entail. Moreover, although Pike and Nida certainly showed promise, the

90. Pike to Eunice Pike, March 7, 1937, 2, PSC.
91. Pike to Townsend, April 12, 1937, 1, PSC.
92. Pike to Townsend, April 25, 1937, 1, PSC.
93. Pike to Family, January 1, 1937, PSC.
94. Pike to Hanley, 1936; Pike to Department of Philology; Pike to Fries.
95. Hibbard, "Quotable Uncle Cam," 3.

former was struggling to find sufficient energy for mind-taxing study and the latter was still smarting from his failed venture among the Tarahumara. Then too, Camp Wycliffe was still nothing more than an upstart summer school convened in various rented farmhouses in rural Arkansas. From the vantage point of early 1937, Townsend's aspirations must have appeared wildly fanciful.

Yet, Townsend's ambitions were timely. The discipline of structural linguistics was still in its infancy. Had the discipline already reached maturity, it is quite possible that linguistic scholars would have brushed off any overtures from an obscure group of missionaries. The rudimentary state of structural linguistics is exemplified by the fact that, as of 1926, there were only eleven general linguistic courses and five American Indian language courses available in all of North America. This dearth of structural linguistic offerings was a significant impulse behind the founding of the Linguistic Institute in 1927, under the auspices of the Linguistic Society of America. The Linguistic Institute was structured around annual summer sessions of six weeks (later extended to eight weeks), held at different universities around the country. The inaugural session of the Linguistic Institute was held at Yale University in the summer of 1928. At each summer session, courses and seminars in a variety of topics were on offer. The institute was not a degree-granting body, it functioned more as an extended academic conference, where a majority of those present already possessed professional credentials. The institute nearly passed out of existence during the early years of the Great Depression, but it was revived and expanded to eight weeks in 1936 under the leadership of Charles C. Fries, a professor of linguistics at the University of Michigan.

The upshot of Pike's inquires as to where he might study linguistics ultimately landed him an invitation to attend the Linguistic Institute being held at the University of Michigan in Ann Arbor.[96] The 1937 session, at which Pike appeared, is historically noteworthy in that an unusually large number of leading linguists were on hand to give lectures. In addition to Fries, the faculty register read like a who's who of linguists, including Leonard Bloomfield, Edward Sapir, Zellig Harris, Bernard Bloch, Edgar Howard Sturtevant, and Franklin Edgerton.[97] If one wanted immersion

---

96. Pike to Hanley, 1937; Sapir to Pike.

97. Hill, "History of the Linguistic Institute," 16–22; Falk, "LSA Linguistic Institutes"; Pike to Blatchley, July 3, 1937, PSC.

in the burgeoning field of structural linguistics in the mid-1930s, the Linguistic Institute was the place to be.

Soon after Pike arrived at the institute in late June 1937, Sapir offered his assessment of the phonetics manuscript. Pike noted in his diary that Sapir "was impressed by it." He also wished to know "if I had not had quite a bit of experience in pedagogy," remarking that "I had quite a talent for emphasizing things which others might take for granted."[98] Sapir's praise was countered by severe criticism from Bernard Bloch of Yale. Bloch rained down pessimism at every point of the manuscript, including its chapter arrangement, phonetic orthography, and writing style. Bloch "doubts my ability to do the job," Pike confided in a letter to his sister Eunice. The underlying reasons for Bloch's blistering critique are unclear, but differences in theoretical approach likely played a part. In any case, Sapir's backing is what counted, since the younger Bloch did not carry the weight of the brilliant and highly respected Sapir. Indeed, the noted linguist offered to write a preface for Pike's book, providing he could complete a first draft of the entire manuscript two weeks prior to the end of the institute. In addition to completing the draft, Sapir indicated that Pike should also round out his work by additional readings in the literature. Pike made a valiant effort to meet Sapir's demands, but he failed to keep up. "About a dozen books are begging on my desk right now," he sighed in the letter to Eunice.[99] In the end, the project proved impossible in such a limited space of time. Some of the vexing realities of postgraduate studies, such as withering criticism and enervating labor, were weighing on Pike, and he struggled under the burdensome load.

Anxiety over the book was only one of several "woes" that he enumerated in his July letter to Eunice. He frankly admitted that "classes . . . in phonetics put an awful strain on my abilities. . . . Good old Camp Wycliffe," he confessed, "is not getting distinguised [sic] by yours truly." He also disclosed that his plans for achieving a workable balance between study and repose were coming unraveled. Inadequate sleep was beginning to tell on him, and although he claimed to be managing at the moment, he warned that "when you see me next I shall be jumpy as a bed bug."[100] In the second week of August, he remorsefully admitted to Townsend that the book manuscript had not been touched, and he saw

---

98. Pike, diary, June 30, 1937, 63, PSC.
99. Pike to Eunice Pike, July 9, 1937, 2, PSC.
100. Pike to Eunice Pike, July 9, 1937, 3, PSC.

opportunity neither to work on it at the moment nor during the coming session of Camp Wycliffe, where his teaching duties would render writing impossible. "Right now I am pretty tired. My days are pushed out of shape so I rarely get to bed before midnight or out before eight in the morning, and it is taking its toll on me."[101] His 1937 sojourn at the Linguistic Institute was threatening to reprise his near collapse and failure at the China Inland Mission candidate camp in 1933.

Apprehension over his performance was fueled by feelings of inadequacy and accentuated by his competitive nature. Surrounded by some of North America's leading structural linguists and other academics, Pike not only wished to hold his own but also to outperform them. "As for these Ph.Ds.," he wrote to his sister Eunice on July 23, "I can hold up my end but I get an inferiority complex because I do not lick the pants off them. In Navaho there are two or three folks who I feel have the edge on me, both analyzing forms and in phonetics. . . . Yet when it comes to teaching folks to make the sounds I am ready to bow to none."[102] Whether it was proving his ability to keep pace with the hardy Indians in Mexico or demonstrating his scholarly prowess in academia, Pike's sense of inadequacy and competitive character were twin impulses behind his drive for mastery and distinction.

Pike rallied as his eight-week stint at the institute came to an end. It appears too that he had at last gained some measure of confidence in his performance. Yes, he was seriously fatigued, but also "quite grateful to the Lord for bringing me here, and giving me so much good material, and for not letting me be put to shame."[103] Indeed, he was far from ready to lay aside academic labors. "Let me add one bombshell," he announced to Townsend on Sunday, August 22. "After [the] summer session I decided to stick around and use the library for some needed reading on phoneimics [sic]." He promised, reluctantly, to leave on Tuesday for Camp Wycliffe. "I rather regret it and wish I had more time in the library."[104] Studying under the tutelage of linguistic scholars at the Linguistic Institute was a momentous event for Ken Pike. If he had previously enjoyed linguistic research, he was now truly smitten. Of his academic experience at the

---

101. Pike to Townsend, August 11, 1937, PSC.
102. Pike to Eunice Pike, July 23, 1937, 1, PSC.
103. Pike, diary, August 20, 1937, 66, PSC.
104. Pike to Townsend, August 22, 1937, PSC.

Linguistic Institute in 1937, he later quipped that "I never recovered."[105] As will be seen, this was a true statement; perhaps even an understatement. The balance between science and religion, in his mind, was shifting.

It was also in the summer of 1937 that Edward Sapir uttered what would prove to be a prophetic statement. He inquired of Pike just how many fieldworkers SIL intended to deploy in Mexico. As of mid-1937, SIL was composed of fifteen linguist-translators, not counting Legters, Nida, and the Townsends. Informed of SIL's current status and future plans to develop all of Mexico's indigenous languages, Sapir speculated the organization might soon "dominate the American Indian linguistic field."[106] By the early 1940s, when the number of SIL members crossed the one hundred mark, the organization most likely had more linguistic fieldworkers—although not very many highly educated ones—analyzing indigenous languages than any other single institution in the world.

As Pike made his way from Michigan to Arkansas to teach at the 1937 session of Camp Wycliffe, classes were already underway. At the conclusion of camp, he returned to Mexico. Once again, he struggled with his own unmet expectations, and this despite Townsend's repeated admonishments to set a measured pace. Near the end of December, he recorded in his diary that "days have gone by and nothing to show in Mixtec or in phonetics . . . just written a few letters—I feel awful." With the upcoming 1938 Linguistic Institute weighing on his mind, Pike voiced his worries to Townsend. "It bothers me to think of facing Sapir, Swadesh or Bloch, or Bloomfield, with nothing to show for the year."[107] His recourse, as he had over the past couple of years, was prayerful confession and seeking spiritual sustenance. "Lord this morning again," reads one 1937 journal entry, "I refuse to think of these things and cast the burden on you."[108] He would have ample occasions for repeating this prayer in the coming years.

Doctoral Candidate

Sometime in the early part of 1937, Cameron Townsend was offered a full scholarship to study under Sapir at Yale for a doctorate. He declined the

---

105. Pike, "Autobiographical Note on Phonetics," 182.
106. Pike to May Granniss Pike, July 5, 1937, PSC.
107. Pike to Townsend, April 12, 1937, 1, PSC.
108. Pike, diary, December 29, 1937, 91–92, PSC.

invitation, and instead proposed Pike and Nida as potential candidates, but for reasons that remain unclear no offer was forthcoming. While at the Linguistic Institute in 1937, Pike had raised the question of doctoral studies with Yale professor Edgar Sturtevant, but again nothing came of it.[109] Pike was not particularly disappointed by these apparent dead ends. In fact, his practical missionary work still took precedence over any academic ambitions. "I had always figured that if the Lord wanted me to get a higher degree," he informed Townsend, "He would arrange it so I would not lose a lot of time from the real work here."[110] In the not too distant future, Pike would often be heard complaining about his fellow linguist-translators drawing sharp boundaries like this between the religious and the scientific aspects of the work. But at this point, his missionary devotion still outweighed his scientific enthusiasm by a good margin, although science was rapidly gaining ground. Townsend, a college dropout, had no inclination—let alone the patience—for advanced studies. Ken Pike was willing but, with the religious task uppermost in his mind, he did not press the idea.

Pike returned to Ann Arbor, Michigan, in June 1938 to attend the Linguistic Institute. While there, he discussed his Mixtec tone analysis with Zellig Harris of the University of Pennsylvania, Edgar Sturtevant of Yale University, and Charles Fries of the University of Michigan, and each suggested that he should present his research during the course of the summer session. Fries scheduled a luncheon at which Pike gave an hour and a half lecture. It created quite a stir. In a historical overview of the Linguistic Institute published in *Language*, the journal of the Linguistic Society of America, Pike was mentioned as one of six "distinguished scholars" on hand in 1938 to deliver lectures at the era's most heavily attended summer institute.[111] Whether this assertion was a case of reading Pike's later scholarly reputation back into the historical record, or whether it rightly attests to the brilliance of the lecture at the time, there is no doubt that Pike had made an impression. He was suddenly catapulted to prominence among North America's leading linguistic scholars.

Immediately following the lecture, Charles Fries, the director of the institute that year, informed Pike that his Mixtec tone analysis was the equivalent of a doctoral dissertation, and indicated that he should receive

---

109. Pike to Eunice Pike, July 23, 1937, 1, PSC.
110. Pike to Townsend, April 16, 1937, 1, PSC.
111. Hill, "History of the Linguistic Institute," 22.

university credit for it. Fries was unable to arrange for this, since he needed to confer with Leonard Bloomfield, who was in a hurry to catch a train. As fate would have it, though, Pike's luck was running hot and he ended up sharing a train compartment with the famous linguist. They discussed Pike's Mixtec work at length, and Bloomfield promised that credit would be forthcoming.[112] All that remained was for him to complete two more summer sessions at the institute, undertake a literature review, and then write up everything in dissertation form. In the space of a single day, Pike unexpectedly found himself on the way to earning his doctorate.

As the train rolled toward Chicago, Pike took the opportunity to explain his Christian faith to the eminent linguist. "I told [Bloomfield] how I believed Christ rose from the dead . . . and so on."[113] Unfortunately, he does not record how Bloomfield responded to his witnessing. In any case, there was little or no hostility toward the Bible translation work of SIL when it came to light at the Linguistic Institute in 1938. Sapir, of course, was already familiar with the organization, but most of the scholars at the Linguistic Institute only discovered the full extent of SIL's religious nature when Pike was pressed to explain how the organization's linguistic workers were supported financially. "Through such things we and our group became definitely earmarked as being in the missionary business," he wrote home. With SIL's missionary purpose now in full view, Pike more than ever sensed the need for the organization to produce first-rate scholarship. "Now," he emphasized, "we have to deliver the goods, or the Lord's name will surely be brought into reproach."[114]

The academic community at the Linguistic Institute had little interest in the missionary aspect of SIL, but some of the scholars present were intrigued by the linguistic research side of the organization. Charles Fries proved to be particularly enthused with the linguistic aspect of SIL's field work, and he went so far as to propose joint sessions between Camp Wycliffe and the Linguistic Institute for 1939, even offering that he might be able to obtain funding from the Rockefeller Foundation to underwrite the project.[115] For reasons that remain unclear, the joint sessions never materialized. Nevertheless, by the mid-1940s, SIL was a significant presence at summer sessions of the institute, with Ken Pike and Eugene

---

112. Pike, faculty seminar, November 29, 1976, 27–28.
113. Pike to Eunice Pike, July 16, 1938, 2, PSC.
114. Pike to Folks, July 10, 1938, PSC.
115. Pike to Mom, Dad, and Sae, July 14, 1938, PSC.

Nida teaching courses and other SIL members often presenting papers.[116] A number of SIL's more gifted linguist-translators also availed themselves of the opportunity to study at the institute.[117] There is no doubting that at least some of the leading linguistic scholars of the 1930s and 1940s looked with favor on SIL's linguistic research, and none seemed to have any qualms over its Bible translation efforts. Only in the late 1960s would this happy state of affairs begin to fall apart as some linguists and anthropologists took a turn toward the Left. In SIL's formative decades, the organization was a respected and welcome member of the North American linguistic community.

Pike's innovative approach to the analysis of tonal languages paved the way for his doctoral candidacy. However, the narrowly focused topic of tone analysis was of insufficient scope and complexity to hold his attention. Therefore, rather than take the path of least resistance by formalizing his work on tone, he instead returned to the uncompleted phonetics volume for his dissertation. In making this move, he established what would become a habit of biting off increasingly larger chunks of language for analysis, while at the same time opening up new intellectual challenges to fend off boredom. The dissertation was an outstanding achievement in that Pike identified and described almost the full inventory of phones (sounds) that occur in the world's over 7000 languages. Only a handful of phones would later be discovered.[118]

His dissertation defense in 1942 was an extraordinary event. Leonard Bloomfield, who was on the committee, remarked that the gathering felt more like a seminar than a dissertation examination.[119] The dissertation was published in 1943 as *Phonetics: A Critical Analysis of Phonetic Theory and a Technic for the Practical Description of Sounds*, and the fact that it remains in print is a testament to Pike's accomplishment.[120] With the publication of *Phonetics*, Pike clearly established himself as a significant player in the discipline of structural linguistics.

At the time Pike completed his linguistic studies, the discipline of structural linguistics was comprised of a very small number of scholars, few of whom actually held academic appointments within the discipline

---

116. Falk, "LSA Linguistic Institutes," 6.
117. Pike to Townsend, June 30, 1935, 2, TA 904066.
118. Pike to Dye, March 14, 1996, 2, PSC.
119. Pike to Goldsmith, November 11, 1996, PSC.
120. Pike, *Phonetics*.

proper. Hence, upon completion of his doctorate, a full-time university teaching position became a very real possibility. Charles Fries, who did more to further Pike's academic career than any other scholar, arranged for his appointment in 1942 as a part-time research associate in the English Language Institute at the University of Michigan.[121] This inaugurated what became a thirty-five-year tenure in various faculty positions at the University of Michigan. This initial faculty appointment, as with those that followed, was important in a number of ways. Keeping a foot in academia not only afforded Pike the opportunity to enrich his own thinking through extended contact with other scholars, but it also took him outside the more narrow confines of the evangelical subculture, which broadened his scholarly outlook. That the position initially paid a $1000 salary was certainly a tremendous financial boon to this chronically under-supported faith missionary. Greater sums followed. A 1945–1946 postdoctoral fellowship netted Pike a $2000 stipend.[122] In effect, he was paid by a major research university to carry out research and writing with direct application to the SIL program, a circumstance not likely found anywhere else in North American evangelicalism. For the spring semester of 1948, Pike was awarded an associate professorship, serving one semester each year at the university with the rest of his time dedicated to SIL work. In 1955, he was promoted to a full professorship on the same rotational basis. Pike's long tenure with the University of Michigan stood him and SIL in good stead, for it ensured his on-going intellectual development while also helping to bolster SIL's academic credibility. By 1950, Ken Pike was not only SIL's leading linguist but also an established scholar in the discipline of American structural linguistics.

In his first few years of Christian service, Ken Pike had shown himself to be an unapologetic faith missionary. The fortitude and active faith he exhibited were in keeping with the ardency expected of faith missionaries. His tenacity in the face of difficulties are proof enough on this point. A broken leg was not an occasion for despondency. Rather, it was taken as a sign from God to reconsider writing the phonetics book. This fortuitous event was a turning point in his life, since it eventually landed him in the company of North America's top linguists. Once on their turf, he held his own. The favorable reception of Pike, as well as SIL organizationally, within the discipline would prove far-reaching. It

121. Watkins to Pike, August 3, 1942, PSC.
122. Fries to Pike, February 21, 1945, PSC.

at once opened the way for SIL to become a serious contender in the field of structural linguistics while, at the same time, raising academic expectations that would propel Camp Wycliffe and SIL in a more scholarly direction than might otherwise have been the case. As will be detailed in subsequent chapters, Pike played a major role in boosting the academic standards at the summer camp, and this at times produced significant strains on some of SIL's less academically inclined candidates. Yet, a smaller but not insignificant number of SIL linguist-translators would follow the trail he blazed and, in time, their scholarship and influence created an institution with unparalleled knowledge on indigenous languages. But all that was yet future. For the moment, Pike was coming to realize that first-rate linguistic scholarship was an absolute necessity if SIL expected to maintain its reputation in academic circles. Moreover, and just as Townsend had boasted, Pike had the scientists sitting up and taking notice. Lest he fall prey to conceit, shortly after the fateful day of the tone lecture he wrote to his sister with a request. "Pray for me," he implored, "to keep my feet on the ground, my eyes on the Lord, and my heart set on his will."[123]

---

123. Pike to Eunice Pike, July 16, 1938, 6, PSC.

3

New Frontiers

The Summer Institute of Linguistics experienced growing pains as it parted ways with the traditional faith mission paradigm in the second half of the 1930s. Much of this had to do with the significant overlap between the fundamentalist movement and faith missions. For the most part, faith missions were populated by and led by fundamentalists.[1] While the adverse effects of fundamentalism on the evangelical mind are sometimes exaggerated, historian Mark Noll's contention that the fundamentalist movement was detrimental to evangelical thinking is accurate.[2] The populist reflexes of many fundamentalists all too often had a leveling effect on fundamentalist institutions of higher learning, and this tendency would make itself felt at Camp Wycliffe.[3]

Along the same line, the rise of the social gospel movement provoked many fundamentalists and faith missions into backing away from social concerns that had been part and parcel of nineteenth-century evangelicalism. This "Great Reversal," an expression coined by historian Timothy Smith, led to an outsized emphasis on evangelism at the expense of social amelioration.[4] Coupled with this shying away from social issues was an antipathy for communism and socialism (although this was by no means confined to fundamentalist circles).

---

1. Carpenter, "Propagating the Faith," 98–108; Frizen, *75 Years of the IFMA*, 85–96
2. Noll, *Scandal*, 109–45.
3. Brereton, "Bible Schools," 114–15.
4. Moberg, *Great Reversal*, 11.

By way of example, William Bell Riley, one of the era's most prominent fundamentalist leaders, in 1934 accused President Franklin D. Roosevelt of "painting America Red." "Disarmament," "Internationalism," and the "Social Gospel," Riley warned, "have become the passwords of the secret order which deliberately plots . . . the downfall of the American government."[5] During the very same period in which Riley and other fundamentalists were giving vent to their fears, Cameron Townsend was actively collaborating with the socialist aims of Mexico's revolutionary government, and thus his enterprise in Mexico was clearly at odds with the social and political sentiments of many North American evangelicals.

There was yet another aspect of the Camp Wycliffe and SIL venture that bumped up against prevailing attitudes: the role of women in pioneering mission work. On this issue, Townsend was not at first in the vanguard. He initially sided with a majority of men in SIL who were opposed to sending women into remote locales without masculine protection. As with anticommunism, traditional sexist attitudes were commonplace among fundamentalist men, and in this respect the attitudes of most men in the early days of SIL's development were no different.

As each of these various areas of concern arose, Ken Pike expressed strong sentiments. An examination of how he thought and reacted to these debates at this stage of his SIL career will tell us much about his cast of mind and reveal his outsized influence on the development of SIL.

Camp Wycliffe and the Linguistic Approach

Cameron Townsend declared that SIL would one day make the linguistic scientists sit up and take notice. In Mexico, he also asserted that SIL linguists were equipped to develop alphabets for unwritten languages, produce grammars and dictionaries, and carry out literacy work. Townsend occasionally boasted beyond his measure, and it would fall to Ken Pike and Eugene Nida to ensure that SIL lived up to his claims. Although cited in the previous chapter, it is worth requoting Pike's January 1937 letter to his mother, since it so vividly demonstrates his conviction that SIL's scholarship must be worthy of the general director's assertions. "Townsend has his plan of action here in Mexico upon the basis of scientific research. In the bargain we will of course plan to do the translating

---

5. Riley, "Protocols and Communism."

which is our goal. But we do not want to masquerade as linguists and be anything else but that. The only answer is to become linguists, in fact, not theory, and deliver the real goods."[6] When he penned these words, it is doubtful that he understood fully what delivering the "real goods" might entail or what exactly should be required of students. By the closure of the 1937 session of Linguistic Institute at the University of Michigan, where he had studied with some of the leading linguists of the day, he had come to some definite conclusions on the matter. On the last day of July, he dashed off a letter to Townsend outlining his ideas. He had in mind nothing less than equipping SIL linguist-translators for competent engagement with scholars in the upper echelons of the academy. "I think to safeguard our reputation," he argued, "we ought to have each of our gang ready to be able to talk with these birds." He also concluded that SIL linguist-translators should master the principal linguistic work of the period, Leonard Bloomfield's *Language*.[7] As the 1937 session of Camp Wycliffe approached, Pike was increasingly concerned about academic standards and prepared to uphold those standards.

Although Eugene Nida had failed as a missionary in Mexico, at Townsend's invitation he was once again on hand to teach morphology at the 1937 session of Camp Wycliffe.[8] His presence was deemed sufficiently important for SIL's co-founder, L. L. Legters, to cover the young man's travel expenditures. As for Townsend, he was ready to fight the devil to keep Nida in the game. "Satan," he avowed to Pike, might be "getting in his licks," but "if we stand together in prayer Satan shall be defeated and this talented life will be saved for Bible translation work."[9] Townsend took the matter of Nida's future in hand, arranging for him to pursue postgraduate linguistic studies at the University of Michigan. He also convinced the American Bible Society to employ him on a part-time basis, with the balance of his time committed to co-directing and teaching each summer at Camp Wycliffe. Nida also continued serving as a board member of WBT-SIL.[10] Although he left SIL in 1953, Nida measured up to Townsend's hopes. During a career spanning seven decades, he was Secretary for Versions at the Bible Society, taught

6. Pike to May Granniss Pike, January 14, 1937, 1, PSC.
7. Pike to Townsend, July 31, 1937, PSC.
8. Discussed in ch. 2.
9. Townsend to Pike, April 7, 1937, 1, PSC.
10. Townsend to North, 1.

linguistics, consulted on translation, and developed what is arguably the most significant theoretical approach to Bible translation of the twentieth century, dynamic equivalence. With wunderkind Nida present at the 1937 camp session, and with Pike just back from rubbing elbows with the scholars at the Linguistic Institute, the stage was set for a much more rigorous summer session than the previous three years.

A withering August heat wave settled over Camp Wycliffe in 1937. The thermometer hit one hundred degrees for days on end, fraying nerves as the sultry weather continued unabated into early September. As if the oppressive weather was not bad enough, Pike and Nida were turning up the academic heat in the classroom. It was not long before an exasperated student body erupted in anger. The turmoil reached full pitch after Nida gave a controversial exam, one that replicated university standards rather than imitating the less demanding Bible college tests with which most students were familiar. Some students were on the verge of quitting. Others threatened to warn their friends off from the camp.[11] A few students were also wondering why they had to bother with what seemed to them some of the more arcane aspects of linguistics. After Pike lectured on the scores of different permutations of consonant sounds found in the world's languages, one perplexed student glumly confessed that "I sure would feel more enthusiastic if I could see just what that had to do with Indian work."[12] For students with only a Bible college education, Camp Wycliffe was proving to be a baffling and stressful experience.

Pike and Nida openly complained that the stragglers lacked sufficient academic experience to keep up. In other words, it was not their teaching but slow minds that were at fault. Quite naturally this unsympathetic judgment was not well-received. Townsend eventually stepped in, and over the course of several days succeeded in finding common ground between the aggrieved students and his two young, and perhaps overly eager, linguistic prodigies.[13] In Pike's and Nida's defense it should be noted that, by this point in time, they probably better understood what was called for in the way of acceptable academic performance than did their college-dropout leader. Their apprehensions were well founded. If academic standards were set too low at Camp Wycliffe, then SIL would

---

11. Townsend to Legters, September 20, 1937, TA 2089.

12. Quoted in Pike to Eunice Pike, September 10, 1937, 1, PSC.

13. Townsend to Elvira Townsend, September 18, 1937, TA 2092; Townsend to Legters, September 20, 1937, TA 2089.

surely founder in Mexico when Townsend's "linguists" failed to produce credible scholarship.

This incident brings into sharp relief what had become common place attitudes in conservative evangelical quarters, where spiritual enthusiasm was prized over intellectual effort. Furthermore, among faith missions and their supporters, soul winning was exulted over most other missionary concerns. One does not have to look any further than Pike's own father, who was an educated physician, to uncover evidence of these attitudes. "Strikes me," he wrote to his son in 1940, that "much of the . . . scientific work is delaying the game."[14] Ken Pike and Eugene Nida found themselves bumping up against the reality of students who were either unable or unwilling to meet greater academic demands. Townsend attempted to chart a middle course between the contending parties.[15] He was of the opinion that the high achievers, such as Pike and Nida, should come alongside determined but less gifted students and make the best of the situation. In other words, students who showed at least some promise should be nursed along rather than eliminated. Townsend argued that by doing so SIL could deploy a greater number of linguist-translators, who could then be aided in turning out respectable scholarship by the likes of Pike and Nida. "We believe," Townsend said of this blueprint in a letter to the Bible Society, that it "will enable mediocre linguists to turn out high class work."[16] Debates over academic standards of this nature persisted off and on for most of Pike's SIL career.

Although the student qualifications issue resurfaced periodically, the founder's formulation, whereby average students willing to work hard were accommodated, became common practice. Once admitted to the summer school, the Pikes and the Nidas could put the thumbscrews to students, but only weeding out the weakest among them. In a September 1938 letter to Leonard Bloomfield, Pike framed it this way: "Two things constantly amaze me here. One, how slow the pupils are to learn, the other, how much they learn if you keep hammering away!"[17] And so it was, SIL would go on to deploy hundreds of "ordinary working linguists," to use a term later coined by SIL's Robert Longacre, and they were assisted by a small cadre of experienced linguist-translators, a number of whom

---

14. Ernest Pike, quoted in Pike to Ernest Pike, March 25, 1940, 1, PSC.
15. Townsend to Lathrop, September 3, 1937, 1, TA 2109.
16. Townsend to North, September 15, 1937, 2, TA 2094.
17. Pike to Bloomfield.

had earned doctorates from major universities, such as the University of Pennsylvania, Cornell University, the University of Chicago, Indiana University, and the University of Michigan to name but a few. At the top of the pyramid, though, were the elite scholars—Pike and Nida being the foremost examples—who would make significant contributions to the discipline of linguistics and thereby lend scholarly gravitas to SIL.

There was another side to the debate on academic standards. During the late 1930s efforts were made to fashion some kind of an official organization with a constitution and bylaws. Townsend believed that the organization should operate democratically. As founder, he would be first among equals rather than retaining absolute and unfettered control. Therefore, a committee was formed to create a constitution. As SIL was formalized, questions pertaining to seminary education requirements came to the fore. In large part, this was due to the fact that the 1935 class of Camp Wycliffe was unusual in that three of the five students were seminarians. Richmond McKinney was a student at the Evangelical Theological College in Dallas (later Dallas Theological Seminary), and Max Lathrop and Brainerd Legters were both graduates of Westminster Theological Seminary.[18] As the SIL constitution was hammered out, these three men reasoned that Camp Wycliffe applicants and candidates accepted for SIL membership should have both a college degree and at least some seminary training, if not a seminary degree. In the course of the next several years a sizable majority of candidates who applied had no seminary education at all, to say nothing of Townsend, Pike, and Nida, each of whom lacked a seminary degree. If the educational standard the seminary men advocated was realized, it would have choked off the flow of students to a mere trickle.[19] Pike, whose SIL career was seemingly threatened by this turn of events, referred to the trio of seminary men as the "faslati [fascist] triumvirate."[20] The seminary men were not yet entirely sold on Townsend's strategy. They were having difficultly breaking free of the older missionary paradigm where seminary education was the acme of missionary preparation. Townsend threatened to steamroll the democratic principle and take back full control over the embryonic

---

18. Svelmoe, *New Vision for Missions*, 254–55.

19. Pike to Townsend, November 24, 1936, TA 2005; Pike to Eunice Pike, December 3, 1936, 1, PSC; Townsend to Lathrop, January 27, 1939, 2–3, TA 2478.

20. Pike to Townsend, November 24, 1936, TA 2005.

organization if the men stood their ground. Cowed by his forcefulness, they bowed to his demands.[21]

The traditional missionary paradigm worked against the Townsend strategy in two ways. In the first place, access to Mexico was gained by fielding "linguists," not "missionaries." Thus, he hardly needed young seminarians flourishing their "Reverend" credentials in anti-clerical Mexico. Moreover, by clinging to the traditional missionary model, these men emphasized preaching and evangelization. Townsend implored his linguist-translators to eschew preaching altogether and even witnessing in Spanish for the most part. To do so would jeopardize SIL's position as a humanitarian and scientific organization in the eyes of Mexican authorities. He pressed them instead to focus on learning the indigenous language, after which they could discreetly engage in personal witnessing of their faith. Richmond McKinney, who was in the habit of crossing swords with the founder, was the most vocal opponent of these restrictions. Against Townsend's warnings, he continued to evangelize openly in Spanish, an action for which he was jailed briefly by Mexican authorities in 1941. In Townsend's words, McKinney had invited trouble by "doing the work of a minister instead of a linguist."[22] Seminary education, and the classical missionary thinking that it engendered, was more of a threat to the Townsend strategy than a help.

In the second place, Townsend also held an entirely different perspective on the relationship between science and Bible translation. "Why," he argued in 1937, "should not missionaries do a more scientific piece of work than the linguists themselves, inasmuch as we are dealing with God's Word?"[23] As this statement indicates, he had combined linguistic analysis and Bible translation under the single rubric of "science." Bible translation was now seen as more of a linguistic or scientific exercise than a strictly religious undertaking. Hence, it was not the seminary men, but those such as Pike and Nida, SIL's rising linguistic stars, who were on the leading edge of Townsend's strategy. And, as it turned out, over the course of the next several decades nearly all the SIL linguist-translators who earned advanced degrees pursued linguistic studies at secular universities. The Summer Institute of Linguistics, as its name implied, was destined to be a thoroughgoing institute of language

21. Townsend, "Hefley Interview," c. 1970, TA 43547.
22. Townsend to "Workers in Mexico," November 14, 1941, 2, TA 2715.
23. Townsend to North, 2.

sciences, even as it carried out Bible translation. This emphasis on science is unmistakable in a 1937 Camp Wycliffe prospectus. Under the heading of "requirements," it was spelled out that the camp "is not interested in the swivel-chair type linguist, but rather in the type which at the cost of hardship and privation is willing to settle among primitive people and thoroughly learn their languages. For such . . . a virgin field (hundreds of extremely interesting languages about which little is known, and long-sought secrets about the relationships of peoples and streams of migration) offers an opportunity for service and discovery seldom surpassed in the realm of scientific research."[24] Linguistics formed the academic backbone of SIL, not seminary training in subjects such as theology and homiletics. Ken Pike, from day one, never had any quibbles with the "linguistic approach," as Townsend dubbed it. Indeed, he would be a steady and vocal apologist for the linguistic approach in the coming decades.

Pike and Nida continued to push for higher academic standards. As the summer camp's curriculum expanded and increased in sophistication, the school garnered a reputation as a rather grueling course of study. While a majority of candidates were of modest academic backgrounds, SIL would eventually distinguish itself by having more personnel with earned doctorates than any other single evangelical institution in the world.[25] Furthermore, from 1937 onward, Pike set a high standard in the classroom, and in the process acquired a reputation for being an awe-inspiring and sometimes fearsome professor.[26] The summer of 1937 was merely a harbinger of things to come. Yet, even at this early date, the Camp Wycliffe and SIL combination was parting ways with the Bible school movement, which valued spiritual ardor and simple piety over intellectual exertion. As Pike and Nida worked toward their doctorates at the University of Michigan, they brought a growing body of knowledge and experience to camp each summer. SIL's association with some of North America's leading linguistic scholars, and the necessity

---

24. "Announcement," 3.

25. "Five Principles," 18; Moore, "Editorial," 3. Note: While the number of PhDs in SIL in 1981, 188, represented only about 2.6 percent of SIL's 4,500 members, it nonetheless surpassed the combined total of thirty-four doctorate professors on the faculties of Asbury Theological Seminary, Fuller Seminary, Gordon-Conwell Theological Seminary, and Trinity Evangelical Divinity School in the early 1980s, see Noll, *Between Faith and Criticism*, 126.

26. This topic is taken up at length in ch. 7.

of providing tangible linguistic results in Mexico, worked against the evangelical propensity for activism over erudition. Yet, academic standards remained a live issue, and Pike would be at the center of future debates over this very question. He was a pacesetter on the academic front in 1937, not a follower, and would remain so.

The Question of Women in SIL

A 1936 Camp Wycliffe brochure encouraged "Single men between the ages of twenty and thirty" to apply. Neither married couples nor single women were invited, since Townsend and Legters had no intention of sending women to work in the isolated and often physically demanding locales where indigenous communities were found in Mexico. Hence the rustic setting of the camp in the Ozark Mountains, selected specifically for its lack of amenities. The camp's atmosphere was akin to that of a hunting lodge. Indeed, the camp brochure informed applicants that "a rifle and fishing tackle will not be out of place." In addition to studies, regular ten-mile hikes were mandatory for physical conditioning.[27] Camp Wycliffe was something of a male enclave, where hardy young men were readied for the rigors of pioneering missionary work.

Efforts to discourage women applicants failed. Two couples and three single women applied for the 1936 session. One of the married couples was L. L. Legters's son and daughter-in-law, Brainerd and Elva.[28] It would have been awkward to block their application, so Townsend and Legters acquiesced. The co-founders continued to rebuff the approaches of single women, but ultimately relented after "many requests had been made . . . to provide the same opportunity for young women as we did for the men." To accommodate them, a women's camp was set up several miles distant from the men's quarters under the supervision of a Baptist missionary, a Miss Helen Yost. Although encamped separately, classes and other activities were held in common. In its third year, the gender barrier of Camp Wycliffe was breached once and for all.[29]

Florence Hansen was probably the most academically qualified of the single ladies admitted to the 1936 session. She had majored in languages and was a Phi Beta Kappa at the University of California at

27. Camp Wycliffe, brochure, 1936, TA 43067.
28. "Camp Wycliffe Chronicle," 2.
29. Townsend, "Camp Wycliffe Activities," 2–3.

Los Angeles. Hansen earned high marks at camp, and Pike touted her as a "language shark."[30] Another of the women was none other than Ken Pike's younger sister, Eunice Victoria Pike. She was a graduate from the Massachusetts General Hospital, with a degree in public health nursing. Of the eight Pike children, Ken and Eunice were the two youngest and the two most interested in spiritual matters. Hence, Ken had prayed for and encouraged his sister to consider a missionary career. Sensing a call to missions, she passed up a well-paid nursing job to attend Camp Wycliffe. As with Hansen, she excelled in her studies, even besting her brother in Cherokee phonetics.[31] With the critical eyes of the men upon them, any academic or physical weakness would have been fatal to the women's aspirations. When they not only passed but excelled in all respects, it could not be claimed that women were unfit for the rigors of camp life and linguistic studies. "The young women's section of camp was highly satisfactory," Townsend reported to the Pioneer Missionary Agency. Convinced by their outstanding academic performance and adaptability to camp life, he now maintained that the admission of women should continue in subsequent sessions.[32]

The acceptance of women was an important and probably inevitable move, since the Camp Wycliffe and SIL combination confronted a long-standing reality: more women came knocking on the doors of missions than did men. "Without women," wrote historian Dana Robert in her *American Women in Mission*, "there would have been no faith missions." These "'worker bees' of the missions," Robert emphasized, "outnumbered men two to one."[33] As mission historian Ruth Tucker has pointed out, "the women's missionary movement itself had become the largest women's movement in the country" during the second half of the nineteenth century.[34] Denominational mission boards in North America responded to the swelling tide of women applicants in the late nineteenth and early twentieth centuries by becoming more discriminating of candidates' qualifications, especially their academic credentials. The faith missions were standing by to absorb this glut of candidates, since their criteria for potential missionaries focused more on spiritual vitality and passion for

---

30. Pike to Beach, October 14, 1936, PSC.
31. Pike to Fisk, June 13, 1936, PSC; Elvira Townsend, "Message," 1.
32. Townsend, "Camp Wycliffe Activities," 4.
33. Robert, *American Women in Mission*, 253.
34. Tucker, "Women in Missions," 252.

winning souls than on educational attainments.[35] By opening the door to women (or perhaps one should say forced open *by* women), Camp Wycliffe was now positioned to tap this overflowing stream of female missionary recruits.

Allowing single women students at Camp Wycliffe was all good and well, but sending them off to remote villages in Mexico was an entirely different matter. Townsend was not in favor of dispatching women into the hinterlands, whether singly or in pairs.[36] He was even less inclined after Legters roundly criticized the idea.[37] The three seminary men, Richmond McKinney, Brainerd Legters, and Max Lathrop, along with the women's chaperon Helen Yost, added their voices to the din of opposition.[38] The only women considered fit for work in rural Mexico were those accompanied by their husbands, who could see to their wives' welfare and safety. Ken Pike was the lone voice crying out in favor of allowing Eunice and Florence to work together in a translation project. It is not altogether clear why he took this position, but confidence in his sister was surely a weighty reason. As already noted of the 1937 session of Camp Wycliffe, where Pike challenged Townsend on academic standards, here he was once again courageously—or perhaps foolishly, considering the odds—defying conventional wisdom.

The attitude of the SIL men toward women was not uncommon in North American missions, as historian Ruth Tucker has concisely summarized: "The fact that Christian women have made their greatest ministerial impact in cross-cultural missions is due more to their vision and persistence than to their male counterparts' encouragement."[39] Around the turn of the twentieth century, many of the more-or-less semiautonomous women's denominational mission boards, which had become well-funded and influential entities, were consolidated with the principal denominational mission boards. This move to rationalize organizational structures was generally claimed as a drive for efficiency, but it was also a barely concealed effort at clawing back power from women. In the wake of these mergers, women were left in the minority and few thereafter held upper-level executive posts. And, even when they

---

35. Robert, *American Women in Mission*, 195.
36. Townsend to PMA, September 8, 1937, 7, TA 2102.
37. Townsend, "Hefley Interview," c. 1970, 1–2, TA 43558.
38. Pike to Evelyn Griset, October 24, 1936, 2, PSC; Pike, "Women in Wycliffe."
39. Tucker, "Women in Missions," 252.

did, upon retirement they were often replaced by men.[40] Faith missions on the other hand welcomed women with open arms, and in theory often promised them equality with men, even going so far as extending the right to serve as evangelists on par with ordained men. But all too often, theory fell victim to circumstance. Missionary women frequently found themselves at the mercy of ordained men, who shuttled them off to undertake domestic duties, orphanage work, and the teaching of native women and children, all occupations of which missionary men would not condescend to undertake.[41] Women suffered yet another setback in the wake of the modernist-fundamentalist controversies of the 1920s. While not every conservative evangelical was a fundamentalist, the fundamentalist movement exerted strong influence throughout much of the middle part of the twentieth century. As the rift between modernists and fundamentalists widened, some of the more vocal pulpit-pounders on the fundamentalist side argued that it was high time to restore the proper relationship between the sexes, with women subservient to men. The appearance of the social gospel and theological liberalism, it was claimed, could at least in part be explained by women usurping their biblically ordained status as subordinate to men.[42] The prevailing mindset among a majority of SIL men in 1936 was not by any means unusual. It was Ken Pike's outlook on the role of women that was remarkable.

Eunice Pike and Florence Hansen paved the way for women to attend Camp Wycliffe, and once there held their own with the men. With that achievement to their credit, they were not about to let male prerogative bar the way to Mexico. Townsend, never shy about sloganeering, often and emphatically exclaimed that SIL "trusted God for the impossible." Faith, for Townsend, was the motor action. In a bit of spiritual reverse psychology the two women played the faith card. How could he or any other man stand in their way when they were certain of God's call? Was God not powerful enough to take care of them too?[43] Cornered, Townsend relented, and the two women were assigned to work with the indigenous Mazatec. Pike accompanied them to Huautla de Jimenez, helped them settle in, and ten days later left them on their own. Hansen undertook linguistic research while Miss Pike put her nursing skills to

40. Hill, *World Their Household*, 166–67.

41. Robert, *American Women in Mission*, 205, 216, 224.

42. Tucker, "Women in Missions," 269–71.

43. Pike to "Friends," May 2, 1941, 1, PSC; Townsend to "Friends," May 2, 1941, 1, TA 2806.

work. Once again the two were on the spot; success or failure would determine the future for women in SIL.

The seminary trio remained indignant. Pike wrote Evelyn Griset concerning the matter. He protested that the seminary men and Miss Yost "sure tried to put the kybosh on the girls [sic] work." "Needless to say," he emphasized, "I hope you know I did not agree with them. I am happy sis is here."[44] Later, in December, he spoke of the men's displeasure in a letter to his sister. "Do not ask me," he wrote, "what the bunch is up to about you folks. I think they would send you girls home now, if they could, or else marry you off."[45] All the handwringing was for naught, since the pair pulled off an outstanding first season afield. In fact, they remained in their village location longer than any other SIL single man or married couple. "Your daughter," Townsend wrote Hansen's parents, "and her companion never faltered in their absolute confidence of God's ability to take care of them. Those of us who were responsible, inspired by their faith and courage, were forced to acquiesce and today rejoice with them over another manifestation of the unlimited faithfulness of our great Leader and close Companion [God]."[46] By the middle of 1937, Townsend had become an ardent defender of female translation teams. "Did Townsend tell you girls," Pike wrote his sister, "how happy he was that you stayed longer in the field than any of the boys had? He was quite exuberant about it when I saw him. Thought you folks had all the rest of the gang skunked."[47] Florence Hansen and Eunice Pike were but the first of many women through the door to pioneering work in SIL.

When the 1937 prospectus for Camp Wycliffe was published, the men-only qualification had vanished never to reappear.[48] A precedent was set, and translation teams composed of two single women would become some of the most celebrated and best publicized. Moreover, although organizational leadership remained firmly in the hands of men for several decades to come, full inclusion of women as translators and linguists opened the way in SIL for women not only to complete New Testament translations but also to pursue scholarship at the highest levels. For example, no fewer than twenty-eight SIL women earned doctorates

---

44. Pike to Evelyn Griset, October 24, 1936, 2, PSC.
45. Pike to Eunice Pike, December 3, 1936, PSC.
46. Townsend to Hansens, September 16, 1937, 2, TA 902092.
47. Pike to Eunice Pike, July 9, 1937, 1, PSC.
48. "Announcement."

by 1980.⁴⁹ Ken Pike, free of the sexist attitude of his colleagues, was once again well ahead of his contemporaries in SIL.

Serving Mexico

Cameron Townsend shaped his venture to fit the political realities of revolutionary Mexico. In doing so, his organization became an extension of the state itself. These moves entailed linking arms with the socialist aims of Mexico's revolutionary government. Townsend, when forced to defend his strategy, argued that SIL was "in Mexico to serve and not dictate policies to the Government. If it wants to teach the children of Mexico to share with one another as sincere socialists should, that is Mexico's lookout [sic] and not ours. . . . I went to Mexico," he emphasized, "not to oppose socialism, but to give the Word to people who have never received it."⁵⁰ For evidence of just how far he was willing to go in accommodating the political context one need look no further than the Inter-American Service Brigade. This was a program that he crafted in cooperation with Mexico's President Lázaro Cárdenas in the late 1930s to encourage young people from North America to undertake humanitarian projects in rural Mexico. Fashioned along the lines of the Peace Corps (which did not come into being until the 1960s), several of Townsend's workers were employed by the government to carry out linguistic research, literacy campaigns, and community development projects.⁵¹ For Townsend, the Pan-American aspect of the venture served the cause of international peace by fostering "respect and friendship" between nations.⁵² The brigade passed out of existence when Cárdenas left office in 1940, and it never expanded beyond Mexico. However, Townsend's internationalist vision would show up time and again as he expanded the work of SIL in Latin America and beyond.

Perhaps the best way to sum up Townsend's mind on serving governments is to quote his speculative thoughts on working in the USSR. "If you and I lived in Russia," he wrote in 1939, at the height of Stalin's repressive regime, "we would find that the life and love of God in

49. The role of women scholars in SIL is discussed at length in ch. 5.
50. Townsend, "Answer to Critics," 2.
51. Townsend to PMA, September 8, 1937, 1, TA 2102; Weathers, "Some Intimate Observations."
52. Townsend to Pike, November 4, 1938, PSC.

our hearts would be ample preparation for living under that regime and it would be less exacting than the Sermon on the Mount."[53] Townsend's optimism sometimes crossed over into naiveté, but his tally of triumphs fostered rather than dampened his idealism. As his organization gained traction in Mexico, he became convinced that it was possible for evangelical Christians to serve communists and socialists, provided one was willing to modify their understating of missionary activity in some rather creative ways. In fact, by Townsend's lights, it was not just possible but imperative.

From the outset, Pike went all in on the Townsend strategy. He took care to warn his family that he was not a missionary, and that they should therefore not address him as such. "I am a linguist, a scientist," he wrote his aunt in typical fashion.[54] Pike knew the score in Mexico, and had few if any qualms over the Townsend approach. "For some years the door [to Mexico] has been closed to new missionaries," he wrote James O. Fraser of the China Inland Mission. "We are admitted because of our linguistic research, while officials rather winked at our plans for Bible translation."[55] Pike understood the political dynamics at work in Mexico, where personal relationships often trumped the letter of the law. Whereas this style of personalist politics and government cooperation might give his fellow SIL members pause, Pike never suffered any pangs of guilt. He was therefore a consistent and welcome voice as Townsend labored to put his strategy into effect.

The establishment of SIL in Mexico as a scientific and humanitarian organization, albeit one with a religious core, created some very real tensions since it recruited many candidates from the fundamentalist wing of North American Protestantism. Some of Townsend's young linguist-translators experienced deep anxiety over cooperating with the Mexican government. Indeed, one couple had already resigned over this very issue. John and Isabel Twentyman concluded that "cooperating with the government was unscriptural."[56] After terminating their SIL membership, they went to Peru under the auspices of a traditional faith mission. Dissension on this point within SIL approached near catastrophic proportions in the late 1930s. The founder could have

---

53. Townsend, "Answer to Critics," 2.
54. Pike to Aunt Kate, April 7, 1936, PSC.
55. Pike to Fraser, October 4, 1938, 1, PSC.
56. Townsend to PMA, September 8, 1937, 1, TA 2102.

attempted to short-circuit the democratic approach to fashioning organizational policy by dint of force but, in this case, he could not risk a large defection for it would have crippled his nascent effort. Beyond that, it would have proved an embarrassment in the watchful eyes of the Mexican government. Townsend therefore scrambled to keep the ship afloat and everyone onboard.

The cozy relationship with Mexican officialdom did lead to some very unusual circumstances for Townsend's group. In October 1936, President Lázaro Cárdenas invited the entire contingent of SIL linguist-translators to a presidential banquet at the Chapultepec Castle. There was an uneasy moment during the reception when drinks were about to be served, but the distress subsided when non-alcoholic apple cider was also offered. The president, a teetotaler, never proposed toasts with liquor, although it was served at presidential functions and was on the table at this particular event. The banquet was a rather private affair. Aside from the twelve SIL members, there were only four government officials present: the president, the governor of the state of Michoacan, the governor of Quintana Roo, and the under-secretary of foreign relations.[57] Cameron and Elvira Townsend sat to the right and left of the president, and Ken Pike sat next to Mr. Townsend. Thus, Pike was later able to report on Townsend's conversation with Cárdenas, especially how he touted the powerful sociological effects of the Bible, and how it could instill readers with a work ethic and cure the evils of alcoholism. Along this line, Pike recalled that "Townsend took the occasion to comment on the fact [that] the President does not drink liquer [sic]. And added that none of us do."[58] If Townsend had cast his gaze at the opposite end of the table, where Eunice Pike was seated, he would have been aghast. After the event she dashed off a letter to her parents. "Perhaps I shouldn't tell you, but I had three sips of champagne. The first to find out what it was. The second to make sure that was what it was, and the third to settle . . . [the] argument."[59] For the traditionally-minded men of Townsend's group, was this not the sum of their fears? Not only had the door been thrown open to women, now one of the sex was imbibing champagne, and at a government function no less.

---

57. Nida to Folks, October 15, 1936, 1–2, TA 2065; Elvira Townsend, newsletter, October 15, 1936, TA 1974; Townsend, newsletter, October 15, 1936, TA 901974.

58. Pike to Folks, October 5, 1936, 4, PSC.

59. Eunice Pike to Folks, October 5, 1936, 3, PSC.

The Pike siblings were both pragmatists when it came to cooperating with the Mexican government. Unlike the Twentymans and the other traditionalists in SIL, they had few if any qualms over serving what was, at least by American standards, a socialist regime. They also displayed flexibility when it came to their missionary identity, willing to assume that of a linguist or nurse practitioner. Many others would eventually follow in Townsend's footsteps, but in the early years of SIL not all would do so with the ease of the Pikes. At a time when other evangelicals downplayed social work, emphasized evangelism, and wrung their hands over what they perceived as the communist threat to the American way of life, Ken and Eunice Pike wholeheartedly embraced the Townsend program in Mexico.

Marriage

When the Townsends took up residence in Tetelcingo in 1935, Elvira's precarious health rendered her incapable of doing much in the way of domestic work. Cameron freed himself from having to take up the slack by inviting his niece, Evelyn Griset, to accompany them. Griset delayed her senior year at the University of California at Los Angeles (UCLA) and passed the 1935–1936 academic year in a Mexican village. It was there that Ken and Evelyn first met, and Pike later recalled it was then that "I began to get interested for some reason which I might not even understand myself," and then admitted that he "rather forgot about it for a year." It was not until mid-1937 that his mind turned once again to Miss Griset, and he struck up regular correspondence with her. Griset, having earned her bachelor of arts degree at UCLA and studied for a year at the Bible Institute of Los Angeles, was anticipating further studies at Camp Wycliffe. As the 1938 session of camp neared, Pike concluded that he had fallen in love. In good evangelical fashion he put out a fleece, praying "that she might not get to camp unless God was in it." Griset appeared and, in Pike's words, "she was willing to be persuaded" to accept his marriage proposal.[60] The couple set their sights on Mexico, where they would work together on the Mixtec translation. They also decided that Mexico City was the ideal place for the wedding.

Evelyn's grandmother, "Deedee" Griset, worried over her granddaughter, since her mother had "never trained her for hardships."

---

60. Pike to Lula Griset, September 24, 1938, 1, PSC.

Evelyn's mother thought otherwise. She admitted her daughter had "not been subjected to many hard things in her life but," she asserted, "I think that she has the capacity to make what some would call hard, easy, because of her attitude toward it."[61] College mate and fellow SIL member Ethel Emily Wallace "marveled at this friend who was always upbeat, [and] impervious to depression."[62] In the years ahead, as Ken Pike shouldered leadership, administrative, teaching, and consulting duties, he repeatedly suffered periods of extreme psychological stress. Providence smiled on him, for without the steady and capable Evelyn at his side, it is very unlikely that Ken would have had such a successful missionary career. But that is to get ahead of the story.

Cause for anxiety was no farther away than the couple's wedding. Townsend was surprised but also delighted with news of the engagement. He was not pleased, however, with the plans for a small church wedding, where only SIL members and a few other missionary friends would be in attendance. Townsend, always on the prowl for opportunities to promote SIL, wanted a large and public wedding with Mexican officials present. Evelyn refused her uncle's designs. Ken was caught in the middle but wisely sided with "Evie," and a small wedding was planned for November 13, 1938, at the English-speaking Union Church in Mexico City.[63] When the marriage paperwork arrived from the government well ahead of the date planned for the religious ceremony, which in Mexico would simply endorse the legal civil union, the couple sealed their fate by immediately concluding the civil marriage. Townsend, still irritable over his thwarted ceremony plans, was aghast at the three-week interval between the civil wedding and religious ceremony. In effect, he reckoned they were only half married at best. "Either I don't know all the facts," he sniffed, "or else your getting married 3 weeks before the religious ceremony was a very foolish piece of business."[64] In order not to draw attention to the glaring time gap and to placate Townsend, it was agreed that the date of the civil union would be left off the religious ceremony announcements. But even this did not go far enough to please the founder, so invitations ultimately were issued by word-of-mouth.[65] Already a member of the SIL family,

61. Lula Griset to Pike, September 28, 1938, PSC.
62. Wallis, *It Takes Two to Untangle Tongues*, 13.
63. Grisets to Pikes, November 13, 1938, PSC.
64. Townsend to Pike, October 31, 1938, PSC.
65. Townsend to Pike, November 4, 1938, 1, PSC; Pike to Townsend, November 5, 1938, PSC.

Ken Pike was now wedded into the Townsend family, and "Uncle Cam" had no scruples over taking him to the woodshed.

The couple had their way on an intimate wedding ceremony, but Townsend dashed their expectations of an undisturbed honeymoon. In 1937, Townsend had organized a linguistic conference in Mexico City. The conference was designed to confer upon SIL academic cachet and to forge ties with Mexican academics.[66] A second conference was organized for 1938, where Mexican scholars and SIL linguist-translators would gather for lectures and the reading of research papers. When it was unexpectedly rescheduled for an earlier date, Townsend demanded the Pikes cancel their planned honeymoon so that Ken could attend all sessions of the conference. The newlyweds therefore passed their honeymoon in a Mexico City apartment, and Pike spent his days at the conference giving lectures and fielding questions.[67] Ken and Evelyn good-naturedly accepted the turn of events and counted themselves fortunate to have secured an apartment on the Paseo de la Reforma, "the most beautiful street in all of Mexico [City]."[68] That they took the change of plans in stride does not, however, alter the fact that Townsend insisted on disrupting their honeymoon. Indeed, in the future such demands from SIL's sometimes overbearing general director left Pike wounded and dispirited. Yet, he remained with SIL and continued to cooperate with Townsend out of a sense of higher duty. "I could not consider leaving," he wrote Edna Legters (L. L. Legters' wife) of the spoiled honeymoon, "without causing [a] serious breach in my loyalty to the work."[69] As will be seen, Pike's willingness to stay the course in SIL over the decades tells us much about his character.

After the Mexico City conference, the Pikes took up temporary residence in a rented cabin in San Miguel, while Ken supervised the construction of another for their permanent home. Evelyn proved resilient and good-natured. Even when in dire financial straits—empty pockets on three occasions in less than a month in the summer of 1939—she maintained her composure.[70] Evelyn was also proving to be an asset to her husband socially. When Ken returned for studies at the

66. Pike, diary, May 2, 1937, 1–2, PSC.
67. Pike to Miss Vandevere, November 15, 1938, PSC.
68. Pike to Gay, Lynn, and family, November 15, 1938, PSC.
69. Pike to Edna Legters, November 15, 1938, PSC.
70. Pike to Townsend, July 31, 1939, 1, PSC.

Linguistic Institute in Ann Arbor, Michigan, in 1939, she went along and thoroughly enjoyed the company of the linguistic scholars, "ole dandies" as she referred to them.[71] Ethel Wallis summed up Evelyn's nature by saying she had "spice and humor; a flair for excitement; a sense of style and spontaneity."[72] Pike considered himself lucky, but he also seemed a bit awed and perplexed by this vivacious woman who was in many ways so unlike himself. "What a strange intellectual mate," he confided to Edna Legters, "yet somehow I believe the Lord is being glorified."[73] In Evelyn, Ken Pike gained the perfect partner, one whose own strengths complemented his weak points. The old cliché that behind every successful man is a good woman was, in this case, no mere platitude.

When reflecting on the 1930s and 1940s period of Pike's life, one is struck by just how swiftly he moved from a failed China Inland Mission hopeful to a hardy pioneer missionary, PhD candidate, university professor, and progressive-minded player in the development of SIL. Of course the basic ingredients were always there, as seen in his life leading up to the China Inland Mission misfortune. Yet, these characteristics were offset by qualities that did not portend success either in the ministry or missions. Nervous, self-conscious, inhibited, and a procrastinator, not to mention easily fatigued by mental effort, taken together these characteristics suggest a young man beset by shortcomings that would confine him to something less than making a mark on the world.

Cameron Townsend sized up the young man, overlooked his flaws, and saw in him the makings of a linguist and Bible translator. Townsend offered him the opportunity to build his confidence and to develop his keen mind, the latter of which in its logical operations was well suited for linguistic analysis. Perhaps, above all else, Pike was reassured in his faith and conviction that he was doing God's bidding—in a sense this was the spiritual bedrock upon which he found stability in times of distress. Of course, such faith in the annals of Christian missions is sufficiently common place as to be unremarkable. Yet, without it few would have persevered. Given the opportunity to flourish, Pike proved to possess a durable alloy of physical stamina, academic prowess, progressive-mindedness, and conventional missionary ardor, the very combination of qualities that Townsend needed for his strategy to succeed.

71. Evelyn (Griset) Pike to Townsend, July 31, 1939, 1, PSC.
72. Wallace, *It Takes Two*, 14.
73. Pike to Edna Legters, November 15, 1938, PSC.

If everything seemed to be coming up roses for Ken Pike, it would not last. In the decades to come he assumed a long list of duties, including that of a linguistic consultant, a teacher at Camp Wycliffe (later folded into SIL), a professor at the University of Michigan, and the president of SIL. As his responsibilities mounted, they exacted a heavy psychological toll, almost to the point of mental collapse at times. Exacerbating the already heavy strain were recurring clashes with Townsend. He would also struggle with his own competitive nature, occasional impatience, and penchant for wounding others with biting logic. Through all of this he was fortunate to have Evelyn at his side. As the narrative unfolds in succeeding chapters, we have a story of a sometimes embattled and anguished soul. But it is also a tale of Pike's part in creating what must be the twentieth century's most unusual faith mission. Parting ways with tradition created almost unlimited opportunities for imaginative approaches to missionary thought and practice. It was, however, a path strewn with obstructions, twists and turns, and more than a few surprises. In retrospect, the latter half of the 1930s would prove to be Pike's halcyon days in SIL. Like Bunyan's Pilgrim, Pike had a long road in front of him.

4

Translator and Leader

It was the fall of 1936 and Ken Pike was living out his missionary dream. Even his hopes for China were rekindled. "Within ten years," he wrote Isaac Page of the China Inland Mission, "I should like to be in China. By that time my work in Mexico might well be finished if the Lord prospers me." Sensing that he had found his niche, he gushed with optimism. "A man who gives his entire time to language work alone, who is young enough to absorb that material quickly, who has special training for the work and can secure bilingual helpers, we figure should do that translation in five years [sic] time."[1] It would take him much longer, even with the help of other SIL translators. From the vantage point of 1936, he could not know all that would transpire over the coming decade. As already discussed in previous chapters, his summers were given over to teaching at Camp Wycliffe and attending the Linguistic Institute at the University of Michigan as he pursued doctoral studies. He also helped his colleagues with their research on Mexico's indigenous languages. This flurry of activity in the late 1930s only portended what would prove an even more eventful decade of the 1940s, at the end of which his future would look very different than he had anticipated.

Bible Translator

Pike first attempted to translate the New Testament into Mixtec entirely on his own. He soon realized the futility of this exercise, mainly due to his

---

1. Pike to Page, October 24, 1936, 1, PSC.

lack of proficiency in Mixtec. "One has to know the language very well indeed," he wrote his aunt, "to make satisfactory work by himself. A better job will probably be done by a native, even if bungled a bit, th[r]ough the medium of Spanish."[2] The assistance of one or more bilingual native speakers was essential. Pike therefore employed several men on various occasions, who were instructed to read a verse in Spanish and then recast it in Mixtec, after which he would write the translated verse on a three-by-five card. Once these first drafts were in place, Pike would check the grammar, reference the original Greek, and make corrections.[3] This was only the beginning of a long and tedious process of further refinement and editing. Not until 1947 would he have a complete draft of the New Testament in place.

On the surface translation might seem a rather straightforward process, but upon closer examination one is left wondering how SIL translators made any progress at all. The obstacles were daunting. In the first place were the enormous complexities they faced in deciphering indigenous languages so completely unlike anything they had ever encountered before. From rising and falling tones that altered grammar to varying vowel lengths that shifted the meaning of words to complex grammatical constructions, all these threatened to defeat their efforts even before beginning translation. Coupled with all this was the still underdeveloped state of structural linguistics. Indeed, SIL linguist-translators were themselves working on the cutting edge of linguistic research. When they finally turned to translation, they were faced with another host of challenges. In the main, the struggle to render an ancient Greek religious text into a language of another place, time, and culture. Why more of them did not give up in despair is a testament to their determination and grit in the face of the seemingly impossible.

In the second place, the men Pike relied upon for translation help were not accustomed to regular employment or keeping fixed hours, since their mode of existence revolved around seasonal agriculture. Frequent periods of inebriation among these men also undermined hopes for steady progress. Formal education was meager at best, and thus the Mixtec men's reading skills were hardly adequate for the work in which they were engaged. Above all else was the fact that few if any of these Mixtec men considered the task before them important. Their religious sentiments

---

2. Pike to Aunt Kate, October 30, 1936, 1, PSC.
3. Pike to "Ta ni taa!," 2.

were an amalgamation of traditional religion and folk Catholicism, neither of which had anything to do with the perusal of religious texts. For Pike, then, living and working in San Miguel was something of a conundrum. He enjoyed the rural life and the company of the Mixtecs, but he experienced near constant frustration over the pernicious social problems caused by rampant alcoholism and the lack of progress on translation. He believed the gospel held the key to personal and social remediation, but at the same time he needed the steady cooperation of at least a few Mixtecs in order to learn the language and to translate the scriptures. None of this was unique. Nearly all pioneering translators working in indigenous language groups faced similar situations.

Pike's early efforts to bring about conversions to Protestant Christianity had little effect. On occasion the men did make an effort to approximate Christian morality, but never with sufficient consistency to win Pike's approval. In one characteristic assessment of his translation helpers, he remarked that "Anecleto seems trying to live right, Nalo is a bit more dubious case. Their father is just as far from the Lord as ever, so far as I can see."[4] For these men, Bible translation must have seemed a rather abstruse undertaking. They were, at this point anyway, probably more interested in earning a little extra money than anything else. Pike's only recourse was to keep plugging away with the hope that, sooner or later, one or more of these translation helpers would experience a religious awakening, and thus come to consider Bible translation as important as did the SIL translator.

Coping with language helpers sometimes brought out the sharper edges of Pike's personality. At twenty-five, still young and somewhat immature, he was unable to recognize when his fangs came out in these early years of his missionary service. Moreover, he did not always comprehend with discernment the cultural context within which he was working. Although he enjoyed living with the Mixtecs, his frustration sometimes exceeded his measure of patience. For example, in early 1938, exasperation got the better of him when a Mixtec co-translator repeatedly misread a portion of John's Gospel. "I pulled his hair hard each time he missed a word," Pike jotted in his diary.[5] Here is Pike the overbearing pedant, seemingly oblivious to his callous treatment of this struggling, unlettered man. On another occasion he voiced frustration with their "little maid," a

---

4. Pike to Robby, December 29, 1937, PSC.
5. Pike, diary, February 23, 1938, 18, PSC.

Mixtec woman whom he accused of being a "dirty and filthy liar."[6] Pike's actions and sentiments clearly constitute cases of cultural insensitivity. In his defense, it should be recalled that all this transpired before the rise of missionary anthropology, a discipline that would go a long way toward ameliorating these kinds of problems. On the other hand, the reverse was also likely true. Mixtecs working for this sometimes testy expatriate missionary surely experienced their own vexations. (A regrettable fact of mission history is that the autochthonous experience is largely lost to us). With the passage of time and through experience Pike would acquire a greater degree of cultural sensitivity, even if he still struggled with his own emotions in some cross-cultural situations.

His mistakes notwithstanding, through immersion in the culture Pike was accumulating a valuable storehouse of insights and wisdom, not only about Mexico's indigenous languages but also about the speakers of those languages. Much of this knowledge was recorded subconsciously, remaining latent in his mind. One day, in the not too distant future, he would discover that the mysteries and vagaries of human experience would not as easily submit to structural analysis as theory suggested. The first few seeds for an entirely novel approach to linguistic theory were being sown even at this early stage. The telling of these fascinating developments must await their turn until chapter 6.

When Pike returned with his new bride, Evelyn, to San Miguel in late 1938, there was little change in the circumstances surrounding the Mixtec translation endeavor. The project was still plagued by a lack of real interest on the part of his translation helpers, but Pike soldiered on as best he could. Translation was held up too by a cabin building project that took up much of his time. While single, he was content to make use of less than ideal quarters. But now, with a wife, a larger and better appointed home was considered a necessity. While most of the manual labor was provided by men hired for the task, much of Pike's time was devoted to securing materials and making sure the cabin was built according to his design. As 1938 drew to a close, very little translation work had been accomplished and the spiritual results among the Mixtecs remained elusive.

In early February 1939, the Pikes began inviting the cabin construction crew to Saturday evening dinners. As the men gathered and waited for the meal one evening, Nalo—the "dubious" case mentioned above—of his own volition pulled a Spanish Bible off the shelf and began reading

---

6. Pike to Townsend, February 26, 1939, 4, PSC.

the creation story from Genesis to the gathering. This reading seems to have piqued their interest, and four of the men subsequently accepted Pike's offer of Bible instruction and literacy lessons. It is not altogether clear why Nalo suddenly became interested in the scriptures, but it would prove to be the breakthrough needed for the translation project to gain traction.[7] As the Pike's left San Miguel in early April for Camp Wycliffe, hopes were high that they were witnessing a spiritual awakening. When they returned in October, their optimism proved well founded. Picking up where they had left off, momentum built into January 1940, when Pike reported that the "carpenters are turned translators."[8] Aiming for a more natural and culturally appropriate translation, he continued the practice of having the Mixtec men make a first draft of the translation. Pike wrote that he wanted "to drain them of their ideas." In other words, he wished to obtain their interpretation rather than superimposing his own reading on the translation. He also sought to create a sense of local ownership through this process.[9] By March there were no fewer than five Mixtec translators laboring on the project.[10] Ultimately, as it turned out, the work done by this group of men proved inadequate, even as a basis for revision. The poor quality of the work was not altogether the fault of the Mixtec men, since much of the failure could be attributed to Pike's inexperience as a translator.

Yet, all was not a loss. The Mixtec men were engaging with the New Testament in a deep and comprehensive fashion. By recasting Spanish biblical texts into the indigenous idiom, the scriptures were being woven into the hearts and minds of these men. In Nalo's case, he went beyond conversion to propagation of the gospel.[11] Narcisco (Nalo's father) and his other son Letu seem to have also experienced a spiritual awakening during this period. While it could be claimed that these men were enticed by financial remuneration and hopes for other rewards that Pike could supply, there is evidence suggesting otherwise. Turning from their local deities and eschewing traditional sacrificial ceremonies were seen by other Mixtecs as both revolutionary and threatening to the social cohesion of the community. Pike recounted in early 1941 that these converts and their

---

7. Pike to Townsend, February 26, 1939, 4, PSC.
8. Pike to Townsend, January 21, 1940, 1–2, PSC.
9. Pike to "Ta nit taa!," 2.
10. Pike to Mr. and Mrs. Abrahams, February 19, 1940, PSC.
11. Pike to "Ta nit taa!," 2.

families not only suffered "oral abuse, loss of inherited land[,] and the harming of [their] domestic animals," but also "threats on their lives."[12] Despite these tribulations, the Mixtec translators agreed to tithe a portion of their meager salaries toward the publication of a Gospel.[13] It is very doubtful that these indigenous co-translators and converts would invite upon themselves these woes only to earn prevailing wages. It is far more plausible that, after firsthand immersion in the scriptures, they and their families found therein something worthy of enduring social ostracism and even bodily harm. All this is very much in keeping with scholarship produced in the last couple of decades demonstrating that indigenous agency was more responsible for the spread of Christianity outside of the Western world than were missionaries themselves.[14]

The turning point in Pike's struggle to produce a translated New Testament occurred when a young Mixtec man by the name of Angel Merecias joined the translation group. Merecias was an impressive and diligent translator. He learned to read Mixtec with preternatural ease and, with six years of schooling, he was the best educated of the group. Soon he was laboring alone, since his work was nothing short of outstanding. He produced a complete first draft of the entire New Testament, written out verse by verse on index cards. Pike then revised the epistles, SIL colleague Donald Stark revised the gospels, and Merecias proofed the orthography.[15] As the translation neared completion in 1946, Merecias accompanied Pike to California, where they could finish the final draft away from the inevitable interruptions of village life in San Miguel. After long days spent revising the text, the indefatigable Merecias passed his evenings typing completed drafts.[16] There is little doubt that Angel Merecias is one of the unsung heroes in the history of Bible translation.

Other SIL translators also discovered outstanding native talent during their translation efforts. In the 1940s, translator Herman Aschmann benefited greatly by the contribution of his Totonac co-translator, Manuel Arenas, who eventually pursued education in the

---

12. Pike to praying friends and churches, January 1941, 2, PSC.

13. Pike to Nida, February 22, 1940, 2, PSC.

14. Sanneh, *Translating the Message*; Kaplan, *Indigenous Responses*; Noll, *New Shape of World Christianity*, especially 77–93, 106–7.

15. Pike to "Ta nit taa!," 2; Pike to praying friends and churches, January 1941, 1, PSC; Pike to the editor of *Intercom*, January 29, 1991, PSC.

16. Pike to Townsend, February 5, 1947, 1, PSC.

United States and Germany and mastered several European languages.[17] Ultimately, the success or failure of a translation project hinged on the willingness of indigenous speakers to cooperate; and finding one who possessed both an interest in translation and a high degree of natural facility in the language could make for a far easier process and a much better translation.

Pike also received considerable help from a cast of expatriate SIL translators. As will be detailed below, he was away from San Miguel for extended periods, since his linguistic talent was called for elsewhere. He simply could not have completed the translation task without additional translators filling the gap. In addition to Evelyn, SIL translator Donald Stark was a key member of the translation team from 1942. SIL members Ruth Mary Alexander, Helen Ashdown, Ann Dyk, and Cora Mak also contributed to the project in various ways, including literacy work. But in a very real sense, it was Angel Merecias who was the star of the team. He created the foundation upon which the translated Mixtec New Testament was constructed. Hence, it was truly a product of indigenous origin and effort. That said, Pike was the major force behind the production of the Mixtec New Testament, and he was intimately involved in it from the beginning through the final editing and polishing process.

It was expected that the American Bible Society (ABS) would publish the Mixtec New Testament. As it turned out, they declined to print it. It was their policy only to publish translations that had passed through a rigorous series of prepublication steps, including orthography testing, translation testing of at least three gospels and some of the epistles for readability and comprehension, and the carrying out of an active missionary effort to establish a church and to insure a body of readers. As the ABS Committee on Versions saw it, SIL had not undertaken sufficient community testing of the translation and had failed to produce a sufficient number of readers.

The crux of the matter was centered on the differing missiological views of SIL and the Bible Society. It was the opinion of the ABS that a wide-ranging missionary program should accompany any translation project. In other words, translating the Bible was not an isolated undertaking but only one part of the larger effort to establish a "self-sustaining" church.[18] In SIL's view, the translated scriptures could, in some sense,

---

17. Steven, *Manuel*; Steven, *Manuel: The Continuing Story*.
18. North to Townsend, December 12, 1950, 1, TA 6498.

replace the missionary. In other words, as SIL saw it, a translated New Testament could, on its own, do the heavy lifting of spreading the gospel in lieu of a full missionary program. Pike would later argue that the "*Scriptures are a means of evangelization*—not just a means of strengthening the church. Hence the Scriptures are exceedingly useful in going ahead of the place where the church exists."[19] To state the matter in somewhat simplified terms, the Bible Society believed that the scriptures should be embedded into the church; according to SIL, the Bible alone could help to create a church. With the two organizations unable to find common ground, SIL had to look elsewhere for getting the Mixtec New Testament published.[20]

When the Mixtec New Testament appeared in 1951, it was one of the oddest Bibles ever put out under the auspices of SIL. Publication was funded by the Tract Club of the Air, a Canadian ministry headed by the Rev. A. J. McAlister.[21] Typed on an early IBM electric typewriter, the final version was printed by Edwards Brothers of Ann Arbor, Michigan, a firm that was not set up to print and bind Bibles. Hence, the Mixtec New Testament came out in hardback with light green boards. The original letter-size typewritten pages determined the final dimensions of the volume. It was large, to say the least. At slightly over eleven inches tall and nine inches wide, Mixtec readers found it unwieldy. "First reports from the field," Pike informed McAlister, "indicate that believers are very happy to have the New Testament. They have suggested that a smaller size might have been helpful so that when trying to read in the sun the shade of their hats would be large enough to cover the entire page."[22] At least Pike could take solace in the fact that it was being read.

The Mantle of Leadership

For Ken Pike, 1942 was a momentous year: he garnered the first doctorate by an SIL member, was appointed as the president of SIL, and became a charter member of the board of directors of WBT and SIL at the time

---

19. Pike, "Our Own Tongue," 4, (emphasis in the original).

20. The ABS-SIL relationship is covered at length in Aldridge, *For the Gospel's Sake*, 96–108. Note: SIL would eventually come, in part, to agree with ABS on this matter, and in recent decades the two organizations have worked together harmoniously.

21. Nyman to McAlister, January 3, 1951, PSC.

22. Pike to McAlister, September 18, 1951, PSC.

of their official incorporation.²³ Down to 1942, the Pioneer Mission Agency (PMA) had served as the home office for the informally organized SIL contingent in Mexico. When the group surpassed one hundred members, the PMA requested that Townsend form his own mission. In addition to incorporating SIL, Wycliffe Bible Translators was created and incorporated as the US-based arm of the WBT-SIL dual organization. Pike and Nida (who was appointed as the vice president) were given full charge of the academic aspects of SIL. Townsend, who much preferred blazing new trails, gladly relinquished this responsibility, and for the most part he left academic decisions to SIL's newly installed president and vice president. On the other hand, Pike's appointment to the board would prove to be a source of frustration for both men. Townsend, as general director, had placed himself under the authority of the board of directors. Hence, on matters of sufficient importance to require board action, Townsend would, in theory at least, be subordinate to Pike. This position, as Pike soon discovered, could be a very uneasy one when the general director threw his weight around.

Pike's leadership status and scholarly visibility—as well as SIL's increasingly sophisticated linguistic research—were recognized by the American Bible Society. In 1943, at the request of Eric North, general secretary of ABS, Pike traveled to South America where he surveyed several Quechuan languages in Peru, Bolivia, and Ecuador. He then co-chaired a conference of missionaries convened to establish a standardized orthography for these languages. The thirty-one-year-old Pike played an incomparable role in the proceedings. Although he later reported suffering "severe nervous tension" in guiding the various parties of the debate to a compromise, he made a good showing of it.²⁴ After the event a number of missionaries sent unsolicited letters to North praising Pike. One attendee, in remarks that conveyed the general sentiment of her fellow missionaries, wrote that Pike "most ably engineered the conference. His quick grasp of the material, and his clear and impartial decisions, inspired one's confidence and respect. His ability to comprehend all sides of the problems in a clear and well outlined manner, took us over many knotty questions in a way that perhaps another personality should not have been able to do."²⁵

23. Townsend to PMA, September 10, 1941, 2, TA 902724; "Consent to First Meeting."

24. Pike, "General Report," 5.

25. Quote from Myers to North, 1; Speed to North; Cammack to North; Case to North; Woodward to North.

The letters sent to North suggest that it was a placid conference, but Pike's correspondence reveals there was contested ground between him and the ABS co-chairman, John Ritchie. Here we catch a glimpse of Pike the pugilist. Moreover, and importantly, this debate also highlights both his understanding of the doctrine of biblical inspiration and his views on Bible translation at this relatively early point in his missionary career. After the conference, he wrote his parents that he had put an "intellectual hammer-lock" on the "fiery A.B.S. representative," who he referred to as a "fighting fundamentalist," over questions related to biblical terms. Ritchie and the Bolivian contingent of translators argued for the elimination from Quechua translations any Spanish or Spanish-derived terms that might connote Roman Catholic doctrines. Pike argued to the contrary that translators should select the word or words most commonly used and best understood regardless of origin, whether Spanish or Quechuan. After all, Pike reminded the conferees, the New Testament quoted the Septuagint, a Greek translation of the Hebrew Old Testament. Therefore, contemporary translators should "trust them [Spanish loan-words] to be purified by Scripture context the way Greek pagan terms were." Pike went one step further, conjecturing that the "Lord" divinely appointed the use of the Septuagint in the New Testament "from choice, just to keep us from being fussy, to the point of nonsense."[26] In this example we have what is probably the first indication of his non-fundamentalist and non-literalist views on the doctrine of scriptural inspiration. At the time, in the mid-1940s, it should be noted that this moderate position was not at all in keeping with a majority of conservative evangelical expositors, most of whom would have taken exception in greater or lesser degree to Pike's perspective. Not until some younger and more progressive fundamentalists undertook to reform the fundamentalist wing of North American evangelicalism in the 1950s and 1960s, would such a position gain any legitimacy, and even then it was cause for bitter internecine battles. Pike maintained this moderate view throughout the rest of his life and, as we will see, he was influential in steering WBT-SIL away from an overly narrow doctrine of biblical inspiration.

Pike's South American excursion proved notable in yet another way when a series of improbable encounters opened the door for SIL to enter Peru. Obtaining a passport and gaining permission to leave the United States during World War II was the first obstacle. Pike carried

---

26. Pike to Mom and Dad, notes from a February 1944 letter, PSC.

with him a letter of recommendation from the University of Michigan linguist Charles Fries to the State Department in Washington DC. When he appeared at the Cultural Relations section, the administrator not only knew of Fries, but also had a copy of Pike's phonetics book on hand in which Fries had written the foreword.[27] His scholarly credentials noted, Pike's passport was duly stamped and he was cleared to embark for South America.

In Lima, he trembled at the prospect of making a personal call on the Peruvian ministry of public education. As was his habit at such moments, he dropped to his knees at bedside to pray. To his SIL colleagues he later confessed that this act of faith produced no confidence, but "I was there—[it was] my job. I had to tackle it."[28] Gritting his teeth, he made the appointed office call where he unexpectedly met an official who had attended one of his lectures at the University of Michigan. During this encounter, Pike was invited to give a series of lectures on phonetics to high school teachers of English while in Lima. Then, after describing SIL's work in Mexico to Peruvian Minister of Education Enrique Laroza, Pike obtained a letter of invitation for SIL to establish a similar program in Peru. Pike's university connection, his scholarly standing, and SIL's willingness to partner with governments all proved eminently useful in opening the way for the organization to enter Peru.[29] Clearly the young man acquitted himself well as he obediently fulfilled the sometimes difficult tasks laid upon him. None of this was lost on Townsend.

By the second half of the 1940s, Pike was one of SIL's most experienced members. With proven leadership abilities, he was an obvious choice for second-in-command to Townsend, who proposed in late 1946 that his top linguist should assume the role of deputy general director. Pike resisted, not wanting to become even more entangled in administration than his present duties demanded. Although willing if forced to assume this role, he was extremely reticent to shoulder the burden. "Executive work and the bearing of responsibility," he informed Townsend, "have been distasteful to me[,] since the tiny tastes of it I have had have cut my technical efficiency very heavily. It has been a source of relief that for ten years I have been able to concentrate on being a linguistic mechanic instead of dealing directly with the plans of

27. Pike, "General Report," 1.
28. Pike, chapel talk, "1943 Peru Visit," 1, PSC.
29. For a detailed account of SIL's work in Peru see Aldridge, *For the Gospel's Sake*, 109–49.

our workers or bearing responsibility for helping to direct our advance or watching over public relations." He also, as he had in the 1930s, considered himself undisciplined, and therefore "unqualified."[30] A perfect example comes from 1943, when he was at his family's home in Woodstock, Connecticut. "I have just finished a very inefficient week at home," he confided to Evelyn. "Where I expected to get a lot done," he confessed, "a hidden . . . lazy streak developed and I didn't. The article I had hoped to write failed to exert its priorities over a wild west story and piddling."[31] How could he, he asked Townsend, "direct others when one cannot adequately control oneself?"[32] Pike nearly always accomplished more than his worries over indolence suggested, but the potential for administrative duties undercutting his ability to produce scholarship was a very real concern. Hence, there was every reason for his wariness over taking on the duties of deputy director.

Although Pike managed officially to avoid the post of deputy general director, Townsend informally regarded him as such; thus, a vague sense of obligation continued to weigh on him. Furthermore, Pike remained the president of SIL, co-directed Camp Wycliffe along with Nida, and served on the board of directors. He was not, therefore, shielded from the two most significant conflicts that occurred in the development of SIL in the second half of the 1940s. The question was whether or not his leadership skills, mental fortitude, and faith would be sufficient to see him through events to which we now turn.

SIL and the University of Oklahoma at Norman

Throughout the 1940s, Camp Wycliffe continued to strengthen its academic program and expand numerically under Ken Pike's and Eugene Nida's direction. By the end of the decade, there were more than two hundred students (both prospective SIL members and non-SIL participants) attending summer sessions.[33] By this time too, a few of SIL's better qualified linguist-translators were embarking on doctoral studies. William Wonderly, who would go on to play an important role in the development of the Spanish *Versión Popular* of the Bible, was awarded a PhD

30. Pike to Townsend, December 18, 1946, 1, PSC.
31. Pike to Evelyn (Griset) Pike, October 8, 1943, PSC.
32. Pike to Townsend, December 18, 1946, 1, PSC.
33. Pike, "Statistics on Camp Wycliffe."

from the University of Michigan in 1948. Richard "Dick" Pittman and Robert "Bob" Longacre earned doctorates from the University of Pennsylvania in 1953 and 1955 respectively. Both of these men were headed for bigger things in SIL. These three were only the first of several hundred SIL men and women to earn doctoral degrees in the coming decades. All this suggested that the organization was on course to become a major contributor to the discipline of structural linguistics. Yet, the attainment of that goal was by no means assured. SIL first had to escape from a backlash of fundamentalist separatism and a spasm of anti-intellectualism.

By the early 1940s, Camp Wycliffe had attained a remarkable level of academic expertise. When Della Brunstetter, a University of Oklahoma at Norman instructor, attended the summer course, she was duly impressed and initiated discussions resulting in an invitation for SIL to affiliate with the university. Pike and Nida were attracted to the idea of garnering academic gravitas and accreditation for SIL courses. A cooperative program would be advantageous to both parties. The state of Oklahoma was home to a large number of Native Americans, whose ancestors had been dispossessed of their aboriginal lands during the nineteenth century. Surrounded by a number of Native American languages, many threatened with extinction, the university was ideally located for the investigation and documentation of these languages before they ostensibly passed out of existence. What the university lacked was expertise in linguistics, and this was something that SIL could supply. Also in SIL's favor was the above average number of Christians on the faculty of the university. The institution was therefore sympathetic, or at least acquiescent, to SIL's religious mission, even though it was a state university.[34] The Summer Institute of Linguistics (the Camp Wycliffe name was officially dropped at this point) and the University of Oklahoma at Norman entered into a formal agreement in 1942. Although the partnership was interrupted in 1943 and 1944 due to World War II, classes resumed in the summer of 1945. The old Camp Wycliffe venture was no longer a provincial missionary endeavor in rural Arkansas; it was now, under the SIL banner, a full-fledged school of structural linguistics.

By ramping up the rigor of its academic program, and by riding on the coat tails of Pike's and Nida's scholarship, SIL was making a name for itself in the field of linguistics. Nevertheless, there was good reason to doubt that it could survive the move to Norman. Many students were

---

34. Pike to Folks, June 27, 1942, 1, PSC.

already struggling with the demanding coursework, and some potential students even feared to enroll. One SIL student with a medical degree, and thus presumably well equipped for studies, was finding the coursework so demanding that he could only manage five to six hours of sleep a night.[35] Students at SIL's recently established summer course in Canada were faring so poorly that closure of the program was considered.[36] Just how difficult was the summer course of study? A trainee returned from the 1946 summer session at Norman to the Bible Institute of Los Angeles bearing such "gory tales . . . about Camp Wycliffe and its stiff curriculum" that it struck terror into the heart of a would-be candidate.[37] Townsend, observing all this, complained to Pike that the present academic program was simply "too intensive for most students." As a remedy, he recommended easier courses for underperforming students and advanced classes for "outstanding pupils who find the course easy." But he was not optimistic about the latter, doubting "if there are any such."[38] Townsend had hit upon a pertinent question: Could SIL attract a sufficient number of qualified students from within the evangelical movement to accomplish its aims?

Likewise, post-graduation performance of SIL graduates on the field was not always up to par. Many were struggling after they took up language learning and linguistic work in Mexico. In 1945, Pike and Nida examined the translation and linguistic performance of all one hundred SIL translators in Mexico. The results were telling. According to Pike, he and Nida "flunked a bunch of the folks and [told] them they might as well get busy or go home." Indeed, some were sent packing.[39] Another indicator of inadequate linguistic competence was the rejection of papers submitted for publication. In early 1946, Pike sent four articles produced by SIL members to *American Anthropologist*, the journal of the American Anthropological Association. "To be quite frank," wrote editor J. Alden Mason, "none of them was up to the professional standard of articles for the Anthropologist." This was hardly happy news, even if Alden did print two shorter pieces in the "Brief Communications" section of the

35. Townsend to Nyman, November 6, 1946, TA 4166.
36. Cowan to Pike, October 30, 1946, PSC; Pike to Cowan, October 18, 1946, PSC.
37. Quoted in Wallis, *Lengthened Cords*, 98.
38. Townsend to Nyman, November 6, 1946, 1, TA4166.
39. Pike to Reginald Pike, November 5, 1945, 1, PSC.

journal.⁴⁰ SIL was mostly attracting practical-minded evangelical students, a majority of whom simply wanted to get on with the missionary task. Yet, the courses at SIL and linguistic research in the field demanded the application of the intellect. Pike and Nida faced an uphill battle getting recruits and new linguist-translators to rise to the occasion.

Joining forces with academia outside of the evangelical subculture was perhaps an even more significant hurdle than was keeping up academic standards. Down to the time of the University of Oklahoma cooperative program, Camp Wycliffe only admitted evangelicals. Course brochures and catalogs of the 1930s bluntly stated that "no modernist need apply." Moreover, Camp Wycliffe had long functioned as a major part of the candidate approval process for those who wanted to serve with SIL. Now, with the admission of any and all academically qualified students to SIL classes, there was confusion over whether or not the door had been inadvertently thrown open for non-evangelicals to become members. In any case, with the move to Norman, SIL could no longer act as the gatekeeper to its courses, since students could now register through the university.

The realities of the new situation were soon felt. In 1946, SIL found itself in the awkward position of having both conservative faith mission boards and liberal mainline denominational mission boards sending new recruits and veteran missionaries to the summer courses. Moreover, the Foreign Missions Conference of North America, an organization that was more broadly based and less doctrinally conservative than most faith missions, recommended SIL to its member missions.⁴¹ The pitched battles between fundamentalists and modernists of the 1920s and 1930s were largely over, but the old battle lines remained. Throwing faith mission students together with the more liberal-minded missionaries was potentially explosive. Upping the stakes was the fact that the thoroughgoing evangelistic and spiritual atmosphere, which had always prevailed at Camp Wycliffe, was toned down to accommodate the public university setting. This curbing of religious expression held the prospect of sparking student unrest, especially at a time when there was a nationwide surge of religiosity among evangelical youth. The postwar rise of the evangelical youth movement, which included Youth for Christ, Inter-Varsity Christian Fellowship, and the Urbana Missionary Conferences,

---

40. Mason to Pike, June 22, 1946, 1, PSC.
41. Pike to Townsend, July 9, 1946, TA 4460.

were all about dynamic religious expression.⁴² For SIL to go against the tide and throttle this youthful religious enthusiasm on campus or in the classroom was risky. After all, these missionary candidates had shown themselves to be the most committed of all by volunteering for foreign service, and therefore likely to be the most vocal of all about their faith and beliefs.

The actual appearance in 1946 of theologically liberal students at SIL Norman sparked some dissension. SIL secretary and board member William Nyman informed Pike that "I positively do not favor accepting modernists as such, even in our schools."⁴³ Townsend hoped to limit or block those of a liberal persuasion by admitting only "pioneering missionaries." He reasoned that few "modernists care to pioneer and fewer to pioneer and translate the Word of God[,] which to them isn't much more than just another book." Townsend expanded his commentary, declaring that,

> God has led us into a broad contact and has used us in it. We have had unique opportunities in witnessing to atheists, communists, Catholics, etc. and it is all through willingness to serve everybody even as our Lord kept company with a lot of folks that Pharisees proscribed. I wouldn't give up this breadth of testimony for anything, but I don't have much of a hankering to work among the Sadducees. If the Lord Himself should send along a few, however (but make it very, very few, please Lord!) I would expect Him to save them or at least protect us from any difficulty.⁴⁴

Pike flatly disagreed, pronouncing that "I am very strongly opposed to any policy which lets them [modernists] in in a routine way, whether or not they be few or many." "I would," he emphasized, "prefer to see us serve fewer people if it amounts to that, or even ultimately break our connection with the University."⁴⁵ All this amounted to a classic case of fundamentalist separatism, and SIL was on the verge of dismantling the cooperative venture with the university.

As it happened, the 1946 summer session of SIL proceeded with only mild grumbling, and the courses ended without any resolution on

42. Shelley, "Rise of Evangelical Youth Movements."
43. Nyman to Pike, July 25, 1946, TA 4579.
44. Townsend to Pike, July 14, 1946, TA 4313.
45. Pike to Townsend, July 31, 1946, PSC.

the question of admitting non-evangelical students. In the interval between the 1946 and the 1947 summer sessions, Pike reversed his stance on the issue. At least part of the reason for his sudden about-face is to be found in California, where he and Angel Merecias were working on the Mixtec New Testament translation. Among the various translations of the Bible they used for reference were the "Goodspeed Bible" and the recently published New Testament portion of the Revised Standard Version (RSV).[46] *The Bible: An American Translation*, more commonly known as the "Goodspeed Bible," was a translation crafted in the 1930s by Edgar J. Goodspeed, a professor at the University of Chicago.[47] Goodspeed also served on the translation committee for the RSV. The translation of the RSV was carried out under the auspices of the International Council of Religious Education, which was later folded into the National Council of Churches (NCC). As the flagbearer of the more liberal mainline wing of North American Protestantism, fundamentalists naturally anathematized the NCC and most anything related to it. When the RSV translators chose to render the Hebrew word *almah* in Isaiah 7:14 as "young woman" rather than "virgin," conservatives read it as an attack on the doctrine of the virgin birth of Christ.[48] In North Carolina, a pastor burned a page from the RSV.[49] With Cold War hysteria in full bloom, even the House Un-American Activities Committee joined in the furor by investigating the RSV translators. Likewise, Senator Eugene McCarthy cast aspersions on the NCC.[50] Pike had the opposite reaction. Working at the translation desk in late 1946 and early 1947, he had "found that the translation by Goodspeed and the new Revised Standard Version were helpful." "I hated to admit," he explained to his colleagues at Norman in 1947, "that I got anything from them and to think that I should consider them enemies. But we owe (them) a debt. We also owe a debt to Goodspeed."[51] Pike was clearly moving away from the typical fundamentalist's one-size-fits-all characterization of liberal Protestantism.

In this same period, Eugene Nida was also distancing himself from fundamentalism. "I used to hate modernists," he once admitted.

---

46. The complete Revised Standard Version of the Bible was published in 1952.
47. Thuesen, *In Discordance*, 71.
48. Thuesen, *In Discordance*, 124.
49. Thuesen, *In Discordance*, 97.
50. Thuesen, *In Discordance*, 102.
51. Pike, "Minutes," 36.

He confessed to calling out theological liberals by name from the pulpit when preaching in the second half of the 1930s, and had even broken off relationships over doctrinal matters. As he took up work with the more moderate and broad-based American Bible Society, he was obliged to work with fellow Christians of a theologically more liberal temperament. This experience widened his perspective on Christian cooperation. "I used to think they were awful," Nida acknowledged, "but now I know them better."[52] Ken Pike and Eugene Nida, the two most important figures in setting the direction of SIL's academic program in the 1940s, were coming to see that Protestants of a more liberal persuasion were not perforce the enemies of Christianity.

By the beginning of the 1947 session of SIL at Norman, Pike and Nida were unapologetically prepared to accommodate the university setting. They therefore ended the practice of opening classes with an invocation. That same summer three students suspected of liberal tendencies were present for SIL courses. There were also Roman Catholic students roaming the university campus, and there was every reason to believe that they might register for SIL's courses. Events quickly spiraled out of control. There was widespread unrest among both students and SIL faculty, with no fewer than six faculty members threatening outright resignation.[53] Pike and Nida were suddenly faced with the very real possibility of their efforts to buttress SIL's academic credibility with the university connection collapsing under an onslaught of reactionary sentiment.

The crisis culminated on the evening of Saturday, July 26. This was the very same day that Pike received confirmation from the university administration that SIL could not bar applicants based on their religious beliefs.[54] Facing the SIL faculty, Pike braced for a grueling session, anticipating the worst. "I don't expect," he declared, "it to be entirely a pleasant evening."[55] With occasional reinforcement from Nida, Pike steadily built his case. At times he pummeled his opponents, in other moments he turned to incisive logic, and once he even gave way to pathos. If there was ever a test of his leadership, of his ability to win the confidence of his

---

52. Nida, "Minutes," 26–28.
53. Pike to Townsend, July 29, 1947, 1–2, TA 4847.
54. Balyeat to Pike.
55. Pike, "Minutes," 1.

SIL colleagues, this was it. The very shape that the SIL academic program would assume in the future hung in the balance.

Pike first argued that if the cessation of classroom prayer was distressing to an individual, then one would not likely thrive in SIL, where the policy of "service to all" necessitated cooperation with non-evangelicals and even non-Christians. Put more simply, the practice of dropping prayer was probably the least offensive issue under discussion.[56]

Having given no quarter on that question, he mounted the argument that it was imperative for SIL to maintain the university connection. In the face of counter-arguments from the floor that SIL could sever the university link and set up its own technical school (something less than a university-level institution), he unstintingly held out for research, scholarly publishing, and more linguist-translators earning advanced degrees. Abandoning the University of Oklahoma cooperative venture in order to establish a practical technical institute was, in Pike's mind, tantamount to intellectual suicide. Having sold Mexico and Peru on SIL's scholarly merits, it was absolutely essential to live up to those claims. "As long as we tell anybody that we are scientists," Pike admonished the faculty, "in my opinion it is absolutely essential that we do not be liars. We claim that we are scientists, we must be scientists. . . . In going to Mexico," he went on to emphasize, "we have committed ourselves to the linguistic approach; now we have to deliver the goods or change our tune and pull in our horns."[57] On the question of academic credibility, Pike was inflexible.

Discussed too was the topic of whether or not it was proper for SIL to share its research, textbooks, and literacy materials with liberal Protestant and Roman Catholic missionaries.[58] One faculty member wished for SIL to lockup textbooks and publications at the home office, only sending copies to evangelicals upon request. Was SIL scholarship only for its own religious ends, or was it to be shared with the scientific community? This question touched on the very nature of SIL. As Pike pointed out, the organization's articles of incorporation stipulated that published research was to be shared with the scientific community and with governments.[59] In effect, the entire SIL enterprise was founded upon the principle of engagement with the academy, both at home and abroad.

56. Pike, "Minutes," 19.
57. Pike, "Minutes," 15.
58. McMahon, "Minutes," 5.
59. Pike, "Minutes," 7.

Pike clearly saw that if SIL took a separatist turn, then the organization would cease to exist as originally founded. Worse yet, by severing the link with academia, SIL would likely experience academic decline. As such, SIL would make a limited scholarly contribution—or perhaps no contribution at all—to the wider world.

There were also pragmatic reasons for remaining engaged with academia. Pike believed that rubbing shoulders with liberals and Catholics at Norman mirrored the realities of Mexico and Peru, where SIL members routinely interacted with non-evangelicals and even non-Christians. Therefore, Pike declared, "make it your business to learn how to get along with people you don't like, whom you consider your enemies and the enemies of the Lord, because those people may be the ones formulating government policies in the country to which you are going."[60] Cooperation with non-evangelicals was a fact of life in SIL, and he insisted that students and faculty might as well practice it in the classroom and on campus.

In the end, the debate centered on the question of whether or not faith mission students, and much more importantly SIL's own students and faculty, could tolerate sharing the classroom with non-evangelicals, which was a given if the university connection were maintained. SIL had for the past decade drawn on the resources of academia, and more specifically from leading linguists such as Leonard Bloomfield and Edward Sapir. There were two questions in play here. Was not research and scholarship a two-way street? And, if so, did this not mean working with non-evangelicals and even non-Christians? Pike was unequivocal, SIL should remain a member of the secular academic community.

At what was perhaps the most tense moment of this long evening, Pike began a recollection of the deceased Edward Sapir, a linguist whom he held in high esteem. Since Sapir had been good to SIL, Pike mused, should not SIL return the favor by supporting the discipline of linguistics? His emotions quickly surfaced, and he wept over Sapir, worrying that the late linguist was "sizzling in hell." "The only thing we can really do to repay them [secular linguists]," he sobbed, "is get them to heaven, and I don't know how to do it."[61] This emotional interlude produced a strong effect on those present. Debate and discussion continued, but resistance to Pike's arguments waned.

60. Pike, "Minutes," 18.
61. Pike, "Minutes," 19–20.

It was after midnight when a tired and subdued faculty finally voted on the issues under consideration. The mood had shifted over the course of the evening. Given the opportunity to voice their concerns, and at last mollified (one is tempted to say punch-drunk) by Pike's arguments, no one moved the resolution to separate from the university. Hence, it was stillborn. A second motion was moved. By a vote of twenty-five to seven, a resolution passed requesting that the SIL board of directors not accept candidates who refused to sign the organization's doctrinal statement for membership unless a majority of five or more directors agreed.[62] The board unanimously approved this recommendation in September 1947.[63] This policy effectively blocked the membership path for non-evangelicals into SIL, while still allowing all comers to gain entry to courses at Norman through the university admissions process. This move ensured that SIL would remain an evangelical organization, while still maintaining its wide-ranging relationship with the scientific community.

Just as he had in Peru during the Bible Society conference, Pike once again proved he could handle a restive assembly and broker consensus. In neither case did he settle for the middle ground. Through a combination of rational argument and passionate emotion, Pike instilled his colleagues with the conviction that SIL was best served by open cooperation with the academy rather than turning inward. The road thus remained open for further academic and scholarly advancements. It also left the door open to Roman Catholics, who in small numbers enrolled for SIL studies in the coming years. Considering the conservative evangelical subculture in which the summer of 1947 events took place, all this was quite remarkable. Yet it was not all smooth sailing ahead. On several occasions in the future, Pike would again have to argue for academic rigor and scholarship. His leadership and stature would be especially important after Nida resigned from SIL in 1953 to serve full-time with the American Bible Society. But all that lay in the future; for the moment, he could push ahead with the linguistic approach and all that this strategy entailed. Indeed, the recent tumultuous events seemed to have created a sense of cooperation among the faculty. The evidence, although inconclusive, suggests that none of the SIL faculty at Norman in the summer of 1947 left the organization over the matters under consideration. In any case, an overwhelming number can be identified as remaining with SIL

---

62. Pike, "Minutes," 39.
63. SIL Board of Directors, Minutes, September 9, 1947.

for several more decades. Free and open discussion in the democratically structured SIL proved immensely useful in this particular case. "The whole thing was very painful to all of us," Pike told Townsend in the wake of July's events, "but without exception, so far as I know, the staff has come out of it with a unity such as we have never had here before and an understanding of each other and the problems involved."[64] Pike had both rallied the troops and slayed his Goliath.

The Missionary Aviation Controversy

Ken Pike had opened the door for SIL's entry into Peru, but it was Cameron Townsend who established the organization's work there beginning in 1946. Taking up work in Peru fulfilled a two-decades-long dream of his. Although he would not attempt a translation project himself, Townsend was nonetheless animated by the challenge of taking the gospel and the Bible to Peru's isolated indigenous people. The logistical problems of reaching the remote tribes inhabiting the Amazon basin offered him the opportunity to resurrect another dream, launching a missionary aviation operation.

With his uncanny penchant for appearing on the scene when important personages or public figures were anywhere in the vicinity, it comes as no surprise that Townsend was in the right spot at the right time to meet United States Army Major Herbert A. Dargue in Guatemala, during the aviator's 1926 Pan-American Goodwill flight that circumnavigated South America.[65] Townsend's imagination was fired, and he concluded that aviation was the key to opening up the isolated Amazon basin for missionary work. While still serving with the Central American Mission (CAM) in 1930, he began pitching an "Air Crusade to the Wild Tribes."[66] The frugal CAM leadership wanted no part of what they considered an expensive and fanciful idea. But now, with his own established mission, Townsend sensed that the moment was ripe to bring his idea to fruition.

But there remained one rather large obstacle in his way. The SIL board of directors saw no reason to establish an aviation program since the recently established Missionary Aviation Fellowship (MAF), formed

---

64. Pike to Townsend, July 29, 1947, TA 4847.

65. Dargue to Townsend, April 11, 1929, TA 1415; Dargue to Townsend, January 4, 1930, TA 1615; Townsend, "Airplane Crusade."

66. Townsend to Legters, April 24, 1930, TA 1529.

by several former military aviators, was already providing aviation services for SIL in Mexico, and was ready to supply the same in Peru. The men, and one woman—Elizabeth "Betty" Greene—who founded MAF were cautious and deliberate.[67] Their military training had taught them the hazards of flying, and they also wished to keep operational costs to a minimum. Townsend had bigger plans in mind. He envisioned a far-reaching, multiple-aircraft service with a team of pilots and mechanics. WBT-SIL's founder was creating an entirely new style of evangelical mission, one that was outside the mainstream of faith mission tradition where penny-pinching was the order of the day. Whether it ever happened or not, the old saw about spendthrift churchgoers sending missionaries used tea bags has a whiff of the truth about it. Thus, MAF envisaged beginning with one aircraft and a single pilot-mechanic in Peru. There was not a solitary aviator among the men of the SIL board. Therefore, the board preferred to rely on the services of MAF.[68]

The makings of a controversy were in place. Twenty-five years later, Pike recalled the events surrounding the MAF issue as one of the most stressful moments in his SIL career.[69] For the first time the relationship between Townsend and Pike would be tested to its utmost limits, since the general director was not about to give up his dream without a fight. When convinced that God was on his side, it was always easy for him to believe that the board members were collectively in the wrong. "There is one thing which I have been very careful about the past three years," Townsend had once exclaimed in the face of internal opposition, "and that is to FOLLOW and not dictate to the Lord about where and how He leads. He has given me many a surprise and upset many an old idea but I have endeavored always to be deaf to my own and others' counsel and listen only to His."[70] Nothing had changed in the interval, and Townsend was just as certain of his actions and God's leading in the 1940s as he had been in the 1930s.

Frustrated with MAF and its economizing ways, Townsend complained in November 1946 to the MAF's secretary-treasurer, Charles Mellis, that a single-pilot operation in Peru fell far short of what he believed was required. He also contended that the MAF leadership suffered

---

67. Buss and Glasser, *Giving Wings to the Gospel*.
68. Goodner to Townsend, April 13, 1948, TA 5545.
69. Pike, "Chief Turning Points," 5.
70. Townsend to Lathrop, January 27, 1939, TA 2478.

from a "lack of vision."[71] Mellis bristled at this, and rebutted to the effect that SIL's general director should confine his efforts to Bible translation and let MAF do the flying.[72] Townsend was not having any better luck convincing SIL's board of directors to authorize his aviation plans. There was general agreement that more than one pilot and perhaps an extra plane should be provided, but the board was committed to seeing these details hammered out in cooperation with MAF.

Annoyed at being rebuffed on all sides, Townsend, who was in Peru in mid-January 1947, ordered Pike to meet with Mellis and instructed him to "find out if you can get him to see my viewpoint."[73] Three weeks later he repeated the demand. "You will not need to try to represent the Board in this case, or even mention your own opinions—simply be my ambassador." The ambassadorial commission was less a diplomatic move than an ultimatum, and Townsend went on to add that until such time as the WBT-SIL board of directors should undertake to replace him in Peru, "I am leading the work here, and there is no choice in the matter."[74]

Pike was in a difficult position. From an executive point of view, Townsend was Pike's superior. But from the board perspective, the general director was more-or-less subordinate to Pike. The general director had backed Pike into a corner. He could either capitulate or come out fighting. Since the MAF-SIL relationship was inter-organizational, not a matter of internal affairs only, Pike took the position that the MAF issue was a board-level matter. Indeed, he saw Townsend's demand for what it was, nothing less than a bald attempt to quash Pike's judgment and bypass the board. "I decline this new commission," he informed Townsend, since "I have already accepted others, as when the [SIL] group put me on their board, and therefore I cannot ignore these responsibilities, even for you, when in my judgment as one of their representatives it would not be to their best interests."[75] Pike was clearly upset, and he complained of Townsend's dictatorial "Stalin plan" to SIL's director in Mexico, Dick Pittman. Pike also sensed that his situation was perilous, fearing that

---

71. Townsend to Mellis, November 30, 1946, TA 4237.
72. Mellis to Townsend, December 18, 1946, TA 4375.
73. Townsend to Pike, January 16, 1947, 1, TA 4770.
74. Townsend to Pike, February 8, 1947, TA 4762.
75. Pike to Townsend, February 14, 1947, 2, TA 4911.

Townsend might charge him with "insubordination."[76] The line in the sand between the two men was clearly drawn.

During a series of SIL board meetings in May 1947, an attempt was made to resolve the growing tension between Townsend and the board. Beyond the MAF question, there were also issues related to the board's oversight of Townsend's appointment of personnel in Peru. Little was achieved. In fact, a despondent Pike came away from the gatherings in Mexico City believing that his relationship with the general director had suffered permanent damage. He poured out his frustration in a ten-page letter to Evelyn. "As far as our personal relationships are concerned, I do not see how they can ever be reestablished on the basis they had previous to last fall." Pike was deeply hurt by Townsend's accusation that he had "sold him down the river" by backing the status quo on the MAF issue.[77] Overcome by emotion during the meetings, Pike at one point verbally resigned and was intent on walking out of the room until board secretary Nyman—an older man with a cooler disposition—convinced him to return.[78] The meeting ended with no resolution of the points under discussion. Townsend took the board's position as a lack of confidence in his leadership; and the board considered the general director's demands for unrestricted action in Peru as verging on autocracy. The crux of the matter hinged on the limits, if any, of the general director's range of action in Peru and the board's desire for a greater level of organizational cohesion and cooperation.

In April 1948, the board of directors met in Glendale, California, with the MAF issue again on the agenda. Pike, who would be absent, cabled that he fully supported the board's previous recommendations and was "absolutely" against ending the MAF relationship.[79] A day later, E. S. Goodner informed Townsend that the directors were unanimously opposed to a break with the MAF, believing that any differences could be ironed out.[80] Feeling himself shackled, Townsend raised the ante. "I cannot return to Peru," he wrote Pike on April 27, "unless I have full charge

---

76. Pike to Pittman, February 18, 1947, PSC.

77. Pike to Evelyn (Griset) Pike, May 19, 1947, 1–2, PSC; Pike, "Hefley Interview," tape two, 11.

78. Pike to Evelyn (Griset) Pike, May 19–20, 1947, 2, PSC.

79. Pike to WBT-SIL board of directors, April 12, 1948, TA 5079.

80. Goodner to Townsend, April 13, 1948, TA 5545; WBT Board of Directors, minutes, April 12, 1948.

of the aviation program."⁸¹ He also informed MAF's president, James Truxton, that he had reached the limit of his patience with MAF's "shoe string" frugality and emphatically demanded full control over the MAF's air operations in Peru, including, rather audaciously, charge of their personnel.⁸² Left only with the unpalatable option of forcing Townsend's hand, the board instead acquiesced and voted unanimously to form the Jungle Aviation and Radio Service (JAARS) under the auspices of SIL.⁸³

The unanimous vote, however, requires qualification. Only four of nine directors, which constituted a quorum under the bylaws, were present at the meeting in California: WBT-SIL secretary William Nyman, home office manager Rolland Cole, Wycliffe deputation secretary Earl Wyman, and California businessman E. S. Goodner. Moreover, to read the board minutes of this vote in isolation would be to miss entirely the prolonged and contentious battle that Townsend waged to gain control of the aviation program in Peru. Pike, to his credit, let the vote and the formation of JAARS pass without comment. Nor did he hold a grudge over the matter. In 1956, he even expressed his appreciation to Townsend for the JAARS operation in Peru, where he was conducting a linguistic workshop. That said, Pike was no pushover. He would fight for what he believed was the right policy. But, as these kinds of controversies recurred, he found them increasingly difficult to manage emotionally. In some sense, that probably accounts for why he washed his hands of the aviation matter after the California-based directors acquiesced to Townsend's ultimatum. It was, in all likelihood, a relief to have the matter behind him.

Whither Bound?

Despite the friction between the two men, Townsend never lost faith in Pike. Nor did he stop insisting that Pike should take up greater administrative and leadership responsibility. In late 1949 and into early 1950, Pike led the first session of SIL courses offered in Australia. He also made a side trip to New Guinea in anticipation of SIL's establishing work there. In Townsend's mind, Pike was ideally suited to lead the advance into New Guinea, and into the Asia-Pacific region more widely. As for Pike,

   81. Townsend to Pike, April 27, 1948, TA 5325.
   82. Townsend to Truxton, April 27, 1948, TA 5321.
   83. WBT Board of Directors, minutes, May 21, 1948.

he continued to insist that he was neither cut out for such an endeavor nor would he find any joy in the task. Townsend brushed aside the younger man's concerns, maintaining he could "develop a technique for handling this work . . . without any more headaches than other executive work you [already] do."[84] For all his confidence in SIL's chief linguist, on this matter it was nonetheless misplaced. In the first place, such a move would have seriously damaged SIL's hard-won academic reputation. Not for the last time, Pike carefully but forcefully reminded Townsend of the labors involved in developing and maintaining SIL's academic credibility and scholarly production. He also took pains to explain that the kind of theoretical linguistic work in which he was engaged would be impossible by "one who is pressed by personnel problems or the weight of immediate responsibility." Pike clearly understood that heavy executive responsibility would undercut his ability to keep up with the scholarly literature and limit his ability to publish. "Such keeping abreast," he implored, "is a serious struggle, Uncle Cam, and cannot be done as it should without lots of time."[85] Townsend simply did not understand that scholarship was more than a sideline for Pike, it was his life and mission.

In the second place, Pike emphasized personal reasons for not taking up an executive role.

> [M]y own personal preferences, and I suspect psychological build, enters into the picture. For some reason or other, I can stand considerable academic controversies and differences of opinion, in a way that the Lord allows me to go ahead without serious loss of efficiency. . . . On the other hand, the pressures of administration and personnel problems very soon eat into my time, energy, drive, punch and contribution to the work of the group. It seems impossible to hope that I could get into [a] difficult administration situation and still continue top academic production.[86]

The battle of scientific ideas was, for Pike, far removed from the delicate arts of executive leadership and personnel administration. He was better fit for the academy than the executive suite, and he therefore pushed for Dick Pittman to lead the advance into New Guinea. Pittman, who was rather more a disciple of Townsend than was Pike, would prove

---

84. Townsend to Pike, April 18, 1950, TA 6457.
85. Pike to Townsend, July 26, 1950, 1, PSC.
86. Pike to Townsend, July 26, 1950, 2, PSC.

eminently qualified for the task. As time and events would reveal, Pike's unmoving stance on this matter was one of the more important decisions he ever made, both for himself and for the organization.

In a way it was Pike's introspective nature that created hazards for his psychological balance. In 1973, when he was sixty-one years old, he reflected on what he called "Chief Turning Points," which were defining events that had occurred over the course of his life. Two particular incidents from the period covered in this chapter stand out. He was the main speaker at a 1948 Inter-Varsity weekend retreat. After one of his presentations, a young lady in the audience posed a question pertaining to Catholic mass. Pike's rejoinder was, in his own words, "very vigorous." The girl was offended by his sharp remarks and she walked out of the conference hall. After the session ended, an Inter-Varsity staff member "gently suggested" to Pike "the need for gentleness." "It about killed me," he recalled. "The shock of seeing myself as tough that way gave extreme pain and helplessness. I asked God to change that—or take me home." This is clearly the prayer of an anguished man. The second episode occurred in 1954. Pike was meditating on scripture when he came across a verse instructing Christians "to pray for those who spitefully use you." As he reflected on this passage it carried him back to the summer session of SIL in 1947, where he took to the bully pulpit in mounting his case that SIL should maintain its collaborative program with the University of Oklahoma. He had taken up "cudgels" to win the debate. "For me it had been 'The sword of the Lord and of Gideon' – and slay. Now I was told to pray for a blessing on these people I had been praying against. . . . I wept."[87] Townsend had thicker skin; such introspective self-criticism was seemingly not a part of his experience. But for Pike, such occasions would recur on his life's journey.

The cooperative venture between SIL and the University of Oklahoma at Norman for which Pike had fought, and the ongoing commitment to research and publication he insisted upon, pushed SIL further along its trajectory toward what would one day become a world-class institution focused on linguistic research and the development of indigenous languages. As SIL had in Mexico, in Peru it also worked closely with various governmental departments in literacy, education, and language development. It was here too that Townsend would turn his flying operation into the equivalent of a nationwide airline service that joined hands with the

---

87. Pike, "Chief Turning Points," 5.

Peruvian military, thus taking the "service to all" strategy far beyond its original meaning.[88] In breaking with traditional missionary thought and practice, WBT-SIL was taking on all the characteristics of what would later be known as a parachurch organization. From shortwave radios to aircraft to linguistics, SIL made full use of technology and science to achieve its ends. Townsend and Pike, in their respective spheres of action, pushed the strategy of "service to all" and the "linguistic approach" to their logical conclusions. As SIL expanded its reach around the world, it continued to forge partnerships with a host of governments and universities; and, by doing so, it had an immeasurable impact on indigenous language development and mother-tongue education around the world.

None of this was visible to Pike in the late 1930s. He had once thought that at the rate of one New Testament translated every ten years, he could, if his luck held, expect to produce perhaps as many as five in his missionary career. As he and Angel Merecias pushed to finish the Mixtec New Testament in California in early 1947, Pike took time out to write Townsend. "Man how I envy you," he rhapsodized over the work in the Amazonian jungles just getting underway. "I would like to be down there on the rivers. Just to think of the boys back in the jungle, the naked savages with their long spears and arrows, and painted inquisitive hostile scowls waiting to crack apart to face-wide grins when you speak their mother's lisp at'em, boy I wish I could be right with them tonight!"[89] He still had fire in his belly for pioneering missionary work (and still beholden to contemporary notions about indigenous cultures). Yet, even at this point, he knew that his future lay elsewhere. The world of linguistics and academia beckoned. There would be no pioneering in the jungles or mountains or deserts. As the decade of the 1940s was coming to a close, Pike's fertile mind was germinating an entirely novel linguistic theory; one that was no less pioneering in the field of linguistics than what Townsend was carrying out on the missionary front in Peru. He was also faced with the prospect of making SIL into a respected international institution of applied linguistics. It is to this story we now turn before taking up Pike's theoretical work in the following chapter.

88. Aldridge, *For the Gospel's Sake*, 129–42.
89. Pike to Townsend, February 5, 1947, 2, PSC.

5

Serving and Defending SIL

CAMERON TOWNSEND WAS THE creative genius behind the WBT-SIL venture. He had shaped his organization to fit the contours of revolutionary Mexico in the 1930s. He had also promised Mexican officials much in the way of linguistic scholarship on indigenous languages, more in fact than he could deliver at the time. But the arrival of Ken Pike and Eugene Nida at Camp Wycliffe boosted SIL's prospects. These two men initially did much of the academic heavy lifting required by SIL's government contracts. As it turned out, Nida spent a large portion of his time at the American Bible Society from the early 1940s until his resignation from SIL in 1953. Therefore, while Nida's contribution to the formation of SIL should not be underestimated, in the long run Pike was the chief architect of the organization's academic advance. In the words of historian William Svelmoe, "the best thing that ever happened to Cameron Townsend was when a skinny, insecure China Inland Mission reject named Ken Pike hitchhiked his way to Camp Wycliffe."[1] As we have seen, Pike actually turned out to be a hardy missionary in Mexico, and then made rapid progress as a scholar and translator. By 1950, he was in his eighth year as president of SIL, had taught at the University of Michigan for as many years, and, with the help of Angel Merecias and Donald Stark, had a completed New Testament translation to his credit.

As Ken Pike began crafting his linguistic theory, tagmemics, in the 1950s (discussed at length in the next chapter), he was also hard at work building the Summer Institute of Linguistics into a reputable international

1. Svelomoe, *New Vision for Missions*, 255.

institution. The summer training program held in cooperation with the University of Oklahoma at Norman proved a roaring success. SIL's own students, other evangelical faith missionaries, mainline denominational missionaries, Roman Catholic nuns and priests, and even those with no religious interests, all found SIL courses eminently useful. Riding a wave of increasing demand, SIL developed cooperative linguistic programs with the University of North Dakota and the University of Washington. It also set up linguistic courses in England, Australia, and Canada in these years. Pike was on the scene in both England and Australia as a leader, teacher, and administrator. He was also largely responsible for SIL gaining notice as a significant player in academia, not only in North America but also in Europe and Latin America. All this was in some sense a culmination of Townsend's vision, which required a radical reworking of traditional faith mission theory and practice. As SIL cooperated with governments, downplayed its missionary nature, and concentrated on developing its linguistic expertise—not to mention transporting Catholics in its aircraft and opening its classrooms to them—other faith missions began to look askance at this odd hybrid of a mission. In the 1950s, SIL increasingly found itself the subject of controversy within the faith mission community, and Pike was drawn into these conflicts. He was at once intellectually suited for helping to steer SIL through this rocky terrain, while at the same time temperamentally ill-suited for these encounters. The price he was paying did not become obvious until the 1960s, when internal SIL skirmishes began to take their toll, revealing that he was perhaps already in the 1950s depleting a reserve of psychological strength that could not easily be replenished. His success at building SIL and his survival through trials are a testament both to his deep commitment to Townsend's overall strategy and his spiritual fortitude. Had Pike not possessed both of these attributes, it is unlikely that SIL would have achieved the international stature that it did, for Townsend could never have pulled it off alone.

Making an International Reputation

Cameron Townsend was an entrepreneur and a pragmatist. For him the means unto an end were just that, provisional undertakings that could be dispensed with when the ultimate goal was at hand. For example, he argued that once a New Testament was translated and an initial literacy effort completed, then any ongoing social service projects should be "dropped into the lap of the national government."[2] SIL, he reasoned, "can't be tied up indefinitely with these tasks that are, as regards us, primarily to get the doors open."[3] He tended to treat scholarship in the same pragmatic fashion, and sometimes underestimated the commitment of time and effort required to build and maintain SIL's academic reputation. Pike, deeply enmeshed in academia, understood what was at stake. He acknowledged that in the 1930s, SIL "got away with murder in the [scientific] conferences and publications, simply because no one knew better."[4] In the late 1930s, Mexican education authorities and anthropologists had little by way of comparison to judge SIL's linguistic work, in large part because the discipline of structural linguistics was in its infancy, and therefore academically underdeveloped. This state of affairs did not endure for long. By the mid-1940s, SIL was compelled to produce better quality scholarship or risk ejection from Mexico.

Under Pike's and Nida's leadership the caliber of SIL publications improved to the point of being regularly published in professional journals. On various occasions, however, Pike was forced to remind Townsend that keeping up with the scholarly literature and producing articles suitable for scholarly journals took more effort than the general director imagined. Townsend's concerns ran in the opposite direction. He feared that an overly academic SIL would limit the participation of ordinary working linguists, thus slowing his drive to multiply translation projects as rapidly as possible. Moreover, at times he worried that high thinking itself was unproductive. In the early 1950s one of SIL's best minds, William Wonderly, began working on a theory of translation that opened up debates over biblical inerrancy. Townsend was no hardliner on inerrancy and considered debates over the doctrine of inspiration of little utility. In his opinion such deliberations were a form of theorizing best left alone. If someone said they believed the Bible was true, that was enough to satisfy him. Wonderly was, in Townsend's mind, committing two sins. He was inciting controversy in SIL over the doctrine of scriptural inspiration, while at the same time propagating an ostensibly superfluous translation theory. "Surely," Townsend wrote Pike, "that theory isn't essential to good translating. Then, why wreck us over it?"[5] In other words, Wonderly

2. Townsend, Report to Board of Directors, 1.
3. Townsend, "What is Our Task?," 3.
4. Pike to Ernest Pike, March 25, 1940, 3, PSC.
5. Townsend to Pike, June 15, 1955, TA 11335.

should quit theorizing and simply get back to the basics of translation. Pike's confidence in Wonderly was unshaken. SIL classrooms were not limited to teaching. They also functioned as linguistic laboratories where new ideas were explored. Pike therefore, against Townsend's wishes, encouraged Wonderly to continue teaching and developing his theory.[6] Pike's concern was the inverse of Townsend's. He fretted over too little intellect in SIL rather than too much.

Pike's insistence on academic rigor and theory development paid off. SIL linguist-translators were making real contributions to the discipline, and there was a strong demand for the research that SIL produced in this era. At a 1953 Linguistic Society of America meeting, Charles F. Voegelin, editor of the *International Journal of American Linguistics*, urged Wonderly to press SIL linguist-translators to write more morphological studies, since they were leading the field in this area.[7] The University of Oklahoma at Norman also noted the improved quality of SIL scholarship. In order to capitalize on SIL's mounting prestige, the school requested that SIL "by-line" the university connection whenever journal articles were published.[8] Perhaps the most unexpected praise came from linguist Bernard Bloch of Yale, who had been a severe critic of Pike's early scholarship. He was also known as a rigorous and demanding teacher. Bloch was obviously impressed with SIL's school at Norman. Writing to Pike after a 1961 visit, he acknowledged that he was "tremendously impressed with the dedication and the seriousness of all your people, and with the excellence of your program."[9] SIL also advanced in the domains of literacy and bilingual education. Townsend had designed his own approach to literacy in the 1920s, the psycho-phonemic method, a simplified approach for helping new readers to gain confidence.[10] Beginning in 1948, SIL's Sarah Gudschinsky joined forces with Eunice Pike to refashion Townsend's approach into a more effective teaching method.[11] In 1951, SIL's literacy work came to the attention of the United Nations Educational, Scientific and Cultural Organization (UNESCO) at a time when it was making a major study of literacy methods and

6. Pike to Wonderly, May 30, 1955, TA 11340.

7. Wonderly to Pike, September 11, 1953, 2, PSC.

8. Cross to Pike.

9. Bloch to Pike, July 22, 1961, PSC.

10. "Biographical Information"; Townsend, "Suggestions"; Townsend, "Psycho-phonemic Method."

11. Gudschinsky, "Literacy."

experimenting with bilingual education. Pike was invited to a major UNESCO conference in Paris, where he read a paper on "The Problem of Unwritten Languages."[12] UNESCO went on to request additional research help from SIL, further increasing the institute's visibility in the international educational and development community. In 1953, SIL established an experimental bilingual education program in cooperation with the Peruvian government, which was subsequently expanded and then continued for the next two decades.[13] By dint of Pike's unflagging efforts, along with the help of Eugene Nida and a small but growing cadre of scholars, SIL was on its way to becoming a respected international institution of applied linguistics by the mid-1950s.

None of this came easy. Expecting SIL linguist-translators, many of them without graduate training, to craft articles for publication in scholarly journals was asking much, perhaps more than could be expected. It was an uphill climb, and many papers were returned time and again by publishers for revision. Yet, Pike and Nida were unrelenting in their push for publication. Their insistence bore fruit. At the 1948 and 1949 annual Linguistic Society of America meetings, Pike noted that approximately a fifth of the twenty to twenty-five papers presented were read by SIL members.[14] By 1955, the organization's linguist-translators had produced materials on seventy languages, including books, monographs, journal articles, and literacy primers.[15] Marking SIL's arrival as a full-fledged scholarly institution was the appearance of the July 1957 edition of the *International Journal of American Linguistics*, in which the entire roster of articles was authored by SIL personnel.[16] The articles therein also demonstrated that SIL was also on the leading edge of grammatical research, the new frontier in the discipline. In Pike's words, "it showed that SIL has begun seriously to move into grammar on a broad front rather than with isolated, occasional articles and monographs."[17] For an organization with its roots in the subculture of North American fundamentalism, this publication record was an outstanding achievement. SIL was clearly

---

12. Pike, "Problem of Unwritten Languages"; Vasquez to Pike, July 31, 1951, PSC; Pike, "Report Concerning SIL," 4.

13. Larson, "Overview," 38.

14. Pike, "Report of the General Director's Appointee," 1–2.

15. Pike to Baker, November 1, 1957, 3, PSC.

16. *International Journal of American Linguistics* 23 (1957) 119–218.

17. Pike, "Report of the President," 2.

leading the way out of fundamentalist anti-intellectualism and proving that evangelicals could produce serious scholarship.

Academic production was given a boost when SIL implemented a program of linguistic workshops, where Pike could lend a hand to struggling linguist-translators and assist them in developing and polishing their papers for publication. In late 1950, a pilot workshop was held in Mitla, Mexico. Although the basic concept proved itself, Pike's demanding schedule prohibited staging another session for several years. For the 1955-1956 academic year, the University of Michigan granted him a sabbatical for the express purpose of conducting a linguistic workshop in Peru.[18] Similar sessions were also held during summers at SIL in Norman, which essentially functioned as graduate seminars.[19] A precedent was set. Over the course of the next several decades, Pike traveled to SIL branches around the world holding multi-month linguistic workshops where he mentored hundreds of SIL linguists. The University of Michigan recognized the scholarly value of these workshops and granted Pike additional sabbatical leaves. The original contributions to the science of linguistics coming out of this program were not inconsequential. Pike listed a number of these discoveries from the Peru session of 1955-1956: the first observation of a five-tone language in South America; finding a never-before documented rounded front vowel in Cocama; and the discovery of a new stress system in the Campa language. Furthermore, a theoretical treatment of verb suffixes in Candoshi would, he noted, impact the teaching of linguistics in North American universities.[20] SIL was on the cutting edge of American structural linguistics at a time when descriptions of Amerindian languages were all the rage. Workshops certainly augmented SIL's publication record, but they also brought Pike into contact with hundreds of indigenous languages. By the 1960s, he was probably the most field-experienced linguist in the world.

The workshop program was also something of an incubator for advancing the careers of SIL's up-and-coming professional linguists. By way of example, twenty-six-year-old Mary Ruth Wise attended the Peru workshop, where she demonstrated above-average aptitude with her analysis of Yánesha, which Pike pressed her to publish. A decade later Wise would be one of the first generation of women in SIL with a

---

18. Pike to Rice, October 18, 1954, PSC.
19. Pike to Matteson, January 26, 1955, 1, PSC.
20. Pike, "Report on Studies," 6.

doctorate. Over the years Pike identified and encouraged countless young scholars. A few of the earliest and most notable were Joseph Grimes, who did path-breaking work in discourse theory and earned a doctorate at Cornell University in 1960; Robert Longacre, who advanced Pike's tagmemic theory of linguistics in a number of directions and earned a PhD at the University of Pennsylvania in 1955; and Sarah Gudschinsky, who specialized in historical linguistics and earned a doctorate at the University of Pennsylvania in 1958. Another, although not as well remembered today in SIL since he moved on to the University of Hawaii, was Howard McKaughan, who earned a PhD at Cornell in 1957 and was a notable SIL teacher.[21] As these and other scholars took up significant roles as consultants at workshops, Pike was freed eventually to lead only the advanced sessions and work on the most difficult of linguistic puzzles.

Under Pike's leadership SIL led the way in another area where evangelicals were slow to innovate, encouraging women to fill professional academic roles. The scarcity of women in Christian academia was not limited to evangelical institutions, few religious schools or seminaries in mid-twentieth century North America accorded women equal status with male faculty.[22] At the time of Fuller Seminary's founding in 1947, women were not allowed in classrooms, not even as auditors.[23] For the 1948-1949 academic year, wives of married students were permitted to take some classes for credit. Women in Christian academia were generally relegated to departments of Christian education, a track that did not lead to the pulpit. Fuller followed this pattern and established a Department of Christian Education. Hence, gender segregation remained a feature of the school.[24] An entirely different atmosphere prevailed in SIL. As a steadily increasing number of SIL women linguist-translators showed promise, Pike placed them in teaching and consulting positions, and encouraged them to pursue graduate and postgraduate studies.

Pike's continued insistence that women should be allowed to pursue scholarship to the limits of their ability paid off handsomely. Just how significant was their contribution to linguistics? A 2011 study carried out by Margaret Thomas, a professor of linguistics at Boston College, found that outside of SIL there were only three women who played a major role

21. McKaughan left SIL in 1963 to take a position at the University of Hawaii, and in 1964 became chairman of the university's Department of Linguistics.
22. Migliazzo, "She Must Be a Proper Exception," 4.
23. Marsden, *Reforming Fundamentalism*, 123
24. Migliazzo, "She Must Be a Proper Exception," 6, 10, 17.

in North American linguistics in the middle part of the last century: Alice Vanderbilt Morris (1874-1955), Gladys Amanda Reichard (1893-1955), and E. Adelaide Hahn (1893-1967).[25] Underrepresented in the discipline at large, women scholars comprised a substantial minority in SIL. Thomas noted that the 880 articles produced by SIL women between 1944 and 1970 amounted to no less than 38 percent of SIL's total output. Some of these articles were in-house publications, but many appeared in refereed journals such as *Language*, *International Journal of American Linguistics*, and *American Anthropologist*. Thomas observed that in "SIL women worked alongside men on a relatively even footing in the profession of missionary linguistics. . . . This fact," she added, "seemed to be taken for granted, so that differential treatment of the two genders is remarkably absent in the execution of SIL's core linguistic-religious endeavors."[26] If SIL had followed the pattern of both the evangelical subculture and the male-dominated discipline of structural linguistics, the loss to the linguistic sciences and education would have been considerable. As it was, SIL women linguists made substantial contributions in linguistics, literacy, education, and anthropology.

Pike's own scholarly career advanced apace in the 1950s. He was promoted to a full professorship at the University of Michigan in 1955, with a double appointment to both the Department of English and Literature and the Department of Anthropology.[27] Since he devoted only one semester each year to teaching at the university and took sabbaticals from time to time, Pike was often away from the campus. The university administration wished for longer periods of residence, and all but offered him a full-time position in 1961.[28] Pike resisted this effort to shift the balance of his academic career toward the university. He was planning another workshop, this time in Papua New Guinea, and he made it clear that SIL remained his top priority. He did agree to put in two consecutive semesters upon his return, but left no doubt that he would always consider SIL his first calling.[29] Warner Rice, the chairman of the Department of English and Literature, was disappointed but counted the university fortunate to have Pike in residence on the usual

25. Thomas, "Gender and the Language Scholarship," 389.
26. Thomas, "Gender and the Language Scholarship," 394.
27. Odegaard to Pike, June 25, 1954, PSC: Peterson to Pike, July 10, 1954, PSC.
28. Rice to Pike, January 13, 1961, PSC.
29. Pike to Rice, April 11, 1961, PSC.

rotational appointment.[30] By 1960, Pike had certainly made his mark as a linguist. It was, therefore, fitting that the Linguistic Society of America elected him to its presidency.[31] Whether the news was welcome or not is debatable—the cable of the appointment arrived while Pike was laid up in bed suffering from a stomach malady and overwork in Ecuador.[32] But he was certainly gratified by the honor and could hardly refuse such a prestigious appointment.

In the 1950s and 1960s a number of prominent evangelical scholars studied in Europe. Figures such as Daniel Fuller, David Hubbard, Clark Pinnock, and Bernard Ramm all made academic pilgrimages to Europe as a means to bolster their scholarly credentials and to garner the prestige of European study. Pike, on the merits of his own reputation, established himself as an equal among European and British linguists. When he traveled to Paris for the UNESCO conference in 1951, he rounded out his European debut by lecturing at the Linguistic Society in Oslo, the Linguistic Circle in Copenhagen, the School of African and Oriental Studies in London, the University College London, and the University of Edinburgh.[33] His scholarship continued to be well received on the continent. In 1956 he was invited, along with a short list of leading linguists from around the world with specialized knowledge of phonetics, to help establish a new international journal, *Studia Phonetica*.[34] As the next chapter will demonstrate, Pike's theory of linguistics was more humanistic than the strongly mechanistic theory of Noam Chomsky, who was in the late 1950s taking the field by storm. Contrary to their American counterparts, European linguists were not immediately enamored with Chomsky's generative-transformational grammar. Hence, Pike's scholarship and theory probably enjoyed greater popularity in Europe in the 1950s and 1960s than in his own country. The crowning moment of his European popularity came in 1978, when the Université René Descartes at the Sorbonne awarded Pike an honorary doctorate.[35] Arguably no other American evangelical scholar enjoyed such prominence on the European continent in these years.

30. Rice to Pike, April 20, 1961, PSC.

31. Hill to Pike, September 19, 1960, supplement, PSC; Hill to Pike, September 21, 1960, supplement, PSC.

32. Pike to Evelyn (Griset) Pike, September 25, 1960, 4, supplement, PSC.

33. Pike to Rice, February 23, 1952, 2, PSC.

34. Zwirner to Pike, May 26, 1956, PSC.

35. Thomas N. Headland, "Tribute," 11.

Of Service to All

Pike's scholarly reputation and SIL's mounting stature were some of the key factors driving the organization's global expansion. Brazil, which was hearing good things about SIL in Peru, is a case in point. Sometime in late 1955, while Pike was in Peru for the SIL linguistic workshop, he received an invitation from Brazil's Ministry of Education to give lectures on linguistics and anthropology at the National Museum. Pike visited Brazil during the second half of April 1956, and ended up giving more than a half dozen lectures. While there he also met a number of officials and academics. But the one that counted was Darcy Ribeiro, since he controlled access to the restricted tribal zones.[36] Ribeiro, an anthropologist and the head of the research section of the Indian Protective Service (SPI), was a rising star who would become an important intellectual in Latin American Indian affairs. As in Peru and elsewhere in Latin America, a new generation of proponents advocating liberalization, state modernization, and indigenismo were coming into conflict with the conservative Roman Catholic hierarchy, which had traditionally exerted more influence over indigenous affairs than the state. Protestant missionaries could, therefore, serve liberal aims by helping to undermine Catholic hegemony. And thus it was that even the fundamentalist New Tribes Mission was already at work in Brazil. However, Ribeiro was not altogether pleased with New Tribes, and complained to Pike that their missionaries were "romántico." The New Tribes missionaries were, in his mind anyway, more interested in effecting conversions and flirting with the idea of suffering martyrdom than doing the humanitarian and scientific work he believed was needed. Ribeiro wanted less emphasis on evangelization and more stress laid on ethics and education. That said, he was not against religion, and he agreed with Pike that the inculcation of Judeo-Christian morals coupled with literacy could function as a bridge to modernity for these peoples. The SPI was underfunded and Riberio was in desperate need of linguistic field research, and this was something SIL could supply.[37] "As this is exactly the field of ethnological research that has been developed least in our country in the last years," he wrote Pike, "we would look with the greatest satisfaction upon any project of the Institute [SIL] undertaken to study the Indigenous languages of Brazil."[38] SIL was not only practically

36. Serviço de Proteção aos Indios.
37. Pike, "Diary of Brazil Trip."
38. Ribeiro to Pike, April 19, 1956, PSC

and ideologically aligned with the liberal modernizers and their aims, but it was also technically competent. As in Mexico, then Peru and Ecuador, and now in Brazil, SIL formed an alliance with the state to accomplish the aims of both parties.

SIL's Dale Kietzman administered SIL's work in Brazil, but the scientific aspects of the program were led by Sarah Gudschinsky, SIL's "right-hand man" in Brazil as Pike put it.[39] By contemporary standards his remark was perhaps sexist, but Pike was not. "Dr. Gudschinsky," he wrote in 1958, "is the most competent of women, and equal to the best of our trained men. She has drive, initiative, capacity, and considerable experience both in research work for descriptive purposes, in the handling of historical [linguistic] problems, and the practical applied work on the field."[40] However, her formidable intellect was matched with an equally demanding personality, making it problematic for other SIL members to cooperate with her. But, Eunice Pike proved a singular exception, and they were able to work well together. Whatever her foibles, Gudschinsky held her own in the world of structural and historical linguistics, and she remained in the top rank of SIL linguists until her passing in 1975.

Working in concert with governments and functioning as a legitimate academic institution did much to shape SIL, molding it into a unique missionary organization. Evangelicals had always displayed considerable adaptability to their surroundings, but no other evangelical organization demonstrated the flexibility of the WBT and SIL combination. The policy of serving everyone, non-sectarianism, and the linguistic approach sometimes combined to startling effect. Openly welcoming Roman Catholics into its classes at the University of Oklahoma—not to mention occasionally underwriting their expenses with SIL-sponsored scholarships—is a prime example.[41]

Probably the best known Catholic to study at SIL Norman was Father Louis Luzbetak, a Society of the Divine Word missionary who came to Norman in 1957, after four years of anthropological fieldwork in the Wahgi Valley of the New Guinea Highlands. Luzbetak had nothing but high praise for SIL after completing a summer of study. "I was certainly edified," he wrote Pike, "by the deep religious spirit and zeal of the instructors as well as the students. A more devoted group you could hardly

---

39. Pike to Needham, January 9, 1959, PSC.
40. Pike to Fejos, April 3, 1958, PSC.
41. Pike to Boetti, May 2, 1962, PSC; Pike to Boetti, June 11, 1962, PSC.

find. You could see that there was more than a hunger for learning that made S.I.L. such a busy, hardworking, and friendly place." Moreover, he had obviously been treated well and experienced little or no enmity. "The students, staff, and especially the Pikes just could not have been nicer to us."[42] Word spread, and Catholics kept coming.

Sister M. Cuthbert, along with two other Medical Mission Sisters of the Society of Catholic Medical Missionaries attended the SIL course in 1960. Cuthbert later conveyed her sentiments to SIL's Velma Pickett, who was on the faculty that summer. "I really want you to know that this summer was a wonderful experience and that I was very deeply impressed and edified by the Wycliffe members and especially by the S.I.L. staff. We felt completely at home with you people and I must admit you gave me a new ideal of teaching as a vocation and an apostolate."[43] While at Norman, Cuthbert demonstrated particular aptitude in her studies. Pike, having noted her ability, wrote her mother superior suggesting that Sister Cuthbert should be given the opportunity to employ her linguistic talents in ministry.[44] That same summer, 1960, a Jesuit priest also took advantage of SIL courses. His letter to Pike exemplifies the atmosphere prevailing at Norman. "This note of gratification," wrote Rev. Andrew Connolly, SJ, "is to express my gratitude to you and the entire faculty of the Summer Institute of Linguistics at Oklahoma. It was a rugged pace, it was a hot summer,—but I was edified by the devotion to work that I witnessed on the part of both the faculty and student body. This was no 'fresh air course.' It was evident that something more than the desire for credits, something more than the search for knowledge for its own sake, was the motivating force. I was gratified at the sacred reverence which all had for the Book."[45] This combination of academic rigor and religious devotion prompted a Cameroonian linguist, who had been educated by Jesuits from high school through university, and who lectured at SIL's school at the University of Oregon in the late 1980s, to remark that "SIL is the Protestant Jesuits."[46] SIL proved that Catholics and evangelicals could cooperate and fellowship together but, at this point in history, it would be difficult—perhaps even impossible—to find another situation quite like that which prevailed at SIL schools.

42. Luzbetak to Pike, September 8, 1957, PSC.
43. Cuthbert to Pickett, September 7, 1960, PSC.
44. Benedict to Pike, August 29, 1960, PSC.
45. Connolly to Pike, September 19, 1960, PSC.
46. Watters, interview.

It will be recalled from chapter 4 that the admission of Catholics and liberal Protestants into SIL courses at the University of Oklahoma at Norman provoked considerable opposition from students and faculty in 1947. Pike successfully resisted the movement to separate from the university. Then, and later, he did so partly out of a sense of respect for Townsend, and his belief that the general director was led by God when insisting on service to Roman Catholics. In 1958, Pike described the difficulties he experienced in following this policy. "I, myself," he wrote Townsend, "have felt these enormous objections to the clergy of the Roman Church. I have reacted with violence inwardly to my own historical antecedents as a Protestant. It has been with a fighting of inner loathing of some of these folks that I have served them." Townsend's perorations of praise for Catholic missionaries were especially troubling for Pike. "Even now," he wrote, "to read some of the letters which you have written to some of these people in South America about turns my stomach."[47] Whatever he felt personally, Pike exercised a great deal of self-control when around Catholics. For example, while he did not require students or faculty to follow his practice, he addressed priests as "Father."[48] This could not have come naturally, but he tamped down his own feelings on the matter in order to serve all students, no matter where they hailed from.

Unswerving in his commitment to Townsend's program, Pike backed another unusual proposition. When setting up the bilingual education program in Peru under the auspices of the department of education in 1953, Townsend agreed—he referred to it as "an emergency measure"—to produce diglot translations of the New Testament based on the Spanish Nácar y Colunga, a version approved by the Roman Catholic hierarchy.[49] Always the pragmatist, he did this at the government's behest; but he also saw it as a way of undercutting the Catholic hierarchy's bitter opposition to SIL's presence in Peru.[50] In 1957, the production of Nácar y Colunga diglots was encoded into law under Supreme Resolution No. 275, which read: "That in the religious education which is given in the bilingual schools with the collaboration of the Summer Institute of Linguistics there will be used as text books 'The Four Gospels' and 'The New Testament'—version translated direct from the Greek by the

---

47. Pike to Townsend, December 8, 1958, 2, PSC.
48. Pike to Kerr, April 20, 1959, PSC.
49. Townsend to unidentified member of SIL, c. September 1953, 4, TA 8824.
50. Townsend, newsletter to US constituency, September 29, 1953, TA 8826.

Rev. Fathers Eloino Nácar Fuster and Alberto Colunga Cueto OP, both of the University of Salamanca . . . with corresponding ecclesiastical imprimaturs accompanying the original books referred to."[51] Producing translations based on the Nácar y Colunga Spanish text was a daring and potentially explosive move by an evangelical organization.

Eugene Nida, secretary for versions at the American Bible Society (ABS) and recently resigned from WBT-SIL, warned Townsend that translations based on the Nácar y Colunga were unacceptable to the ABS, and would therefore not be published. Nida asserted that there was unequivocal evidence for the influence of Catholic penitential theology on the translation, which "has heresy in it." He was bewildered by WBT-SIL's decision to translate the Nácar y Colunga and called for a "radical change in Wycliffe policy."[52] The SIL and ABS relationship was already strained by the latter's unwillingness to publish SIL translations unless a sizable readership could be ensured.[53] Now this controversy threatened to leave the relationship in tatters. "The fears expressed in your letter of 12 November," Townsend wrote Nida, "I am happy to say are quite unfounded." As he saw it, there was enough semantic elasticity in terms such as the Spanish "penitencia" to render it as "repentance."[54] This was slippery ground, since what he suggested amounted to recasting the Catholic elements of the text into language acceptable to Protestants. Nida rightly pointed out that this approach would violate SIL's promise to faithfully translate the Nácar y Colunga into Peru's indigenous languages.[55] Townsend brushed aside this concern, and even produced a Catholic dictionary that seemed to conflate the terms penitence and repentance, thus paving the way for SIL to rework translations along this line.[56] In January 1957, the general director received some welcome support from his top linguist. Pike thought Townsend's counter argument was "magnificent."[57] He concluded that there was in fact sufficient latitude to massage the translation into an acceptably Protestant form.[58]

51. "Ministry of Public Education Textbook Authorization."
52. Nida to Townsend, November 12, 1953, 2, TA 9214.
53. Aldridge, *For the Gospel's Sake*, 98–100.
54. Townsend to Nida, November 16, 1953, TA 8780.
55. Nida to Townsend, November 27, 1953, TA 9209.
56. Townsend to Nida, December 28, 1953, 1–2, TA 8763.
57. Pike to Townsend, January 7, 1954, 1, TA 10862.
58. Pike to Townsend, March 28, 1957, 1–3, TA 13513.

To get around the ABS stricture on publishing, Pike felt out the Scripture Gift Mission in England on the possibility of their publishing SIL translations, but their policy forbade publication of "Roman Catholic versions in any form whatever."[59] SIL was clearly in uncharted waters, but Pike was again willing to sail along with Townsend in this venture.

In 1957, Pike was faced with another weighty question related to SIL's non-sectarian status. Seattle Pacific College (SPC), founded by the Free Methodists, vied with the University of Washington for an SIL summer school, something along the lines of the University of Oklahoma at Norman program.[60] Were SIL a typical evangelical organization, SPC would have won the contest hands down. Seattle Pacific was a reputable, fully-accredited Christian liberal arts institution, and it therefore met SIL's high academic standards. Moreover, as an evangelical school, it would presumably make for a good fit with SIL.

Linking up with Seattle Pacific also held the potential for solving a growing problem SIL faced in that part of the country. Rumors were surfacing among evangelicals in the Northwest that SIL was becoming a liberal institution, what with its acceptance of liberals and Catholics at its summer school. The leadership at SPC believed SIL could allay these fears by establishing a program on its campus. Indeed, in arguing against cooperation with the University of Washington, SPC's president, C. Hoyt Watson, dropped what amounted to a veiled threat. "Among faculty and students if you should choose to go to the University [of Washington]," he wrote, "quite frankly, we would be very much disappointed. This would, in part, be due to the fact that we would feel it would not be to the best interest of the Institute [SIL] itself. It would become increasingly difficult to build into the minds of the evangelical wing of the Protestant church in this area that your program is definitely evangelical."[61] From a public relations perspective, choosing an evangelical school looked like a wise move.

Alternatively, the University of Washington offered substantial academic heft, with the opportunity for launching a graduate program to boot. A cooperative program there would also be much more in keeping with SIL's commitment to remain non-sectarian. Additionally, the Washington University link would carry more weight in the eyes of

---

59. A. H. Long to Pike, May 12, 1955, 1, TA 11801.
60. Pittman to Pike.
61. Watson to Pike, December 16, 1957, 3, PSC.

governments with which SIL related. Pike struggled with the decision, but ultimately favored Washington for several reasons. The prestige of the public university figured heavily in his determination, especially when considering SIL's relations with foreign governments. And, going with an evangelical college would have made it difficult for Catholics and non-Christian students who might wish to attend SIL classes. At the end of the day, Pike concluded that something along the lines of the University of Oklahoma at Norman program better served SIL's needs, and therefore the University of Washington best fitted the bill. Townsend concurred, and SIL's Benjamin "Ben" Elson, a recent PhD who would head the school, likewise believed it was a good match.[62] Pike left no doubt that he was willing to continue pushing SIL deeper into secular academia, even if it might injure the organization's reputation among North American evangelicals.

As the next chapter will demonstrate, Pike remained an evangelical throughout his life. This was true of an overwhelming majority of WBT-SIL members. Yet they were breaking down barriers and fashioning relationships across formerly forbidden lines of separation. Time and again, Townsend said WBT-SIL was just following the commands of Christ to "love your enemies" and to "love your neighbor." Yet, for many evangelicals, and especially fundamentalists, cooperating with or serving liberals and Catholics constituted heretical acts. Then too, there remained an undertow of anti-intellectualism in many quarters of North American evangelicalism, and thus SIL's intense focus on science was suspect. Down to the early 1950s, WBT-SIL was accepted as a full-fledged, if somewhat unusual, member of the faith mission community. But, as SIL's unusual strategies and policies became public knowledge, its place within evangelicalism was challenged.

Under Fire

The SIL strategy was unprecedented. Modeled as a faith mission enterprise, Townsend conceived a number of departures from the standard evangelical mission. The linguistic approach yoked science with faith as partners in a program of Bible translation, serious scholarship, and understated evangelism. SIL linguist-translators did not preach, baptize converts, or plant churches in any formal sense. Indeed, they

62. Pike to Nyman, December 17, 1957, PSC.

were even reluctant to call themselves missionaries on foreign soil. Their daily activities included language learning, working on linguistic analysis, writing linguistic sketches and papers, developing dictionaries, preparing primers, and of course translating the Bible. Personal evangelism was quietly and unobtrusively woven into the fabric of these activities, but it was nothing like that of a typical missionary's heavy focus on preaching and church planting. Moreover, Townsend had long insisted on a non-sectarian stance. SIL would not favor any denomination or sect nor propagate such. Broadly evangelical in nature and makeup, SIL was careful to avoid any hint of sectarian bias. Townsend even went so far as to discourage SIL members from associating too closely with other expatriate evangelicals or appearing at large gatherings of faith missionaries when on the field. The organization would, however, serve just about anyone. Indeed, under the banner of "service to all," SIL shared its products and offered its services to Roman Catholic priests and nuns and other non-evangelical missionaries. Moreover, Catholics, government officials, military personnel, miners, and lumbermen, among others, were carried in SIL's Jungle Aviation and Radio Service aircraft.[63] Missionaries in the conventional sense of the term, SIL members were not.

To have placed the entire SIL strategy before evangelicals in North America would have invited serious repercussions. The dual-organizational structure was designed to solve this problem. When in North America, SIL members assumed their identity as Wycliffe missionaries and accented the religious aspects of their work. They did not deny their SIL identity; they simply did not emphasize it in their home countries. The reverse was true abroad. They did not deny their religious intentions, but neither did they give it prominence. The dual organization, which sanctioned these shifts of emphases depending on context and constituency, became a major source of criticism. Without the flexibility that it offered, though, it is doubtful that the SIL strategy would have enjoyed the measure of success that it did.

From WBT-SIL's earliest days, Cameron Townsend had sought to build a network of relationships with the movers and shakers of the fundamentalist movement. Not long after taking up with the Central American Mission in the early 1920s, he left the Presbyterian Church to join the Church of the Open Door of Los Angeles, a major fundamentalist base on the West Coast. His first wife, Elvira, was a member of Moody

---

63. The formation and development of the Jungle Aviation and Radio Service is briefly covered in ch. 4, and at length in Aldridge, *For the Gospel's Sake*, 129–42.

Memorial Church in Chicago.[64] After Townsend became friends with Charles Fuller, the evangelist publicized Wycliffe on his nationwide radio broadcast. WBT-SIL's membership in the Interdenominational Foreign Mission Association (IFMA) is perhaps the most important indicator of the organization's acceptance within fundamentalism. The IFMA was formed in 1917 by some of the largest faith missions, such as the China Inland Mission and the Africa Inland Mission, and specifically as a fundamentalist counterweight to the theological liberalization occurring in denominational missions. The association functioned as something of an informal "accrediting" agency, with membership signifying that a mission was in good standing with the fundamentalist network. When WBT-SIL joined the association in 1949, a few questions were raised over its scientific work, but these concerns were promptly dispelled and the organization was duly accepted. Down to the early 1950s, WBT-SIL was seen as a somewhat unusual missionary enterprise, but it was nonetheless considered a full-fledged fundamentalist faith mission. Nothing could have been further from the truth.

In 1952, WBT-SIL circulated a note in its publicity organ, *Translation*, mentioning its cooperative relationship with United Nations Educational, Scientific and Cultural Organization (UNESCO).[65] This public notice appeared at a time when McCarthyism was in full bloom and when there was no shortage of Cold War fearmongering that the United Nations was part of a plot for world domination by communists. Fundamentalists had their own worries about UNESCO. One critic of WBT-SIL responded by quoting a *Sunday School Times* article that asserted the atheistic and evolutionary character of UNESCO.[66] Another letter came from John G. Mattingly, pastor of the "Independent" and "Fundamental" Emmanuel Bible Church in Colorado, Springs. "It is hard for me," wrote Mattingly, "to see how you can justify helping such an outfit." He too referenced the *Sunday School Times* article.[67] For a growing number of critics, SIL was mixed up with the wrong kind of company.

The *Translation* piece also inadvertently laid a trap for WBT-SIL's North America director, Turner Blount, who walked headlong into an ambush at the May 1952 Independent Fundamental Churches of America

---

64. Elvira (Malmstrom) Townsend died of a stroke in 1944.
65. "United Nations Seeking Linguists," 9.
66. Stone to WBT, June 9, 1952, TA 8422.
67. Mattingly to WBT, October 4, 1951, TA 7205.

(IFCA) national convention in Los Angeles. Although WBT-SIL was not a member of the organization, Blount was on hand to strengthen relations with church leaders. During the event, a formal condemnation of Wycliffe over its cooperation with UNESCO was proposed. This move was parried by William McCarrell, the executive secretary of the IFCA and pastor of the well-known Cicero Bible Church near Chicago, who went out on a limb and vouched for Wycliffe. McCarrell's overture notwithstanding, a pall was cast over Wycliffe.[68] In the wake of the IFCA convention, WBT-SIL secretary William Nyman cautioned that the organization should henceforth "soft-pedal" its connection with UNESCO.[69] Nyman was correct in warning that prudence was called for when publicizing SIL's atypical programs, but this would not stem the rising tide of criticism. These incidents were mere skirmishes foreshadowing the battles to come.

The year 1956 in Ecuador was the occasion for SIL's first major clash with other faith missions. Ken Pike, close at hand in Peru conducting a workshop, was called in at the height of the crisis in May. In the wake of his visit, he confided to Townsend that "Ecuador was one of the biggest strains I have ever undergone—depressing, nerve wracking, morale ruining. I did not feel I could take that strain very long. Fortunately it let up towards the end—but I have a headache this mo[r]ning just remembering."[70] Pike was not exaggerating, he truly was experiencing profound psychological stress. Sometime in the late 1950s, he began taking tranquilizers on a doctor's advice. There is no evidence that he took them on this occasion, but it was events of this nature that eventually drove him to seek medical relief from the near debilitating tension produced by such conflicts.

In part, the trouble in Ecuador came from the fact that SIL implemented the Mexico-Peru strategy when it was not entirely necessary. After all, faith missions operated freely in the country. Earlier success with the SIL strategy in Mexico and Peru convinced Townsend that it was providentially ordained, and therefore it was the template for SIL everywhere in the world. It was also important to maintain consistency; it would not do to have an SIL branch operating as a normal faith mission in a country, since it could tarnish SIL's reputation as a quasi-secular institution in other places. As other missions had opportunity to observe

68. Owen to Pike, June 23, 1952, 1–2, TA 8421; Nyman to Townsend, May 27, 1952, 1, TA 7298.

69. Nyman to Townsend, May 27, 1952, 1, TA 7298.

70. Pike to Townsend, May 26, 1956, 1, supplement, PSC.

SIL in Ecuador, it appeared less and less like a normal mission, and thus became the object of suspicion.

SIL initially set up its Ecuadorian base of operations at Llushin, on the Pastaza River, well away from other evangelical missions. Hence, the organization initially attracted little attention. However, recurrent floods rendered the site impracticable and, at the suggestion of the Ecuadorian Air Force, SIL relocated to Shell Mera in the foothills of the Ecuadorian Andes.[71] An abandoned Shell Oil Company base, Shell Mera was the hub of operations for a number of evangelical missions in the 1940s, including the Gospel Missionary Union (GMU), the Christian and Missionary Alliance, and HCJB Radio.[72] Working in close proximity to these missions was destined to give SIL a great deal of trouble.

It was from Shell Mera too that the Plymouth Brethren missionaries Jim Elliot, Ed McCully, Peter Fleming, GMU missionary Roger Youderian, and Mission Aviation Fellowship pilot Nate Saint launched "Operation Auca," an effort to establish contact with and evangelize the isolated and feared Waorani.[73] A small tribe of about six hundred, the Waorani aggressively defended their territory. On January 6, 1956, the five men established contact with the Waorani at "Palm Beach," their appellation for the camp site they set up on a sand bar in the Curaray River. Two days later, several Waorani men speared the five missionaries to death, and the incident became big news in North America. Newspapers and radio stations across the country carried the electrifying story of the "Auca martyrs." *Time, Newsweek, The New York Times Sunday Magazine*, and *Reader's Digest* all covered the event in detail.[74] At the time SIL relocated to Shell Mera in August 1955, it was already a hotbed of evangelical missionary activity. Now it was a household name in North America.

Townsend was adamantly opposed to Shell Mera as a base of operations for SIL, and he pushed the board of directors to prevent SIL's Ecuador branch remaining there.[75] He believed—and time would prove him prophetic—that close proximity to these evangelical missions would be a recipe for disaster as SIL's atypical strategies became known. He preferred some isolated location where serving Catholics, spending

---

71. Townsend to Crowell, May 24, 1955, TA 11345; Burns to Townsend, August 16, 1955, 2, TA 11322.

72. Townsend to Nyman, November 10, 1955, 2, TA 11205.

73. "Auca" is an epithet meaning "savage," thus "Waorani" is preferred.

74. Long, *God in the Rain Forest*, 1–44.

75. Lindskoog to Townsend, December 30, 1955, TA 11550.

large amounts of time on scientific tasks, and working closely with the government would not attract attention. The first sign of trouble came in late 1955, when Philadelphia radio preacher O. R. Palmer paid a visit to the base. He sniffed something odd in SIL and began to raise questions about its nature and work.[76]

Events surrounding Operation Auca also precipitated anxieties. SIL linguist-translator Rachel Saint, the sister of Nate Saint, was working closely with a displaced young Waorani woman by the name of Dayuma, in an attempt to learn her language and analyze its structure. The Plymouth Brethren and GMU missionaries naturally felt that the Waorani was their "tribe," and the martyrdom of their men reinforced this sensibility. When Rachel Saint was heard speaking of the Waorani as her "tribe," it was felt that SIL was encroaching on the GMU's rightful territory. Townsend, who was in California, wrote Saint insisting that she should avoid any action that "might appear to be a race for getting to the Aucas first." She should, he cautioned, quietly focus on language work with Dayuma.[77] He did not exactly heed his own advice. Taking note of the media ferment surrounding the "Auca martyrs," Townsend proposed having Rachel Saint, and perhaps even Dayuma, tour the US raising funds for a new SIL base in Ecuador. He hoped that, what with all the fanfare in North America over recent events in Ecuador, the said tour could generate as much as $10,000.[78] An article appearing in *Translation* inadvertently gave the impression that only SIL was doing any missionary work of significance among Ecuador's indigenous tribes. The other missionaries in Ecuador were incensed with the *Translation* piece, and with SIL's apparent willingness to capitalize on the sacrifices of other missions.[79]

By early March 1956, a beleaguered Don Burns, the SIL Ecuador branch director, reported that the "opposition to our work by other missionaries has reached its climax."[80] Burns and the chairman of the Ecuador branch executive committee, John Lindskoog, discussed matters with Abe Van der Puy, the director of the HCJB radio station. Van der Puy was well connected in the missionary community, and probably had a

---

76. Townsend to Lindskoog, January 9, 1956, 1, TA 12142.
77. Townsend to Saint, February 14, 1956, TA 12130.
78. Townsend to Burns, January 23, 1956, TA 12386; Watters to Saint, January 28, 1956, TA 12595; Long, *God in the Rainforest*, 59–60.
79. Burns to Townsend, March 6, 1956, 2–3, TA 12350.
80. Burns to Townsend, March 6, 1956, 1, TA 12350.

better feel for the situation than anyone else on the scene. In early March, Van der Puy wrote Burns setting out the major issues behind the turmoil. It was believed by some that SIL was more interested in linguistics than evangelization and, paradoxically, by others that linguistics might simply be a front behind which SIL hid its religious intentions. Clearly there was confusion about the nature of the dual organization. Serving and associating with Catholics was viewed as the most serious issue, since anti-Catholic sentiment at Shell Mera was potent.[81] "We have to go extremely careful here in Ecuador in our relationship with clergy," Burns informed Townsend in 1955, "because of the extreme antagonism (which borders at times on hatred) of the clergy by American missionaries."[82] To all this was added the perception that SIL publicity traded on the martyrs and exaggerated SIL's role among the indigenous tribes.[83] The controversy threatened to metastasize beyond Ecuador, when the editor of the widely read *Sunday School Times* came into possession of Van der Puy's detailed letter, or at least became aware of its essential points.[84] SIL suddenly had another fire to put out.

Philip E. Howard Jr., editor of the *Sunday School Times*, was deeply disturbed by SIL's strategies in Ecuador. Making matters worse, during the dustup another brainchild of Townsend's came to Howard's notice.[85] In late 1955, Townsend became mesmerized by a newly developed short-take-off-and-landing aircraft, the Helio Courier.[86] At a price of $22,000, they were several times the cost of the typical airplane used by missionaries. WBT-SIL could hardly afford such expenditures, but Townsend had a plan. Although "the flesh flinched at the thought," he warned the board of his intention to seek "non-evangelical assistance" in developing the necessary financial resources for the Helios.[87] To this end, he launched one of his most unconventional enterprises, the "Inter American Friendship Fleet." Civic and business leaders in major cities across the United States were organized by SIL to raise funds for aircraft, which were then donated to lesser-developed nations as gestures of international goodwill.

81. Van der Puy to Burns, March 3, 1956, 2, TA 12566.
82. Burns to Townsend, June 23, 1955, TA 11625.
83. Van der Puy to Burns, March 3, 1956, 2, TA 12566.
84. Howard to Townsend, April 27, 1956, TA 12322.
85. Howard to Townsend, June 6, 1956, 2, TA 12289.
86. Merrill Piper, "Hefley Interview," c. 1970, TA 43702.
87. Townsend to WBT-SIL board of directors, November 21, 1955, 1, TA 11291.

Over the next twenty-six years, twelve Helio Couriers and eleven other aircraft of various types were donated to eight different nations under the auspices of what eventually became known as the International Goodwill Fleet.[88] SIL attracted a variety of public figures to speak at the christening ceremonies of these airplanes, such as Chicago Mayor Richard J. Daley, Vice President Richard M. Nixon, evangelist Billy Graham, and former President Harry S. Truman.[89] All this echoed President Roosevelt's 1930s "Good Neighbor" policy, for which Townsend had high praise.[90] Once delivered, the donated aircraft were operated by SIL on behalf of the recipient nations and also for its own use. Altogether it was a bold plan, and the WBT-SIL board initially balked before finally relenting under the general director's campaign to have his way. At the *Sunday School Times*, Philip Howard was left scratching his head over this latest development, and he informed Townsend that SIL could not cooperate so intimately with non-Christians "without compromising your testimony and hindering the work."[91] The true nature of WBT-SIL was becoming public knowledge among fundamentalists abroad and at home, and they were not pleased with what they were discovering.

Intra-organizational strife compounded problems in Ecuador. Burns, and especially Lindskoog, argued for remaining at Shell Mera against the wishes of Townsend and the board. Lindskoog's take on the controversy was also quite different from the general director's view. He composed a seven-page evaluation of the controversy. Although he felt that he was more-or-less representing the SIL group's sentiment in Ecuador, he aimed to keep the matter private. Rather than writing in his official capacity as the chairman of the executive committee, he sent the communiqué as a personal and confidential letter to Townsend. Lindskoog laid much of the blame for the controversy at SIL's feet. Avoiding contact with the missionaries at Shell Mera, he believed, was not the answer to the problem. Better relations depended on SIL taking time to explain its unusual policies and the reasons for them. Trying to hide would only

---

88. Steven, *Yours to Finish the Task*, 271–72.

89. "Gift of Plane to Peru"; Townsend to Burns, November 13, 1955, TA 11296; Bollinger to Townsend, November 16, 1955, TA 11295; "Chicago Sending Plane to Ecuador"; Townsend to Crowell, June 11, 1956, TA 12038; Townsend to Watters, June 11, 1956, TA, 12037; Townsend to Schneider, July 30, 1956, TA 12008; Townsend to Truman, January 22, 1958, TA 14840.

90. Townsend to Roosevelt, September 16, 1940, TA 2591.

91. Howard to Townsend, June 6, 1956, 2, TA 12289.

exacerbate matters, Lindskoog insisted.[92] It was a reasonable and cogent appraisal of the situation as it stood in April 1956.

Townsend took Lindskoog's letter as an unwarranted reproach and exploded with a stinging six-page, point-by-point rebuttal, and his reply was carbon-copied to a number of SIL leaders and the board. He also circulated copies of Lindskoog's missive.[93] The general director was effectively cutting the executive committee chairman off at the knees. Lindskoog now felt he had to defend himself publicly. He issued a follow-up seven-page letter that was firm and insistent but still respectful, and it too made the rounds.[94] Townsend did not take it any better. He grumbled to Pike about receiving another "unkind" letter from Lindskoog, and complained he could not sleep for "thinking about Ecuador."[95] The controversy between SIL and the other missions, and the internal dissension within SIL was taking its toll. "We are," wrote one SIL Ecuador branch member at the time, "a sick branch."[96]

At this juncture, Ken Pike was thrust into the fray. It was not a task he relished, but he dutifully accepted the commission. Arriving in Ecuador in early May 1956, Pike gathered the fretting SIL members and encouraged them to air their concerns and frustrations. It soon became apparent that the previous branch director had insisted that SIL members were not missionaries, but when Don Burns subsequently assumed the directorship, he allowed that SIL folks were in fact missionaries. Seeds of confusion were thus sown within the SIL group and mistrust provoked among the other missionaries. Pike's first move was to reach for his Bible. He opened it and read some passages demonstrating that Jesus sometimes obscured his identity and hid his intentions. Pike quoted Matthew 12:16, where Jesus charged his disciples "that they should not make him known."[97] Pike, in doing this, was simply following Townsend, who had long argued that Jesus' equivocations were a model for SIL.[98] Pike understood the nuances of the dual organization and, like Townsend, realized that the term "missionary" was freighted with meaning that in some

---

92. Lindskoog to Townsend, April 12, 1956, TA 12328.
93. Townsend to Lindskoog, April 16, 1956, TA 12088.
94. Lindskoog to Townsend, May 5, 1956, TA 12317.
95. Townsend to Pike, May 14, 1956, TA 12072.
96. Sargent to Townsend.
97. Matt 12:16 AV.
98. Townsend to unidentified member of SIL, c. September 1953, 2, TA 8824.

ways failed to apply to SIL. Yes, WBT-SIL shared the evangelistic aims of the faith missions, but its strategies were otherwise quite different. The "missionary" nomenclature, in its traditional sense, was not especially helpful in describing SIL linguist-translators. If Jesus found ambiguity necessary, then it was permissible for WBT-SIL members to do the same, so argued Townsend and Pike. In any case, Pike's explanation, and his allowing the group to get the matter off their chests, seemed to help. It was also another case where his force of personality and stature halted the downward spiral of events, thus avoiding a potential catastrophe.

Pike then turned his attention to the other missions, in particular the Gospel Missionary Union. GMU was holding its annual meeting at Shell Mera, and Pike made his appeal to the entire group in two separate meetings, one lasting well past midnight. He carefully walked them through WBT-SIL's history and development, explaining Townsend's rationale for the linguistic approach, the non-sectarian policy, and the strategy of serving everyone. He also admitted that SIL had caused confusion over its missionary identity, and he attempted to clarify how SIL perceived its linguist-translators in their restricted roles, which forbade many ecclesiastical functions normally carried out by missionaries. Pike did not back away from confronting the issue of serving Catholics. The "big question" posed by the GMU, he reported, was whether "we intend to identify with the evangelical movement, or the enemy?"[99] He explained that "science demanded" sharing scholarship and that Christian ethics required "loving one's enemies." For Pike and SIL it was not an either-or question. One could remain evangelical and serve others, even Roman Catholics. On the topic of publicity, he went on to acknowledge that WBT-SIL, and especially Townsend, should exercise more caution when publicizing its work, and he promised that they would in the future be more generous and tactful.[100] Pike was firm, but gentle; careful, yet convincing. His explanations effectively dissipated much of the lingering fear and anxiety felt by the GMU missionaries. GMU could not share SIL's outlook, but perhaps coexistence was possible. After many tense hours, sometime after 2:00 a.m., the GMU president stated that he was "satisfied."[101] It was another exemplary performance by SIL's president

99. Pike, "Report to General Director," 5.
100. Pike, "Report to General Director," 11.
101. Pike, "Report to General Director," 7.

in the realm of diplomacy. Although ephemeral, his efforts did much to restore at least a modicum of harmony at Shell Mera.

Townsend had but faint praise for Pike's labors in Ecuador. "I feel," he wrote, "that you should have taken greater care to avoid the impression that might be given by certain statements in your report that I have anything but a kindly and cooperative attitude toward our sister organization."[102] He went on with two more pages of complaints about Pike's actions in Ecuador. Townsend could only see the world one way, his way. As a man of action, he was not given to reflection. Nor was his confidence in his own powers of perception in short supply. Lindskoog had tried to reason with his boss on this very point. "You and our Ecuador directors have been accused of untruthfulness. I know how you react to charges of this sort, that you resent them fiercely, and that you feel you are scrupulously honest. I don't know where the discrepancy lies, perhaps varying philosophies of truth, but at any rate you will have to accept that you have left serious doubt in the minds of several people, within and without the group, regarding your absolute truthfulness."[103] Lindskoog was not the first to perceive that the general director tended to bend the truth to suit his own ends. Former Wycliffe president Bernie May once asserted that Townsend was a "power player."[104] The general director was possessed of a single-mindedness, where the ends sometimes seemed to justify the means. Pike had no illusions about the man's flaws, yet he was able to look beyond these less admirable characteristics to see the larger man. Perhaps what Pike saw, and this is nothing but informed speculation, was something less than premeditated manipulation on Townsend's part. One does get the impression that Townsend was blind to his faults, that he was largely unaware of how he shaped his words to fit his version of reality, and thus his conscience was unburdened. He probably meant well even when he was unwittingly clobbering a colleague or overselling his latest idea. Whatever the case may have been, Pike made allowances for Townsend and even defended him. In Ecuador he confronted Lindskoog, insisting on Townsend's *absolute integrity*."[105] Judging historical figures based on extant evidence is difficult, and with Townsend the difficulties are multiplied. It is clear, however, that Ken Pike was learning to

102. Townsend to Pike, May 28, 1956, TA 12050.
103. Lindskoog to Townsend, April 12, 1956, 4, TA 12328.
104. May, interview.
105. Pike to Townsend, May 26, 1956, 1, TA 12298 (emphasis in the original).

manage the vagaries of the Townsend personality with a fair degree of wisdom and sophistication.

Pike put out the fire in Ecuador, but he could not stop its spread elsewhere, since fundamentalists in North America were growing increasingly suspicious of WBT-SIL. As SIL's radical strategy became more widely known among the Christian public at home, the organization was increasingly forced to spend more time and effort mounting a defense of its approach to missions. It was a Sisyphean task.

The IFMA Controversy

The first tremors of the earthquake that would eventually dislodge WBT-SIL from the Interdenominational Foreign Mission Association (IFMA) were set off by some missionaries serving with the Association of Baptists for World Evangelism (ABWE) in Peru. These ABWE missionaries leveled charges against WBT-SIL with the association in February 1957, protesting that SIL carried Catholics in its aircraft, that SIL members appeared at diplomatic affairs where alcohol was served, and that SIL shared literacy materials and Bible portions with Catholic missionaries. These missionaries were also convinced that the dual-organizational structure was a deceptive ruse.[106] All this was essentially a rehash of the criticisms dating back to the early 1950s.

The controversy with the IFMA reached its peak at a moment when North American evangelicalism was in the midst of significant turmoil. A younger generation of self-styled "neo-evangelicals" were inaugurating a movement to break away from the classical fundamentalist coalition formed during the first half of the twentieth century. Institutions such as the National Association of Evangelicals (NAE) and its missionary auxiliary, the Evangelical Foreign Missions Association (EFMA), were fashioned along progressive lines eschewing the militant and separatist proclivities of organizations such as the Independent Fundamental Churches of America and the the IFMA. Billy Graham was the most visible figure of the neo-evangelical movement. And, in the words of historian George Marsden, when Graham cooperated with liberal Protestants during his 1957 New York Crusade, "it was all over for the classical fundamentalist coalition, although the shouting continued for

---

106. Key to the ABWE, February 11, 1957, TA 14143.

two more decades."[107] WBT-SIL's clash with the IFMA was exacerbated since it occurred during a period of upheaval within North American evangelicalism.

As the drama with the IFMA unfolded, WBT-SIL received several overtures from the EFMA. It certainly would have been a better fit. Billy Graham joined the WBT-SIL board of directors in January 1958, an unmistakable affirmation that the organization was respected within the neo-evangelical movement. Graham's taking a seat on the board was also a clear signal of WBT-SIL's actual, if unstated, location in the religious spectrum. Townsend was impatient with the opposition, and thus ready to make a break with the IFMA and join the EFMA.[108] Pike thought otherwise. "Ever since feeling the enormous weight of resistance that I ran into slam bang with pain in Ecuador," he wrote Townsend in December 1958, "I have assumed that what we have met so far was the first ripple of a stone dropped in the pond, and that this would not be over until it spread all over the States. . . . To be realistic I think we must realize that we are in for objection and criticism for a long time." In Pike's view, it was to be expected that many fundamentalists would recoil when they learned of SIL's radical strategies, especially that of cooperating with Catholics. Pike himself, as we have seen, experienced his own sense of unease over serving Catholics at times. Townsend never seems to have suffered this kind of angst, and he therefore had difficulty understanding all the hostility coming his way.

Pike leveraged his position as a member of the board of directors to throw cold water on the idea of joining the EFMA. Jumping ship at the height of the crisis, he thought, would only raise suspicions. He was probably correct in this assumption, but events would prove that Pike overestimated the threat to WBT-SIL from breaking with the fundamentalist wing of evangelicalism. Townsend, always perceptive and often on the leading edge of socio-religious developments, seemed to understand intuitively that the times were ripe for breaking with the past.

Rightly or wrongly, Pike was once again going up against Townsend, never an easy move. Even as he did so, Pike reassured the older man of his unshakable faith that the general director was led by God. "I nevertheless go along with the program that you have pointed out for us, on the

---

107. Marsden, *Reforming Fundamentalism*, 165.
108. Townsend to Pike, November 29, 1958, 2, TA 14337.

basis of God's will and the getting out of the Scriptures."[109] Like so many other WBT-SIL members, Pike saw in "Uncle Cam" a visionary worthy of following, even if this forced him to struggle with his emotions. But Pike was also willing to work against the general director when he sensed that prudence dictated. And in this case he felt that a more measured approach to the crisis was appropriate.

As the controversy reached a boil, Townsend hoped that Pike would step in and "carry the ball."[110] Pike did not have the stomach for it, and felt that he had other more pressing priorities. "I have been deliberately schooling myself to keep from allowing such matters to get beneath my skin to where they interrupt the work which—it would seem to me—God has specifically called me." Already heavily involved with developing SIL as an academic institution and expending considerable effort crafting a novel theory of structural linguistics, he could not afford getting bogged down in bureaucratic infighting or another inter-organizational conflict. For Pike, his vocation as a scholar ranked above all else. "I rejoice," he wrote Townsend, "in the opportunity to put my shoulder to the wheel in this way [scholarship], but shall continue to try to keep out of some of these other nerve-wracking situations excepting as, from time to time, by moving in and out fairly quickly."[111] He was willing to speak with the upper leadership of the IFMA informally, but he refused to involve himself any more deeply in the matter.

Ultimately the board of directors forced Pike to engage with the IFMA matter by having him craft a series of work papers defending and explaining the organization's strategies. Here was an errand ready made for his constitution and abilities. Completed in September 1959, this twenty-three page exposition was well reasoned and grounded in scripture throughout. It was the most detailed and nuanced explanation of the organization's principles and practices down to that time. A scholar's touch was evident as he mounted what was a decidedly progressive argument.[112]

WBT-SIL, Pike argued, rejected separatism, preferring instead to enter fully into the socio-political milieu as a means to further the gospel. The thoroughly progressive nature of its program was evident in its

109. Pike to Townend, December 8, 1958, 2, PSC.
110. Townsend to Pike, November 29, 1958, 1, TA 14337.
111. Pike to Townsend, December 8, 1958, 3, PSC.
112. Pike, "IFMA Issue."

three-pronged strategy comprising "a spiritual contribution worked out especially through our Bible translation activities," "scientific research and publication," and "cultural (e.g. educational, medical, and literacy) service." Mirroring the renewed emphasis on social concerns by neo-evangelicals, Pike stressed that the "*whole man*, we feel, must be affected by the Gospel—his spirit, intellect, and culture."[113] This was not the sort of language that fundamentalists were comfortable hearing. To their ears such talk smacked of the social gospel and theological liberalism. Moreover, as they saw it, such a broad mission strategy threatened to undermine the primary missionary task of evangelism.

The IFMA leadership proposed having two leading fundamentalists evaluate Pike's manifesto. They selected John F. Walvoord, the president of the Dallas Theological Seminary, and Charles J. Woodbridge, a former Fuller Seminary professor who resigned when the progressives took control of the school. Hoping to balance the scales of justice, Pike submitted Fuller Seminary progressives Paul Jewett and George Eldon Ladd as potential evaluators.[114] The rift between the old guard fundamentalists and the neo-evangelicals was patently obvious in the choices proffered, and Pike left no doubt where SIL stood. There is no evidence that any of the four men ever examined Pike's work. In any case, the IFMA was unmoved by the arguments presented.

Fearing that expulsion from the association would create a public relations disaster, the WBT-SIL leadership chose to withdraw from the association in December 1959.[115] These leaders had not wanted to choose sides as the old fundamentalist coalition broke up, since WBT-SIL did not self-identify as either fundamentalist or neo-evangelical. With its non-sectarian posture, it simply hoped to remain neutral and avoid taking sides so that it could get on with its three-fold social, scientific, and religious program. But the yawning gap between the classical fundamentalists and the neo-evangelicals made this all but impossible. The IFMA, from day one, was a thoroughgoing fundamentalist association. As for WBT-SIL, it was doctrinally conservative, but it was never marked by the separatist and militant proclivities frequently found within fundamentalism. In short, WBT-SIL was a poor fit for the IFMA, and the controversy and subsequent rupture were almost a given from the outset.

---

113. Pike, "IFMA Issue," Work Paper, VI.1, (emphasis in the original).
114. Cowan to Townsend et al., October 19, 1959, TA 16987.
115. Cowan to IFMA.

WBT-SIL's departure from the association proved anticlimactic. The neo-evangelical movement carried the day, and the holdouts for classical fundamentalism dwindled year by year. The shifting terrain was reflected within the evangelical missionary community. In 1946, the IFMA mission representatives had unanimously refused an overture from the EFMA to enter into a cooperative relationship. The IFMA's essentially fundamentalist character was the main factor behind its call for continued separation.[116] The EFMA repeated its proposition in 1960, and this time the IFMA accepted the offer. Winds of change were reshaping the evangelical landscape, and the IFMA took its first cautious step toward embracing mainstream evangelicalism in order to maintain its relevancy.[117] By the mid-1960s even social concern was in vogue with the IFMA. An IFMA-EFMA joint congress in 1966 echoed Pike's work papers when it declared that "we urge all evangelicals to stand openly and firmly for racial equality, human freedom, and all forms of social justice throughout the world."[118] Townsend was ahead of his time, and thus so too was WBT-SIL. The organization was caught in the crosscurrents of change, but it ultimately benefited from its progressive posture. Ken Pike, having mostly shed the last vestiges of fundamentalism in the 1940s, was already in lock-step with the neo-evangelical movement as it emerged. Yet, with that said, he nonetheless remained very much the idealistic faith missionary.

Pike the Classical Faith Missionary

Townsend had the vision and chutzpah to put his radical project into motion, but it should be clear by now that Pike was a major factor in SIL's successful expansion. It is just as obvious that Pike, his differences with the general director notwithstanding, was a cheerleader of Townsend's unique approach to missions. He also had a deep and abiding respect for Townsend, and this despite sometimes being treated roughly by the general director and disagreeing with him over how to implement various strategies. Nevertheless, Pike was repeatedly forced to resist efforts to enter more deeply into administration at the expense of scholarship. By doing so he was able to become a world-class scholar and, as the next

---

116. Frizen, *75 Years of IFMA*, 249–50.
117. Frizen, *75 Years of IFMA*, 257–59.
118. Frizen, *75 Years of IFMA*, 372.

chapter will explore in detail, develop an extremely complex linguistic theory. However, as we have already observed, he did not confine himself to the ivory tower. Pike possessed a good measure of what might be referred to as the faith mission ethos—a combination of missionary idealism and ardent activism that is abundantly on display in popular missionary hagiographies. That Pike was imbued with the missionary ethos proved an exceptionally important factor in his lifelong commitment to Townsend, and to WBT-SIL.

A fine example of this fact came in September 1956, when Pike was unexpectedly thrust into the events surrounding the commissioning of the "Friendship of Orange County" Helio Courier, an Inter-American Friendship Fleet aircraft being donated to Peru under SIL auspices by Orange County, California. In typical fashion when in a new and exciting situation, he fired off a breathless five-page single-spaced account of this event to some of his SIL colleagues and family. He had arrived in California expecting a two-week rest before attending the ceremony, but panic ensued when Vice President Richard Nixon suddenly canceled plans to appear. Press releases announcing the event and publicizing Nixon as the guest of honor were already circulating in Southern California papers. Frank Gelinas, the secretary of the Orange County Chamber of Commerce, who was largely in charge of the event, was faced with an impending disaster. Pike, the only high-ranking SIL leader on hand at this point, was suddenly thrust into the process of coming up with a revised program.[119]

Nixon's cousin, Sheldon Beeson, and evangelist Billy Graham had been instrumental in convincing the vice president to speak at the commissioning event. But with his father suddenly on the verge of death, Nixon decided to cancel at the last minute. Pike, communicating through the office of Ambassador Simmonds, the chief of protocol in Washington DC, attempted to secure ex-president Herbert Hoover to fill the gap, while working feverishly with the planning committee to revamp the itinerary.

Bill Retts, a real estate developer and committee member of SIL's aviation arm, the Jungle Aviation and Radio Service, went into action. He phoned Nixon's secretary and protested that "you're not just dealing with a bunch of farmers out here." Retts spent the next half hour convincing the vice president's office that the event was truly of international

---

119. Pike, "Family Report."

significance, for which he had some tangible evidence. The occasion would be covered by *Life* magazine; Fernando Berkemeyer, the Peruvian ambassador to the United States was slated to appear; and Mrs. Teresa de la Puente, wife of the consul general of Peru, was to christen the aircraft. Along with these notable figures, local civic, educational, and government leaders, including the mayor of Santa Ana, a State Department official, and a retired admiral, would participate. A no show by Nixon at this auspicious event in his home county would, Retts argued, be a political misstep. The vice president's secretary phoned back, at the very moment the Orange County planning committee was in an "emergency session," to inform them that the vice president had reconsidered. "Hurrah!," a jubilant Pike wrote, "Jumping up and down! We came back into the committee meeting, and what a session, you have never seen! The secretary of the Chamber of Commerce, Frank Gelinas, finally calmed down enough to say, 'Men, I think we ought to pray.'" "Imagine it," Pike exclaimed, "prayer at the Chamber of Commerce of an American city! From then on, the sky seemed the limit."[120] It was a spiritual high, and Pike was exulting in the moment.

Townsend, "always able to think up gimmicks for a time such as this," as Pike put it, arranged for the aircraft to be christened with a mixture of California orange juice and Amazon River water. This was followed by a demonstration of the short-field performance of the Helio taking off from a local baseball diamond. Pike unabashedly reveled in the affair. His more demure sister Eunice would not likely have shared her brother's fervor. When she was dining with the Townsend's in December 1955, the general director described his grand ideas for the Friendship Fleet. Eunice was appalled. "Inwardly I shuddered at the publicity plans," she wrote her brother. "It seemed to me that all precaution had been thrown aside."[121] Through Pike's eyes, however, the event was a roaring success. "The ceremony made a big impact on the people who watched," he wrote after the event. He also reported that the Calvary Church of Santa Ana was duly impressed, and that "they were very pleased by the balance between spiritual emphasis given by Uncle Cameron and the technical materials, reports, etc." Many postwar evangelicals, like many Americans, welcomed public displays of religion and American technological prowess. The Friendship Fleet project was well timed by Townsend

---

120. Pike, "Family Report," 2.
121. Eunice Pike to Pike, December 12, 1955, PSC.

to coincide with the Cold War cultural milieu that was in some sense embodied at the time by Nixon himself. When it was all said and done, Pike concluded that "The name of the Lord was clearly glorified in the ceremony."[122] On full display was yet another facet of the Pike personality, a boyish enthusiasm. Townsend's big ideas could be infectious, and Pike was caught up in the passion of the event.

Pike's scholarly colleague, Eugene Nida, on the other hand was by his very nature immune to such unbridled passion. As he matured, he displayed less and less the faith missionary ethos, and was thus not given to enthusing over Townsend's ventures. Always somewhat more reserved and urbane than Pike, he did not quite fit into the energetic and activist faith mission style. Likewise he was not as tractable when it came to managing the inherent contradictions of the dual-organizational structure. In September 1953, Nida wrote the WBT-SIL board that his "conscience has been deeply troubled . . . during the last few years." In fact, he now concluded that only resignation from the organization would relieve the inner tension he suffered. At the top of his list of reasons for resigning was the dual-organizational strategy, which he felt resulted in a "tendency toward a degree of misrepresentation in the explanation of the SIL-WBT program." Nida complained that "our role as missionaries is not only denied in some instances, but our primary objective of winning people to Jesus Christ is spoken of in veiled terms of 'spiritual objectives.'" Nida essentially argued for WBT-SIL to do away with the dual structure and form a single organization. As he saw it, there was no call for emphasizing either the religious or scientific goals in differing contexts. Nida worried too that WBT-SIL was on a path that would isolate the organization from other faith missions.[123] The loss to SIL's academic program by Nida's departure was softened by the fact that he was already spending much of his time at the American Bible Society, where he was much more at home. With its narrower focus on Bible translation, publication, and distribution, the ABS was a much better fit for Nida. Its New York address too, rather than the Southern California base of WBT-SIL, made for an organizational cultural more amenable to Nida's genteel personality. By way of contrast, then, Pike possessed the flexibility to work within the sometimes chaotic and free-wheeling world created by Townsend. Yes, he struggled at times, but he was imbued with a good measure of the zealous

---

122. Pike, "Family Report," 5.
123. Nida to WBT-SIL board of directors.

missionary ethos, and was therefore disposed to stay the course with the sometimes irascible but visionary Townsend.

The 1950s were heady years for Pike and SIL. By 1958, the organization had branches in Bolivia, Brazil, Canada, Ecuador, Guatemala, Mexico, New Guinea, Peru, Philippines, and the United States, and its linguist-translators were working in 150 different languages.[124] Largely under Pike's direction, SIL schools proliferated and matured academically. He had also helped to guide SIL through some stormy waters when fundamentalists violently reacted to SIL's unusual strategies. His leadership and steady hand on the tiller were essential to SIL's ongoing success. By any measure it was a full decade. Yet, amongst all the activity, Pike somehow managed to develop a linguistic theory, one that would catapult him onto the world stage in academia. But it was no ordinary theory, since his theoretical ideas were bound up with his faith in some fascinating ways, and it is to that story that we turn in the next chapter.

124. Pike to Roller, July 20, 1957, 1, PSC.

6

With Heart and Mind

THE TITLE OF THIS chapter is taken from a collection of religious and philosophical essays, *With Heart and Mind*, published by Ken Pike in 1961. He has often been characterized by such dualistic formulations. Eunice Pike's biography of her brother is a case in point, carrying the title *Scholar and Christian*. Pike viewed his own life in such terms, albeit with a synthesizing twist. A Chinese scholar once asked him whether he was a missionary or a linguist. "I thought fast," Pike later recalled, "and told him I was a hybrid—a mule." He went on to clarify that "sometimes I'm a horse and sometimes I'm a donkey, but I'm always a mule."[1] A perusal of his linguistic scholarship appears to accent dualism over synthesis, for only on rare occasions in his linguistic writing did he mention his Christian belief, and then only in passing. All this, in one way or another, is a legacy of the post-Enlightenment tendency to dichotomize facts and values, faith and reason, religion and science. With one foot in secular academia and another in Christian mission, Pike was forced to live in two worlds. As he did so, to what extent was his Christian thought and scholarship integrated? Was his linguistic theory informed by his faith? What about his philosophy of language? Did he keep his evangelical faith in one box and his academic and scholarly career in another? Or, perhaps, did Pike shed elements of his evangelical Christianity for a more liberal form of Protestant Christianity? If he largely compartmentalized his religion and linguistics, then there are simply two separate stories to be told. If, on the other hand, his faith and scholarship were integrated, we have a story

---

1. Quoted in Simons, "Call to Academic Community," 83–84.

of synthesis. A persuasive argument can be made that Ken Pike achieved a fusion of heart and mind, what one might even refer to as evangelical Christian humanism, a truly unique manifestation of the evangelical mind in the twentieth century.[2]

By any standard the Pikean mind was, for an evangelical, an unusual one. In 1976, evangelical philosopher and theologian Vern Poythress referred to him "as the greatest living Christian Speculative Philosopher."[3] A former student of Pike's and a professor of linguistics, A. L. Becker, described him "as one of the last—maybe the last—of the New England transcendentalists and pragmatists—Emerson, Thoreau, William James, [and] . . . Charles Pierce."[4] Becker's classing Pike with these figures certainly counts as odd company for an evangelical missionary. Another scholar who studied Pike's theoretical work labeled him a philosophical phenomenologist, one who "has developed a theory that, if not unique in an absolute sense, is at least conspicuous within the range of human sciences. While dependent on, and linked to, many of the theories of various areas within the humanities, tagmemics has an origin, an application, a conceptualization, and a guiding philosophy like no other."[5] To one degree or another all these characterizations have some validity. Pike was not merely a linguist or a typical missionary, and thus the scope of his thought was not limited to linguistics or conventional evangelical concerns. In fact, intellectually he ranged far beyond most of his SIL colleagues. But it is in the very midst of this depth and complexity that we find the integration of his philosophy of language and religious faith.

Reforming Fundamentalism

Ken Pike's intellectual development paralleled and, at some points, anticipated moves taking place within North American evangelicalism of the mid-twentieth century. As we saw in previous chapters, he was more than a little touched by the fundamentalist ethos. He could even be somewhat anti-intellectual in his early days before taking up postgraduate studies.

---

2. This chapter serves as a corrective to my previous characterization of the Pikean mind as largely divided between faith and reason in Aldridge, *For the Gospel's Sake*, 73–80.

3. Poythress, *Philosophy*, 171.

4. Becker, "Foreword," xiii.

5. Radney, "Confluence," 34.

But, as he developed intellectually over the course of the 1940s, Pike trended away from fundamentalism and into what would become known as neo-evangelicalism. He was, in fact, somewhat ahead of this new movement to reform fundamentalism, having mostly adopted a progressive posture by the middle of 1947, a point at which the neo-evangelical movement was just getting underway. Hence, Pike's intellectual journey of faith, his struggle to escape from the strictures and narrowness of fundamentalism, seems to have come about independently from the mainstream currents of neo-evangelicalism.

The fundamentalist movement, by which Pike had been influenced in his younger days, had done much to push conservative evangelicalism into an anti-intellectualist frame of mind. As fundamentalists withdrew from the mainline churches and retrenched in the 1920s and 1930s, the life of the mind and first-rate scholarship all but vanished within evangelicalism. In *The Scandal of the Evangelical Mind*, historian Mark Noll incisively charted the baleful effects of the fundamentalist movement on the evangelical mind. He observed that in the wake of the modernist-fundamentalist controversies, evangelicals failed to sustain an older Protestant scholarly tradition reaching back to the Reformation. The anti-intellectual proclivities of the fundamentalists severely damaged evangelicalism. "The scandal of the evangelical mind," Noll asserted, "is that there is not much of an evangelical mind."[6] It was not enough that some Christian scholars had carved out successful careers in secular academia. What went missing was a true integration of faith and scholarship; that is, specifically Christian thinking applied to all academic disciplines, including linguistics. "Failure to exercise the mind for Christ in these areas has become acute in the twentieth century," Noll charged. "That failure," he emphasized, "is the scandal of the evangelical mind."[7] Another well-known historian, George Marsden, arrived at essentially the same conclusion. "Indeed," Marsden wrote, "by 1950 the American evangelical scholarly community was in disarray. Scattered evangelical academic institutions boasting a few competent scholars survived, but only in ethnic, regional, and denominational pockets or in the intellectually suspect fundamentalist movement. Few outsiders took these institutions seriously or realized they existed. Some competent Christian scholars could be found in American universities, but evangelical thought would

6. Noll, *Scandal*, 3.
7. Noll, *Scandal*, 7.

seldom have been counted as part of American academic life."[8] The state of the evangelical mind in the mid-twentieth century was at low ebb.

Beginning in the late 1940s, a handful of progressive-minded North American fundamentalists rallied to recover the evangelical intellectual tradition. This neo-evangelical effort was largely centered on Fuller Seminary, which was established in 1947. Reforming fundamentalism proved challenging. Many first generation neo-evangelicals tended to be rather more conservative than truly progressive. "Scratch a neo-evangelical," historian Molly Worthen wrote, "and underneath you would likely find a fundamentalist who still preferred the comforts of purity to the risks of free inquiry and collaboration."[9] By and large the evangelical mind after fundamentalism was locked into a framework that tended to restrain rather than encourage intellectual imagination. There were, however, a few progressives that parted ways with the fundamentalists and charted new territory.

Edward J. Carnell of Fuller Seminary was one of the first to break ranks with the fundamentalists. He was also one of the brightest neo-evangelical theologians of the mid-twentieth century, evidenced by his earning doctorates at Harvard Divinity School and Boston University concurrently. It was Carnell's ambition to craft an entirely neo-evangelical apologetic, one that would transcend the fundamentalist habits of mind. As a doctoral student he had studied the works of Søren Kierkegaard and Reinhold Niebuhr, and, in his 1957 volume entitled *Christian Commitment*, he endeavored to grapple with existential aspects of Christian life and thought. "Ultimate reality," Carnell argued, "cannot be grasped unless rational knowledge is savored by spiritual conviction."[10] Over against rationalist forms of apologetics, he contended that faith and salvation involved the whole person, and that there was the need for child-like faith to reach Christ. Truth was not merely about rational proof, since there was a subjective aspect to genuine Christian belief. "God is a living person," he insisted, "not a metaphysical principle. Evidences may point to God, but God himself must be encountered in the dynamic of personal fellowship."[11] Therefore, for Carnell, knowledge did not precede faith since truth could only be rightly apprehended when the apologist's

---

8. Marsden, "Collapse," 219.
9. Worthen, *Apostles of Reason*, 46.
10. Carnell, *Christian Commitment*, 13.
11. Carnell, *Christian Commitment*, 302.

affections were rightly ordered. "The moral must precede the rational," he reasoned, "for individuals are motivated by power as well as mind."[12] Carnell also shifted ground on the doctrine of biblical inspiration. While he never repudiated inerrancy *per se*, he did put some daylight around the term, arguing that errors of fact might have entered the text when errant materials were quoted in the original composition of the scriptures.[13] Carnell was clearly moving away from the rationalist and evidentialist cast of mind that marked most fundamentalist thinking to a presuppositionalist position, or a faith before knowledge epistemology.

Bernard Ramm was another well-known fundamentalist theologian who changed course. He began his theological career as a proponent of evidentialist apologetics and inerrancy, but later came to realize he was operating more out of fear than confidence in his apologetics. After studying with Karl Barth during a 1957–1958 sabbatical, Ramm became critical of the fundamentalists' proclivity for approaching the Bible as a repository of facts or proof texts, and instead stressed the role of the Holy Spirit in mediating the verities of scripture. Despite this shift of thinking and his defense of Barth, Ramm's theology and apologetics remained essentially evangelical. Thus, he continued to emphasize biblical inspiration, a point where he believed Barth was weak.[14] As with Carnell, Ramm came to a more Kantian position on perception and somewhat Kierkegardian existential understanding of the role of faith and spirit in revelation.[15] Although the more fundamentalist wing of evangelicalism disdained the moves made by these men, Carnell and Ramm demonstrated the potential for developing credible evangelical apologetics that profited from the insights of Barth and Kierkegaard while not lapsing into liberalism.

Other progressive evangelicals took the same path. George Eldon Ladd, Paul Jewett, Donald Bloesch, Daniel Fuller (the radio evangelist's son), and Clark Pinnock, each in various ways, gave up on the narrowly empiricist and highly rationalist approach to scripture and apologetics. They instead allowed for some subjectivity to enter the picture, although without ever abandoning any of the historic doctrines of Protestant belief. These moves created a rift within evangelicalism, with the

---

12. Carnell, *Christian Commitment*, 21.
13. Dorrien, *Remaking Evangelical Theology*, 92.
14. Ramm, "Helps from Karl Barth," 123–29.
15. Ramm, *After Fundamentalism*, 66.

fundamentalists on the one side and the neo-evangelicals on the other. As the tensions rose, Fuller Seminary found itself in the forefront of this battle. "The seminary," Marsden wrote, "had been built on a fault, a fine ideological fissure that underlay the attempted fusion of the more malleable positive emphases of the new reformist evangelicalism and the hard rock of stricter fundamentalism."[16] The seminary eventually fractured in the mid-1960s, with the fundamentalists departing.[17] The internecine warfare notwithstanding, the adversaries were siblings. Resemblances among evangelicals were stronger than their differences, and their shared opposition to liberal theology was sufficient to weld them into a loose coalition. By way of example, Billy Graham, the evangelical of evangelicals, affirmed Ramm's position on biblical inspiration. Graham also remained on Fuller's board of trustees throughout the shakeup.[18] For all its internal strife and variety, evangelicalism remained a more-or-less cohesive movement throughout the mid-twentieth century, and it was a movement to which Pike belonged. But, as will become evident as this chapter unfolds, Pike was very much in the progressive camp and thus shared much in common with the likes of Carnell and Ramm.

Pike's Faith and Belief

From his youth, Pike was a deeply committed Christian with an abiding trust in the sovereignty of God. We have certainly seen ample demonstration of his faith and belief on a number of occasions in previous chapters. His diary and letters contain many more examples. Even as Pike established his scholarly career, which included a professorship at the University of Michigan, he remained an evangelical. He therefore maintained a high regard for the scriptures. The Bible truly is the "Word of God," he declared in a rousing 1959 chapel talk. Coming to the end of his oratory, his high-pitched voice rising and quivering with emotion (pounding of the lectern is audible in the recording), Pike exclaimed of the Bible that "I will submit to it, I will not rebel. It is orders from God to me."[19] He

---

16. Marsden, *Reforming Fundamentalism*, 147.

17. D'Elia, *Place at the Table*, 150–51, 161–63, 170; Marsden, *Reforming Fundamentalism*, 220–8; Nelson, *Making and Unmaking*, 117–21.

18. Marsden, *Reforming Fundamentalism*, 158, 290; Dorrien, *Remaking Evangelical Theology*, 124.

19. Pike, chapel talk, audio recording, July 2, 1959, PSC.

also emphasized conversion. One must, he believed, be "born again" to enter into relationship with God.[20] We have already seen too that he was a strong proponent of the active Christian life; he was, after all, a missionary. But his was—after some early insensitive missteps—a careful and thoughtful activism. In one chapel talk he framed it this way: "The law of love seeks the neighbor's good positively; the law prevents the neighbor's ill negatively."[21] His was clearly a Bible-based, active, and heartfelt faith. Hence, throughout his life, the main contours of Pike's faith remained essentially evangelical.

As with a few other notable neo-evangelicals, Pike's Christian apologetics also transitioned from evidentialism to a faith-before-knowledge presuppositionalism in the 1950s. Failed attempts to persuade unbelieving scholars that Christian revelation was true on evidential grounds convinced him that mere rationalistic argumentation (knowledge before faith) was an insufficient apologetic.[22] "Yes, there are true statements," he told students at chapel in 1961, "but I can only find them by faith, I can't prove any one of them to someone who doesn't want to believe it."[23] "Logical argument," he therefore concluded in another 1960s sermon, "cannot be expected to persuade the agnostic." Pike had come to realize that his own life, the way he lived it, was a better authentication of Christianity than endless arguments. He thus went on to suggest that only "goodness working out in human character under stress" would convince the unbeliever that Christianity was true.[24] This was an outlook that led Pike to one of his more interesting assertions (one that echoed Carnell), that the choice of an epistemology is a moral choice. "Adherence to an epistemology is not something which merely 'happens to' a person," he argued, "but instead it reflects a component of his moral development. In some sense he is, in my judgment, morally responsible for adopting an epistemology even though it can be neither proved nor disproved to the satisfaction of those who oppose it."[25] Hence, life, truth, and faith all functioned in concert in his Christian thought. "Truth," he once wrote, "comes from the person first, and Christ is at

20. Pike, *With Heart and Mind*, 5.
21. Pike, chapel talk, audio recording, July 3, 1958, PSC.
22. Pike, "Why I Believe in God," 5.
23. Pike, chapel talk, audio recording, June 13, 1961, PSC.
24. Pike, chapel talk, audio recording, August 16, 1962, PSC.
25. Pike, *With Heart and Mind*, 14.

the heart of all. I am not a Platonist who looks for ultimate reality in ideas floating around in the abstract. I am a Christian who believes that Christ is the embodiment of truth, and that His words are therefore truth. Propositional revelation is true because it comes from a person who is true."[26] One did not begin with evidence and work up to God; one began with a belief in Christ as a foundational proposition.

He never equivocated when it came to believing revelation was true, and that truth was embodied in relationship to Christ. But he did admit that there remained a troubling gap between perception and apprehension of truth, scientific or religious. When confronting this problem, he probably pushed the margins of acceptable evangelical thought with something that came close to a Kierkegaardian leap of faith. Concluding an essay on the nature of truth, Pike wrote that "fruitful discourse in science or theology requires us to believe that *within the contexts* of normal discourse *there are some true statements*. Man *must*, sometimes, act as if he believed it—or die."[27] Yes, there was truth, and in some sense it could be grasped, but his epistemology was a humble one that affirmed we only see as through a glass darkly.

Pike's approach to biblical inspiration was similar to that of his apologetics. It was a moderate position, one that landed him on the conservative end of the spectrum of neo-evangelical thought. Inerrancy, the doctrine that the original autographs of the scriptures were free from error of any kind, was both a primary doctrine and a litmus test of orthodoxy within the conservative wing of evangelicalism. As such, inerrancy came to police the borders of fundamentalism and conservative evangelicalism more effectively than any other doctrine.[28] A small cadre of neo-evangelical theologians, such as E. J. Carnell and Clark Pinnock, contested this view and opened up space within evangelicalism for granting the possibility of minor errors of fact. The Bible, for these theologians, was God's inspired Word, but it was not absolutely inerrant in every respect. This did not mean that they viewed the Bible as fallible, for they continued to insist on scriptural infallibility. In Pinnock's words, "the Bible *contains* errors but *teaches* none."[29] Pike never spoke of errors in the scriptures; he only allowed that there were "indeterminacies."

26. Pike, *Stir, Change, Create*, 11.
27. Pike, *With Heart and Mind*, 46 (emphasis in the original).
28. Dorrien, *Remaking Evangelical Theology*, 159; Worthen, *Apostles of Reason*, 53.
29. Pinnock, "Inerrancy Debate," 11–12 (emphasis in the original).

When he set forth his views in 1966, he stated that "the Bible is not to be treated as a textbook of science, but as teaching faith and practice in the Christian life." Indeed, Pike cautioned that a "rigid legalistic view could lead to great distress of mind." There were, if one were at all honest, difficulties to be found in the biblical text. Consequently, Pike argued that "we should be as concerned about over-rigidity in a legalistic but non-realistic view of the nature of Biblical language, as we are in a liberalistic view."[30] When it came to the doctrine of biblical inspiration, Pike chose a Socratic golden mean between the extremes. Hence, while never denying the doctrine of inerrancy, he was cautious in not making claims for the maximal precision of language in the scriptures.

Ken Pike remained evangelical in his theology and apologetics, but he clearly moved in the same direction as other neo-evangelical scholars. Such an outlook offered Pike greater intellectual geography to explore than would ever have been possible if he had remained within the more fundamentalist wing of the evangelical movement. By the early 1950s, if not earlier, Pike began to open up his understanding of science to Christian thought, and in some very interesting ways that were unique for an evangelical. Before exploring his philosophy of language though, we first need to examine his development as a linguistic theorist.

Pike's Early Scholarship and the Linguistic Background

Ken Pike began his academic career at an exciting moment in the development of structural linguistics. From the late eighteenth century down to the turn of the twentieth century, linguists mainly devoted their energies to tracing the genealogy of languages; that is, they endeavored to discover the common roots of various classical and modern Indo-European languages. This "comparative method" primarily involved the reconstruction of the historical (diachronic) development of languages. During the early part of the twentieth century, the discipline of linguistics entered a period of ferment. Largely under the impetus of Leonard Bloomfield and Edward Sapir, the study of languages in North America in the 1920s and 1930s shifted away from diachronic reconstruction of Indo-European languages to synchronic descriptions of Amerindian languages. Put another way, linguists now wanted to understand the structure of individual languages in the present—synchronically that is—and

---

30. Pike to Leal, 6.

these structural linguists therefore aimed to develop a methodology for analyzing and describing what were mostly little known, unwritten indigenous languages in the Americas.

Bloomfield and Sapir were the two leading figures in the early years of structural linguistics, but they differed somewhat in their respective outlooks. Bloomfield was determined that the emerging linguistic paradigm would be built on a thoroughly scientific foundation, after the fashion of the physical sciences. "It was Bloomfield," wrote linguist Bernard Bloch, "who taught us the necessity of speaking about language in the style that every scientist uses when he speaks about the object of his research: impersonally, precisely and in terms that assume no more than actual observation discloses to him."[31] Such an approach imposed some rather narrow restrictions. Bloomfield emphasized that linguists should not rely upon either their own subjective insights or native intuitions about the structure of language, but rather only upon what could be objectively established. One did not ask speakers to explain the grammar of their language, nor did one impose their own unexamined notions about language on the analysis. Committed as they were to empirical examination of what could be observed, those who worked in the Bloomfieldian tradition often had behaviorist and positivist tendencies. The combination of these proclivities generally left them somewhat chary about the place of meaning in analysis, for it would take them into the subjective world of the mind or "mentalism."[32] Instead they focused almost exclusively on what came out of the speaker's mouth, what could be transcribed and then analyzed objectively, and without recourse to questions of social context, psychology, and native intuition. It was, in a word, mechanistic.

Oriented toward structural description and away from meaning as they were, Bloomfieldian linguists had a propensity to neglect syntax, and instead devoted a larger share of their energies to elaborating the lower levels of language: phonetics (charting individual sound units), phonology (the methodology of discovering the patterning of those sound units), and morphology (rules governing word formation). These lower levels of the linguistic hierarchy could be analyzed without delving deeply into meaning or semantics, which would entail at least some degree of mentalism. Hence, as one historian of mid-twentieth century

31. Bernard Bloch, quoted in Hockett, *Leonard Bloomfield Anthology*, 531.

32. Harris, *Linguistic Wars*, 25–26; Hymes and Fought, *American Structuralism*, 107–8, 139–41.

linguistics put it, "Bloomfieldian work was heavily sound-based, rarely extended in any systematic way to units as big as sentences, and was congenitally nervous about meaning."[33] There was among these linguists also the notion that one should study each level in the linguistic hierarchy in isolation. For example, when analyzing the patterning of sounds, phonology, one would not refer to morphology, but rather keep it out of the picture. Again, the aim was mechanistic, or to be as scientifically objective as possible by not mixing levels of analysis.

Unlike Bloomfield, Edward Sapir and Benjamin Lee Whorf sustained an abiding interest in the relationship between language and the mind, and the way in which language shaped culture. Together they formulated the Sapir-Whorf hypothesis, which in principle maintained that language determines perception. "We dissect nature along lines laid down by our native languages," argued Whorf in 1940. "The categories and types that we isolate from the world of phenomena," he added, "we do not find them there because they stare every observer in the face; on the contrary, the world is presented in a kaleidoscopic flux of impressions which has to be organized by our minds—and this means largely by the linguistic systems in our minds."[34] Sapir and Whorf both died at the turn of the decade, in 1939 and 1941 respectively, and their work therefore garnered less attention than that of Bloomfield and his disciples in this period. Thus the Bloomfieldians, with their more tightly circumscribed and less wide-ranging approach to linguistics, dominated the discipline into the middle of the 1950s.[35]

In summary, structural linguists from the 1930s to the mid-1950s most generally applied a bottom-up methodology and were determined to ground their theoretical approaches to linguistics on a thoroughly scientific basis. Bloomfieldian linguists in this period concentrated most of their efforts on phonetics, phonology, and morphology, and they largely shied away from syntax, since it would have carried them into the realm of semantics. This level of analysis, they believed, would have taken them beyond a strictly scientific structural analysis, and into the imprecise and therefore unscientific realm of human action or mental activity. This "mentalism" was largely considered off limits by a majority of structural linguists in this period. Syntax was not entirely ignored,

33. Harris, *Linguistic Wars*, 75.
34. Whorf, "Science and Linguistics," 213.
35. Carroll, *Language, Thought, and Reality*, 21, 29; Hymes and Fought, *American Structuralism*, 93–95; Harris, *Linguistic Wars*, 22.

but it was commonly assumed that thorough analysis of syntax lay in the future, when advances in theory and methodology would provide a strictly scientific or mechanistic accounting of this level of human language. Anyone with more than a passing knowledge of linguistics will, of course, note that this account is oversimplified. There were varying schools of thought, and far more complex aspects of linguistics were pursued and debated. Nevertheless, there was a recognizable and dominant Bloomfieldian approach to linguistics that more-or-less followed the pattern set forth above, and this brief account is of sufficient detail for us to locate Pike and his innovations within the developing field of North American structural linguistics of the mid-twentieth century.

Pike's doctoral dissertation, written under the direction of Charles Fries at the University of Michigan, concentrated on phonetics. It was therefore situated well within the narrow parameters of structural linguistics of the late 1930s and early 1940s. Entitled "A Reconstruction of Phonetic Theory," it set out to do exactly what the title implied. In the first place, he drew a rather sharper distinction between phonetics and phonology than many of his scholarly contemporaries. By focusing specifically on a detailed method for describing the features of, and symbolically representing, nearly all possible sounds occurring in the world's known languages, his dissertation regularized the collection and notation of discrete sounds or "phones." Pike aimed to help linguists produce more detailed and accurate phonetic transcriptions, which in turn would produce better phonological analyses.

Inaugurating what would become a habit in his long linguistic career, Pike challenged conventional wisdom with his dissertation. "If it is generally accepted," he conjectured in a letter to SIL colleague Eugene Nida in early 1940, "it will cause plenty of comment, since it steps on lots and lots of toes."[36] Indeed, the grandee Leonard Bloomfield, who was on Pike's doctoral committee, was somewhat dismissive of charting phonetic units in such fine detail, at least at this point in the development of structural linguistics. "A description of the non-distinctive features," wrote Bloomfield in his 1933 volume *Language*, "might be of great interest, but for this it would have to be more complete and more copious than any that have so far been made."[37] Pike's dissertation was ambitiously targeted to fill this gap. With his characteristic wry humor, Pike noted

36. Pike to Nida, February 22, 1940, 1, PSC.
37. Bloomfield, *Language*, 129.

in a letter to his father that linguist George Trager had once warned: "A doctoral thesis should never challenge any old well established position. In that case, if he is correct, I better start trying to peddle papers instead of being a phonetician."[38] If his dissertation failed, he took solace in the fact that it would still be useful to his colleagues in SIL.[39] He need not have worried. Bloomfield was impressed with the work, the dissertation defense was successful, and the degree was conferred by the University of Michigan in March 1942.[40] Pike staked out new territory, and held the ground.

The thrust of Pike's early academic labors were eminently practical in aiding SIL translators to crack the mysteries of indigenous Amerindian languages. However, the combination of deep immersion in an indigenous social context and the profoundly heuristic nature of SIL fieldwork pushed Pike partly outside the boundaries of the standard Bloomfieldian box and toward a more Sapirian approach. Oddly enough, this actually came to him as a surprise. In 1947, he published a key work on phonology, *Phonemics*, which he thought was well within the Bloomfieldian mechanistic tradition. A year or two after the publication of *Phonemics*, he received a letter from the distinguished Czechoslovakian Prague Circle linguist Josef Vachek (these Czech linguists shared much in common with Sapir).[41] Vachek applauded Pike for his moves beyond the prevailing conceptual confines of phonology. It would seem that only upon receipt of this letter did Pike begin to realize that he had more in common with Sapir than he realized.[42] Yale University linguist George Trager, a year before the publication of *Phonemics*, had perceptively noted elements of Sapir in Pike's outlook.[43] The shadings of Sapir were faint, yet portentous. Pike had a toe over the line, but he was about to spring headlong into a paradigm of his own making.

38. Pike to Ernest Pike, April 20, 1941, 5, PSC.

39. Pike to Nida, February 22, 1940, 1, PSC.

40. Montgomery to Pike; Pike, "A Reconstruction of Phonetic Theory," later published as Pike, *Phonetics*; Pike to Goldsmith, November 11, 1996, PSC.

41. Hymes and Fought, *American Structuralism*, 94; Newmeyer, *Linguistic Theory in America*, 31–32.

42. Pike to Wood, December 23, 1950, 2, PSC; Pike, faculty seminar, February 21, 1977, 3.

43. Pike to Wood, December 23, 1950, 2, PSC; Hymes and Fought, *American Structuralism*, 85.

Tagmemics

Beginning in the early 1950s, Pike set out to craft his own theory of linguistics, one that was profoundly humanistic. "Tagmemics," as he called it, differed significantly from the more mechanistic theory fielded by the well-known linguist Noam Chomsky, whose generative-transformational theory of grammar dominated American linguistics from the 1960s. With tagmemics, Pike maintained that the social aspects of language could not be divorced from the study of linguistic structure. Language, for him, was bound up with what it meant to be a human being. Creativity, the intellect, and moral purpose were all part and parcel of language itself, and thus the study of language was inseparable from meaning. Perhaps the most fascinating side of all this is how an American evangelical crafted an approach to structural linguistics that garnered the attention of linguistic scholars around the world. His theory of language was especially appealing in Europe, where humanistic approaches to linguistics had not yet been overtaken by Chomsky's more mechanistic theory.[44] Pike was a maverick, as we have already seen. He therefore charted his own course, and it was one that put him on the leading edge of structural linguistics.

It was in the late 1940s that Pike began to lose interest in analyzing the lower levels of the linguistic hierarchy.[45] As he looked beyond phonetics and phonology, he did so from a unique perspective conditioned by his experience in SIL. He also, to great effect, mined Edward Sapir's work for insights. Given his penchant for independent thought, Pike ranged further and further from the conventional norms of Bloomfieldian linguistics. Pushing the theoretical frontier, he staked out entirely new conceptual ground in structural linguistics with tagmemics (originally grammemics). Tagmemics was one of a small number of linguistic theories that appeared on the scene between the 1950s and 1980s in North America, which included Montague grammar, stratificational grammar, relational grammar, case grammar, and the most significant of the bunch, Noam Chomsky's generative-transformational grammar, of which more will be said below.[46]

---

44. Newmeyer, *Linguistic Theory in America*, 39.

45. Pike, "Toward the Development," 94; Pike, "Draft Lecture," 13.

46. Tagmemics: "the name *tagmemics* is related to the Greek word from which we get the English word *tactics*," quoted in Pike, *Linguistic Concepts*, 11.

A major factor behind the development of Pike's thinking came from a particular feature of Cameron Townsend's approach to translation projects. He feared that if SIL linguist-translators first learned Spanish, they would then come to rely on it rather than mastering the structurally complex indigenous languages. He therefore insisted that they first learn the local language into which they expected to translate the New Testament. This presented a formidable challenge, since these languages remained unwritten. Research was thus undertaken without the aid of dictionaries and grammars. As such, Pike was often compelled to acquire knowledge of Mixtec from monolingual speakers mostly by way of observation and listening, by pointing to objects in hope of eliciting nouns, by gesturing in expectation of obtaining verbs, and so on in an *ad hoc* fashion. Implicit in this monolingual approach to language learning was the intimate relationship between language and behavior. Bloomfieldian linguistics, with its strict adherence to investigating only spoken language abstracted from the social context in which that speech occurred, ignored behavior and mental activity altogether. Pike, however, by circumstance was forced to go beyond these limitations into at least tacitly linking language and human behavior. In the situation in which he found himself, it was unavoidable. Once he had obtained language material—transcribed words, clauses, and texts—he then analyzed them very much after the Bloomfieldian fashion, a mechanistic approach, as would any other linguist of the day. But, latent within the monolingual method was the essential relationship between language and human action, or behavior, and this reality would prove to be one of the most important factors in the development of Pike's linguistic theory.

In 1947, Pike mounted the argument that phonological analysis must include reference to grammar, an explicit violation of the Bloomfieldian interdict against mixing levels of analysis.[47] His experience analyzing various languages in Mexico, along with the practical necessity of creating alphabets for these previously unwritten languages, convinced Pike that the proscription against mixing of levels in analysis simply to maintain a mechanist scientific methodology was, in fact, oddly unscientific. If units of language at one level could be shown to affect units at another level, it was illogical, in Pike's way of seeing things, to circumscribe the analysis. To understand the structure of a language in all its complexity required, in his view, attention to the totality of what was operating in the language

---

47. Pike, "Grammatical Prerequisites to Phonemic Analysis."

at all levels in concert. It was a tall order, but Pike was a very tenacious linguist. As Pike turned his gaze toward grammar, the stage was set for an entirely novel theory of linguistics to emerge from his mind. Once launched, the project took on a life of its own. In time it would expand well beyond linguistic analysis to encompass an entire theory of human behavior.

When Bloomfieldians first began to consider grammar, they conceived of it only as descriptive relationships within the sentence, or syntactical structure. In 1948, Pike took a hard turn away from this outlook and began to speculate on the possibility that there might be a "phoneme of grammar." This is a very complex topic. Nevertheless, it can be simplified by saying that he was not just talking about labels applied to grammatical units in a structural description, but positing the fundamental reality of psychological grammatical categories in the mind. Here was nothing less than full-on mentalism. One of SIL's top linguists later commented upon this novel aspect of Pike's work. "Following his mentor Sapir," wrote George Huttar in 2003, "Pike was also unabashedly mentalist in his view of language, long before mentalism made its way back into favor [among] . . . American linguists in the latter half of the last century."[48] Moreover, as already noted, he was departing from the Bloomfieldian mechanical mapping of structure to imagine instead linguistic units, chunks of language, all conditioned by and conditioning one another in a concert of relations. Where Pike was headed was far enough outside the conventional approach as to seem ludicrous. But he was far from finished. Like St. Paul coming "to visions and revelations," he would glory in the complexity of language and human behavior before he was finished.[49] Units functioning within and across the varied levels of the linguistic hierarchy to carry meaning, and meaning explicitly involving human action and thought, together opened the way both for conceptualizing yet higher levels of linguistic interaction, and for recognizing the role of the person or persons in those interactions.

If sound units, Pike conjectured, are distributed into words (each sound occupying a slot), and words into sentences, and sentences into paragraphs, and so on, what was language itself distributed into? Could language itself be conceptualized as a unit in context? As already implicit in the monolingual approach, it seemed obvious that language

---

48. Huttar, "Scales of Basicness," 119–20.
49. 2 Cor 12:1 AV.

was inextricably linked to behavior. Pike made this connection explicit, and then extended it by suggesting that language itself was distributed into the larger realm of human behavior. Language, he reckoned, was only a sub-unit of all human action, verbal and nonverbal. These speculations set the research agenda for the rest of his life, and it had far-reaching consequences. Grappling with linguistic complexity without reductionism is where Pike applied his efforts in the 1950s and beyond. What he developed was an immensely complex system, even for the most competent professional linguist. Indeed, this would prove to be one of the drawbacks to tagmemics; it could overwhelm the analyst.

Pike opened his major treatise on tagmemics, *Language in Relation to a Unified Theory of the Structure of Human Behavior*, with an illustration of why a unified theory was necessary. He took as his example a song sung at a party, *Under the Chestnut Tree*, where a stanza was repeated but with the deletion of a word each time substituted by a bodily action. In one instance, the word "spreading" was replaced by participants extending their arms and waving them around. After a number of repetitions most words would be replaced by bodily actions, but the meaning conveyed remained intact. As Pike pointed out, a linguist recording the song for analysis would do fine in the first repetition, but would become increasingly incapable of capturing data as it shifted into nonlinguistic behavior. The event also lent itself to illustrating the unit in context. "This gesture song," Pike explained, "constitutes a single complex unit, a total experience which is perceived by the participants as beginning, as ending, and as constituting a unified whole—a single game. After it is finished, a different unit of the party may begin. Certainly," he emphasized, "the gesture-song is in some way a single unit of activity, an event which must be studied as a cohesive set of actions."[50] Here was a simple, yet convincing, argument for the relationship of language and human behavior.

A fundamental aspect of tagmemics was Pike's contention that linguistic form and meaning were fused: a "composite" as he put it. Combining meaning with form was not always neat and tidy. Things could get messy, and he did struggle with meaning for a long time. But Pike, steeped in the monolingual approach, more than most linguists understood the cost of reductionism. One might have an orderly structural description of the forms, but it would not hold up well when one was

---

50. Pike, *Language in Relation*, 25.

working with authentic speech uttered in actual settings. "In addition to form," Pike argued, "a meaning, relevance, value, significance, deduced cause, result of deduced cause, or some other *observer-related component* is always demanded in our affirmation of the existence of any unit of rational behavior, of the existence of the observability of any concrete object or event, or of any object or event as deduced by man or imagined by man."[51] One might analyze and describe linguistic or behavioral forms in a quasi-mechanistic fashion, he allowed, but "lurking somewhere in the background" was meaning. At the bottom of all this was his unwillingness to lose sight of the person, the speaker of language. With tagmemics, one was forced to keep human beings, the makers of meaning through linguistic and behavioral forms, always in sight.

Insistence upon reference to meaning is a key aspect behind what is arguably the most enduring and classical element of tagmemics, Pike's distinction between what he termed the "etic" and the "emic," which were extensions or generalizations of the words *phonetic* and *phonemic*.[52] The phonetic inventory of a language is the total, concrete, observable number of individual sounds in that language. The smaller phonological or "phonemic" inventory of psychologically real sound units is derived from a native speaker's internal unconscious knowledge. Pike dropped the "phon-" from *phonetic* and *phonemic*, and applied the terms to cultural behavior in much the same way that the original terms applied to sound systems. "The etic viewpoint," he wrote in *Language*, "studies behavior as from the outside of a particular system, and as an essential initial approach to an alien system." Etic observations were those open to casual observation by the uninitiated. For example, one without any knowledge of baseball might easily observe the players and various actions of the game, but would have no understanding of the rules or strategies or goals of the game. To understand the game meaningfully requires inside knowledge that the uninitiated observer must acquire. Thus, as Pike explained, "The emic viewpoint results from studying behavior as

---

51. Pike, *Linguistic Concepts*, 111 (emphasis in the original).

52. Philip Stine claims, in *Let the Words Be Written*, 96–97, that it was Nida who first conceptualized the etic-emic paradigm, although he provides no evidence. Nida himself seems to have laid the matter to rest in a 1997 letter to Pike, in which he wrote: "Just the other day I was writing up some material on translation and of course came to the issue of emic and etic contrasts, a concept for which I am extremely thankful to you" (Nida to Pike, December 3, 1997, PSC).

from inside the system."[53] Once described, the terms seem quite simple, but when the etic-emic distinction first appeared it was a significant innovation, one that aided anthropologists in getting at or focusing on meaning from within a cultural system.

The etic-emic distinction led Pike to a Kantian understanding of perception. "I have refused," he asserted, "to talk about the 'thing in itself' as reality out there."[54] Perfectly objective descriptions of the world outside the mind were therefore impossible to come by, since observer variation precluded uniformity. "All phenomena," he wrote in *Language in Relation*, "all 'facts,' all 'things,' somehow reach him [the observer] only through perceptual and psychological filters which affect his perception of the structuring of and relevance of the physical data he observes. . . . This fact, in turn, leaves us always with the empirical possibility of a plurality of equally-true—or equally-false—observations, coming from different standpoints and from different observers."[55] By the mid-1960s, if not before, he had parted ways with the common-sense variety of knowing that was almost universal in conservative evangelical thought.

Pike did, however, aim for some kind of bridge between mind and matter, between Kant's noumenal and phenomenal. "No item of human behavior," he asserted, "can be completely abstracted from all physical settings, or from all physical components; no purely abstractional system can serve it, whether of ideas or of systemic relational elements. Each must have its physical component."[56] He was attempting, with his theory of language, "to bridge both mind and matter, idea and thing, will and act."[57] The mind, through language, attempted to make sense of what was external to it. But the world outside was not chaos, it was an ordered world just as language was an ordered system. "God," Pike declared, "insisted on having no loose edges outside His control." There was an ordered world outside the mind which human perception attempted to grasp, but the gap between mind and matter was never wholly eliminated because humans are finite. The common-sense variety of knowing was,

---

53. Pike, *Language in Relation*, 37.
54. Pike, faculty seminar, October 25, 1976, 33–34.
55. Pike, *Language in Relation*, 658–59.
56. Pike, *Linguistic Concepts*, xii–xiii.
57. Pike and Harris, *Etics and Emics*, 35.

in Pike's way of looking at it, overly confident. "We can't," he emphasized, "know everything because we're not God."[58]

Did this form of relativism, then, take Pike outside the acceptable boundaries of evangelical thought? Arguably, it did not. First he maintained that there was an objective reality, as well as truth, beyond the mind. "This truth, in my view," he explained in *Language in Relation*, "would be the emic perception experienced by God, who in turn could focus upon the emic perception of individual men as a component of the total reality available to His observation."[59] Aspects of this truth, that which God chose to reveal, were, in Pike's theology, opened up to believers through relationship with Christ. "We know God through Christ. We know truth through Christ. He said, 'I am the truth,' and then when praying to the father, 'Thy Word is truth.' This is central to the nature of truth." Recall, that for Pike, commands found in scripture were unequivocal; God, through the Bible, reached human perception with a very high degree of comprehension, so long as one was inclined to hear it. As with his insistence that the choice of an epistemology was a moral choice, one also had to be predisposed to receive truth. The orientation of the heart regulated the mind, and it was revelation and faith together that closed the existential gap between perception and truth. "It is only by revelation, and faith in it," Pike therefore reasoned, "that we can find God. He that comes to God must believe that he is—and that makes a difference."[60] Hence, his philosophy of the mind was more-or-less Kantian, but his theology of revelation was evangelical. One's perception of the world outside the mind was imperfect, but God's revelation received in faith led to truth.

Language as behavior, the necessity of meaning, emic knowledge, and observer perspective all pointed to the person, a human being. Implicitly underlying all this was Pike's faith and belief, his Christian thought shaped his view of language and what it meant to be a human being. As to the nature of language, for Pike it was theistically grounded. "Language," he believed, "is in the creative image of God."[61] Language was not merely structure to be examined and parsed. Rather it was bound up with creative acts, both human and divine. In the early 1960s, Pike

---

58. Pike, "Value of General Principles," 1.
59. Pike, *Language in Relation*, 658–59.
60. Pike, *Stir, Change, Create*, 45.
61. Pike, *Stir, Change, Create*, 11.

observed in his research notes that "the study of speech patterns or forms by themselves becomes empty of impact on life and character. Meaning and pattern, for deep humanistic purposes, need to be tied together."[62] His entire philosophy of language flowed from an innate belief that language and human beings, both created by God, must be studied as living entities, not as abstractions. "Life is deeper than language," he insisted, "and life is deeper than the intellect that works through language."[63]

If one takes Pike's theory of language as mere structural linguistics, then one has truly underestimated just how deep his faith had penetrated his mature thinking on theoretical linguistics. Pure abstract theory was abhorrent to him. "Pure reason, with no faith, no adequate assumptions, no careful assumptions based on experience, and inner trust to feed into the logic machine," was, for him, nothing but a "hamburger machine."[64] The faith-reason and religion-science binaries had no place in his theory of language. "Faith," he insisted, "does not begin where logic leaves off."[65] Indeed, a "theory," Pike maintained, "is *not* completely *mechanistic*, since it has purpose, meaning, significance and human relevance tied to it; and is *not* completely *abstract*, since it has a physical component for every unit."[66] The point to note here is he never lost sight of the person in pursuit of a theory of human behavior. "It was axiomatic for Kenneth Pike," wrote SIL linguist George Huttar, "that people are coherent wholes, that their language behavior is a coherent part of their purposeful behavior as human beings, and that the language of a community of people is an integral part of their culture and norms of behavior."[67] As both a Christian and scholar, he had a strong aversion to putting people under the microscope as specimens or seeing them as laboratory rats in an experiment. Person, as Pike often said, is above logic.

Pike's reticence to include more than a few direct references to Christianity or theism in his scholarly publications and in non-SIL lectures has obscured the profound relationship between his Christian belief, his tagmemic theory, and his philosophy of language. Pushing evangelical religion in the academy likely would have been fatal to his

62. Pike, "How Do You Know When You've Thought?," 3.
63. Pike, *Stir, Change, Create*, 12.
64. Pike, chapel talk, audio recording, August 16, 1962, PSC.
65. Pike, *Stir, Change, Create*, 12.
66. Pike, *Linguistic Concepts*, xii–xiii (emphasis in the original).
67. Huttar, "Scales of Basicness," 119.

scholarly career outside of SIL, and by extension damaging to SIL itself. Moreover, he was no Bible thumper, choosing instead to share his faith quietly and discreetly in the secular public space. If Pike was cautious, he was not afraid of declaring his religious beliefs. A classic case of how he handled this occurred in 1978, at the Interdisciplinary Colloquium on Language Development in France, where he read a paper delineating his philosophy of language as part of the reception ceremonies granting him an honorary doctorate at the Sorbonne. At one point, his discussion of linguistic hierarchy reached into the realm of metaphysics. "Eventually," he stated, ". . . there is no stopping place in the hierarchy until one reaches some kind of mechanistic, pantheistic, or theistic whole."[68] Presumably most everyone present knew Pike was a Christian, or at least a theist of some sort, and would therefore understand that he was alluding to his religious belief. If not, he did point them to his *With Heart and Mind* should they wish to know more about the relationship between his faith and scholarship. That said, his most important statement on the matter was made in his magnum opus, *Language in Relation to a Unified Theory of the Structure of Human Behavior*, where he stated his "belief in an ultimate designer of nature."[69] And we should recall, as already quoted above, that it was in *Language in Relation* in which he also wrote that ultimate "truth, in my view, would be the emic perception experienced by God, who in turn could focus upon the emic perception of individual men as a component of the total reality available to His observation."[70] Pike neither hid nor pushed his faith in the academy, but he unambiguously asserted a theistic foundation for his theory of language.

Characterizing Pike's body of thought is difficult. The task is complicated by the unfortunate fact that the term "evangelical," as of late anyway, has accumulated political overtones arising from the contemporary culture wars. If we keep in mind Pike's historical setting, where the term did not carry today's socio-political connotations, then it is perhaps still useful to retain the terminology, at least in its historical sense. As already suggested above, with his deep sense of moral purpose and commitment to person above logic, Pike's philosophy of language and behavior is perhaps best described as a form of evangelical Christian humanism. In some sense, Pike saw the philosophical aspects of his

---

68. Pike, "Here We Stand," 14.
69. Pike, *Language in Relation*, 58.
70. Pike, *Language in Relation*, 658–59.

theory in this light, and worried that some theologians might consider him "too humanist."[71] As we continue to see in the next two chapters how Pike's thinking played out in different settings, this characterization of his thought will hopefully become more obvious.

Tagmemics was nothing if not comprehensive. "The activity of man constitutes a structural whole," Pike asserted in *Language in Relation*, "in such a way that it cannot be subdivided into neat 'parts' or 'levels' or 'compartments' with language in a behavioral compartment insulated in character, content, and organization from other behavior. Verbal and nonverbal activity is a unified whole, and theory and methodology should be organized or created to treat it as such."[72] By the 1970s, Pike was well known among linguists for his all-encompassing approach to linguistic theory. Reviewing a volume of Pike's writings, Norman A. McQuown of the University of Chicago wrote that it "epitomizes the career of a 'whole' man, one who does not separate body from mind, or mind from soul, or linguistics from theology, or phonology from morphosyntax, or language theory from language application."[73] Everything from the smallest units of language, sounds and the sub-features of those sounds, up to the totality of human behavior was a staggering lot of material to include under a single theoretical outlook. Tagmemics could, therefore, be threatening for those who sensed the need for greater concision and less mutability from a theory. In *Linguistic Concepts*, Pike admitted that tagmemics could be "disconcerting." He went on to elaborate. "Nothing it seems is stable, everything seems everything else, and observer freedom seems to be the death of scientific detachment and precision."[74] Pike was not afraid to grapple with the messiness of social life in hopes of shedding more light upon human language and behavior than would have been possible with a less sweeping and vigorous theoretical approach. For those who could live with the apparent chaos, or better yet for those who flourished under the intellectual flexibility and liberty afforded by tagmemics, it was an exciting theory in which to do structural linguistics and to push the frontiers of linguistic analysis. For those who found tagmemics too bewildering or unwieldy, there was a strong competitor with a much

---

71. Pike, "Questions Concerning," 4.
72. Pike, *Language in Relation*, 26.
73. McQuown, review of *Selected Writings*, 931.
74. Pike, *Linguistic Concepts*, 109.

more linear approach, Noam Chomsky's generative-transformational grammar.

The Chomskyan Revolution

As Pike was developing tagmemic theory, Noam Chomsky was constructing a theory of grammar that, in a variety of permutations, was destined to reshape the discipline of structural linguistics. First at Harvard, and then from 1956 at the Massachusetts Institute of Technology (MIT) where he taught, Chomsky worked out a generative theory of grammar. In a sense, he stood the traditional approach to linguistics on its head. Rather than concentrating on structural descriptions of indigenous languages, Chomsky instead worked to devise a rules-based methodology that would generate only grammatical sentences of a language. To carry out this project he focused exclusively on English, since he was more interested in the universal properties of the mind and its language generating processes than any particular language.

In a nutshell, he began with what he referred to as phrase structure rules, a set of mathematical-like ordered operations that specified (or "generated") a language's most basic syntactical structures, or sentences. These phrase structure rules were taken to represent the way in which the mind built the basic sentences from which all other sentence types, including the more complex, were derived. The move from basic sentences (referred to as the base or deep structure) to more complex sentences (the surface structure) was carried out by a second set of rules referred to as transformations. Thus, for example, the phrase structure rules would generate an active sentence, which a transformational rule would then turn into a passive one. The central design feature of Chomsky's system was the crafting of said rules in such a way as to eliminate the possibility of generating a non-grammatical sentence. Generative-transformational grammar was a highly abstract theory that purported to represent the functions of the human mind, a rather stark turnabout from the description of language data in the Bloomfieldian tradition.[75]

What generative-transformational grammar did share in common with the Bloomfieldian enterprise was the aspiration of being thoroughly scientific. On this point Chomsky held out a most promising approach. "Syntactic investigation of a given language," he wrote in his 1957

75. Harris, *Linguistic Wars*, 89–96; Newmeyer, *Linguistic Theory in America*, 55–78.

landmark *Syntactic Structures*, "has as its goal the construction of a grammar that can be viewed as a device of some sort for producing the sentences of the language under analysis."[76] What, after all, could be more scientific than a computer-like "device" that could spit out grammatical sentences while excluding non-grammatical ones? Chomsky's method was not only rigorously scientific, but his work was centered on syntax in all its complexity. Once the possibilities and potential of generative-transformational grammar were understood, the Chomskyan revolution was unleashed and his theory, in a number of varieties, more-or-less swept the field of North American linguistics from the early 1960s. For the next two decades, all other linguistic theories were forced to vie for attention in the shadow of Chomsky and his colleagues at MIT.

There were few similarities between Pike and Chomsky's theories. For example, generative-transformational grammar was a tightly constrained system. "From now on," Chomsky wrote in the early pages of *Syntactic Structures*, "I will consider a *language* to be a set (finite or infinite) of sentences."[77] Pike's approach was just the opposite. "In linguistics, I personally choose to enter *not* at the level of the sentence, . . . but at the level of *social interaction* of person with person. This leads directly to dialogue, personal response, and definition of the sentence in relation to dialogue."[78] The differences on this point between the two men's outlook was stark.

The place of meaning in linguistic analysis was another point of significant departure between generative-transformational grammar and tagmemics. It will be recalled that Pike insisted on the fundamental relationship between form and meaning with what he referred to as the "form-meaning composite." One might temporarily examine a linguistic form independent of meaning, but in the final analysis meaning had to enter the picture. Not so for Chomsky. "Grammar," he insisted, "is best formulated as a self-contained study independent of semantics. In particular, the notion of grammaticalness cannot be identified with meaningfulness."[79] Thus, besides the main generative versus descriptive emphasis between the two theoretical points of view, there were

---

76. Chomsky, *Syntactic Structures*, 11.
77. Chomsky, *Syntactic Structures*, 13.
78. Pike, *Linguistic Concepts*, xiii (emphasis in the original).
79. Chomsky, *Syntactic Structures*, 106.

substantial differences between Chomsky and Pike on both the scope of linguistic analysis and the place of meaning.

Moreover, Chomsky did not concern himself with the social context of language. His interest was the mind and, more specifically, the formal structure and universal properties of the mind that governed language. To get at the mind he took English as his language for analysis. It was, after all, already resident in his own head. Suddenly linguistics was less about fieldwork—the collection and description of linguistic data—and rather more about the development of rules and logical operations underlying English syntax, which at the level of abstract theory would presumably get at the universal properties of the mind behind all human language. Hence, whereas Chomsky searched for an abstract representation of the mind, Pike searched for a dynamic understanding of language in its larger social reality.

Excluding the social aspects of language and the singular focus on English by Chomsky and his followers of various stripes eventually drew some rather sharp criticism, especially from anthropologists. "Within linguistics in the United States, the almost exclusive study of their own language, English," wrote well known anthropologist Dell Hymes in 1974, "by so large a proportion of the world's linguists, has seemed to the participants a source of deepening insight into the underlying structure of all languages. Leaving aside the methodological difficulties that have become increasingly apparent, we must consider that to many other communities, including those of American Indians, such a concentration may seem an expression of ethnocentrism at best, and a hostile turning of the back at worst."[80] Pike, and SIL as a whole, came in for their own share of criticism in the 1970s from anthropologists, but neither Pike nor SIL could ever be faulted for neglecting indigenous languages and peoples. In fact, tagmemics drew its life blood from deep engagement with indigenous languages and the social context of those languages.

Pike frequently and forcefully took exception to Chomsky's linguistics. In his mind generative-transformational grammar was too reductive in its drive for efficiency, and in the main too mechanistic. Chomsky himself had written in *Syntactic Structures* that, in the generative-transformational "conception of language . . . we can view the speaker as being essentially a machine of the type considered."[81] "Tagmemics," Pike

---

80. Hymes, "Introduction: Traditions and Paradigms," 21–22.
81. Chomsky, *Syntactic Structures*, 20.

lectured in 1960, contrasting his outlook with Chomsky's, "does not grant that the innards of a translation machine necessarily have any correlation with the behavioral correlates of man—which may be much more complex."[82] The centrality of the human being, his Christian faith, his deep immersion in Mixtec society while translating the New Testament, and his ongoing contact with language communities, taken together, imbued Pike with a profound sense of the social dimensions of language, as well as the necessity of keeping meaning and personhood always in sight. Indeed, for him, Chomsky's approach was essentially anti-humanistic. In the same 1960s lecture, Pike pounded the lectern on this very point. "My current words are chosen carefully," he explained to the class so that there would be no misunderstanding of what was coming. The theory of generative-transformational grammar is, he maintained, "an inhuman machine." It "is," he emphasized, "*exclusively* a machine operation, a logical operation, a hamburger factory."[83] Pike was clearly no enthusiast of generative-transformational grammar.

Although Chomsky's theory enjoyed greater popularity than its competitors, Pike's tagmemic theory was designed for the study of previously unwritten languages, and had a proven track record in performing this very function. Moreover, SIL linguist-translators were working deep within a social context and attempting to translate a complex text in that arena. Tagmemics offered the multi-dimensionality and flexibility to manage the linguistic, cross-language communication, and social dimensions of such projects. In addition, with its built-in anthropological component and theistic understanding of human experience, it would seem that tagmemics was ideally suited to the SIL program. Pike certainly believed this to be the case.

It is therefore perplexing that tagmemics eventually gave way to generative-transformational grammar in SIL. In addition, tagmemics was only one of a number of theories taught and worked on in SIL, and it was never strictly taught at SIL's non-US schools.[84] At the SIL and University of North Dakota cooperative program, generative-transformational grammar was the only theory on the syllabus, and at the University of Washington tagmemics was only one of a smorgasbord of theories that included generative-transformational grammar, stratificational grammar,

---

82. Pike, "Transformations Versus Tagmemics," 14.
83. Pike, "Theory of Meaning," 18–19, (emphasis in the original).
84. Karl Franklin, personal communication, September 19, 2016.

and scale and category grammar.[85] From the 1970s, SIL linguists increasingly published research from the generative-transformational perspective, in both its classical form as well as in its generative semantic form.[86] How and why was it that tagmemics had to share a place with other theories and ultimately declined in SIL? And what were the effects on SIL, not to mention on Pike himself? On the surface, all this looks like an unmitigated disaster, what with SIL coming to favor a mechanistic theory seemingly at odds with its essentially religious nature, not to mention one sharply criticized by Pike. How, then, could tagmemics have been sidelined, and with most of the ground ceded to generative-transformational grammar in one or more of its configurations? To answer these questions, we must explore the ongoing development of SIL as an institution and the relationship of the Pikean heart and mind to the organization he served. These topics, in turn, are taken up in the next two chapters.

The future of his theory aside, Pike's linguistic research and the development of tagmemics secured for him a respected place in the discipline of structural linguistics and beyond. In the decades since Pike first postulated a distinction between the "etic" and the "emic," scholars have employed the terms and the associated theory not only in ethnography but also in psychology, sociology, medicine, education, and in the study of the phenomenology of religion.[87] Pike's etic-emic conceptual framework is perhaps his most significant and durable contribution to the wider academic world. Likewise, tagmemics proved quite useful for describing unwritten languages, and the structure of hundreds of languages worldwide have been analyzed from a tagmemic perspective by structural linguists. Yet, in a number of ways, tagmemics was only the beginning. Pike would eventually move into philosophy proper, with Christian thought and tagmemic theory forming the foundation of his philosophical ideas and speculations. The arc of his intellectual development was far from over with the development of his linguistic theory.

---

85. Brend and Pike, *Works and Contributions*, 63.

86. Brend and Pike, *Works and Contributions*, 96–97.

87. Headland, "Introduction," 16–24; McCutcheon, "Kenneth L. Pike," 28–36; Goodenough, "Anthropology," 434–35.

7

The Obedience of a Christian Man

ALAN S. KAYE, a professor of English, comparative literature, and linguistics at California State University, Fullerton, interviewed Ken Pike in 1994 for the journal *Current Anthropology*. In a lengthy introduction, Kaye summarized Pike's academic career, noting that he had been the President of the Linguistic Society of America in 1961 and of the Linguistic Association of Canada and the United States from 1977 to 1978, and had been awarded honorary doctorates from Huntington College, the University of Chicago, Houghton College, l'Université René Descartes, Gordon College, Georgetown University, and Albert-Ludwigs University, Freiburg. Kaye also reminded readers that Pike was a member of both the American Academy of Sciences since 1974 and the National Academy of Sciences since 1985. On top of all this, SIL's president and foremost linguist had lectured in no fewer than forty-two countries and had published more than a dozen books.[1] For a man who counted himself lazy, it was quite a record.

Then too there was Pike's professorship at the University of Michigan. When he returned from Papua New Guinea in 1962 for a full academic year at the university, he was awarded one of the Department of English Language and Literature's highest salaries, $14,000. And not for the first time he was pressured by the university administration to reduce his SIL responsibilities in favor of more time teaching.[2] He agreed to a program of two academic years at the university followed by an unpaid

1. Kaye, "Interview," 291.

2. Rice to Pike, July 2, 1962, PSC. Note: The $14,000 salary is more than $120,000 in 2020 dollars.

year away for SIL work.³ In 1974, the College of Literature, Science, and the Arts awarded him a named professorship, the Charles Fries Professor of Linguistics, and later that same year offered Pike the chairmanship of the Department of Linguistics.⁴ "I have now received," wrote acting dean B. E. Frye to Pike in December, "confidential letters concerning the chairmanship of the Department from a great majority of the faculty members of the Department as well as from a number of student representatives, and it is clear that you are the overwhelming choice of your colleagues for Chairman. It is clear that you are universally liked and respected, that you are regarded as one of the most prominent figures in the Department both in the area of scholarship and international reputation as well as in the area of teaching."⁵ The executive committee of the university concurred and Pike accepted the appointment in January 1975, and held the position until he retired from teaching in April 1977.⁶ Officially retiring from the university in May 1979, Pike was subsequently named Professor Emeritus of Linguistics in 1980.⁷

There was more, much more, but touching only on these main points demonstrates that Ken Pike was a respected international heavy hitter in the discipline of linguistics. He had come a long way from Camp Wycliffe, Townsend's rustic linguistic school in the backwaters of Arkansas in 1935, and it was the period from the 1960s to the 1980s that Pike reached his full measure of scholarly maturity and influence. He had helped to build SIL into a world class institution of applied linguistics and had made a deep and lasting impression on a generation of younger linguists. During these three decades, out of a robust sense of duty and Christian obedience, he probably pushed himself harder than at any other period, and he would suffer the consequences for his dedication. He also had to endure seeing interest in his tagmemic theory decline within SIL itself. Then there was his foray into mathematical linguistics, at which he mostly failed. Hence, the 60s, 70s, and 80s were a compound of outstanding accomplishment, disappointment, and personal struggle.

---

3. Pike to Rice, July 9, 1962, PSC.

4. Pike to Eunice Pike, March 21, 1974, PSC; Eunice Pike, *Ken Pike: Scholar and Christian*, 176.

5. Frye to Pike, December 16, 1974, PSC.

6. Pike to Frye, January 9, 1975, PSC; Frye to faculty and student representatives, January 22, 1975, PSC; Frye to faculty and students, March 30, 1977, PSC.

7. Award of professor emeritus.

Pike the Mule

Pike often characterized his dual career as a missionary and scholar with the metaphor of a mule, an animal produced by crossbreeding a donkey with a horse. He explained that he was sometimes a horse and sometimes a donkey but always a mule.[8] During the 1960s and 1970s, Pike divided his time by serving as SIL president, teaching at the University of Michigan and the University of Oklahoma, and conducting extended linguistic workshops around the world. He also guest lectured at universities, engaged in government and university relations work on behalf of SIL, mentored and furthered the scholarly careers of SIL academics, developed his theory of tagmemics, and wrote numerous articles and books. Pike rarely stood still, and whatever he put his hand to—whether in missionary service or in academia—he gave it his utmost.

He expected the same from students, and not a few found themselves overwhelmed. We can get some idea of what they experienced by quoting an early 1950s opening statement Pike made on the first day of classes at SIL Norman: "Our first lecture is an attempt to give you a tie-in with your previous experience and understanding of the basic metaphysical base upon which we are operating. Our first point is this, that any item in the universe, if you wish to know it well, needs to be thoroughly explained, but can be explained only in terms of the entire universe."[9] Students could be forgiven for feeling as though they were forced to drink from the proverbial fire hose. In the classroom, Pike not only displayed erudition but also projected a formidable personality, one with great intensity. When interviewed, former students offered up words like "scary," "intellectual dynamo," "passion," and "enthusiasm" to describe their teacher.[10] His high velocity mind churned as he scrawled linguistic descriptions on the chalkboard with blinding speed. After he began using an overhead projector, it became even more difficult for slower students to keep pace as he flashed previously prepared transparencies across the screen in rapid sequence.[11] One former student quipped that an "ordinary guy could barely hang on."[12] As Pike developed his tagmemic theory, his lectures became increasingly abstruse, and teaching assistants often had

8. Pike quoted in Simons, "Call to Academic Community," 83.
9. Pike, "Phonemics Lecture," 1.
10. Lyman, interview; Sheldon, email.
11. Bartholomew, interview.
12. Rupp, interview.

to explain the material to bewildered students. One assistant observed that "he went so fast, . . . he didn't worry much about pedagogy, about what it takes to get the concept across; . . . he was so intellectual [that] I don't think he could see it."[13] Perhaps, though, there was something of a method behind all this intensity. For him, SIL students were not just any students. "You are called by God to be scholars," he told them at Norman in a 1961 chapel talk, and "that is why you are here."[14] Linguist A. L. Becker once remarked that "Pike would often say that for many of his students the final exam was survival in that strange place, and that survival meant learning an unknown language very quickly. He'd say 'I am tough on you so you'll survive.'"[15] For the more advanced students, Pike's lectures could be a source of intellectual stimulation, but for the average pupil they could be harrowing. Whether a student understood little or much, no one who sat through Pike's classes ever doubted that they had come into the presence of a recondite mind. They also discovered that they were going to be pushed to the limit, and perhaps beyond.

Pike delivered chapel talks during summer sessions at Norman with even more gusto than his teaching. Passionate with swelling oratory, he sometimes shed tears. His arms swung as he rousingly led hymn singing. His daughter Judy said of her father that he was a "showman," an observation confirmed by many others who had witnessed Pike at the podium or in the pulpit.[16] His talks were not the stuff of commonplace homilies, most were filled with philosophical ideas and deep questions concerning the spiritual life. More than a few students came away from chapel scratching their heads in wonder or confusion. Expecting devotional pep talks, young evangelicals instead found themselves hard pressed to follow Pike's high-flown rhetoric. In the mid-1980s, an SIL couple recruited for non-academic support work, after hearing Pike in chapel for the first time, expressed their complete befuddlement and declined ever again to attend. However, they later met Pike in the dining hall where he recited his poem "My Blue Refrigerator," which apparently convinced them that he was worth listening to after all.[17]

13. Lyman, interview.
14. Pike, chapel talk, audio, June 13, 1961, PSC.
15. Becker, "Forward," xiii.
16. Judith Schram, interview.
17. Franklin, interview.

My blue refrigerator
Stands in spotless corner
Matched by towels and sink.
  * * *
— Now let's think
  * * *
Both bugs and dirt
'll soil rug and skirt,
'n my esthetics'll hurt.
I'd build bridges to heaven
With trestles of sweat
And cultural blunders I bet.
   Money'd go blow —
   Don't I know the peace corps
   Or missions'd leave me sore
Wounded in purse (or, worse, hearse)? and
Override materialism, and
Two-eyed blearialism?
  How on foot or earth
  Could I climb mountain ridge
  Or exchange fridge for — Bridge?
   * * *
Serve in Viet?
Nyet. Not yet.
Go? No.
  I'LL SURE PRAY
  But stay if I may.
  Hip Hurray![18]

Others took to Pike's talks with relish. Linda Ann Boice (nee McNamara) came to Norman after studying at the University of Pennsylvania. Pike's erudite discourses resonated with this intellectually inclined young lady, who went on to pursue graduate studies at Harvard and later married the well-known Bible teacher and pastor of Tenth Presbyterian Church in Philadelphia, James Montgomery Boice.[19] Pike was a gifted speaker, and he rarely failed to challenge his listeners to pursue their faith with both their hearts and minds.

The mule metaphor, symbolizing the combination of faith and science, was exemplified in the linguistic workshops that Pike led in

---

18. Pike, "My Blue Refrigerator."
19. Bartholomew, interview.

various SIL branches around the world. During sessions running from a few weeks to several months, he assisted struggling linguist-translators with a multitude of knotty linguistic problems, sometimes working in as many as twenty or more languages simultaneously. "I would jump down into the ditch with them," he once described it, "and try to boost them out."[20] As was the case in his classrooms, workshops were rigorous and thoroughly academic affairs. "The biggest thing to me was the general stimulation to the whole branch that came through this," one Mexico workshop participant recalled. "It was like having another second year course all over again[,] but this time about twice as intensive and very stimulating."[21] Thoroughly academic on the one hand, Pike nonetheless suffused the workshop program with spiritual intent. After an early 1960s workshop in Africa, the founder of SIL's work on the continent, John Bendor-Samuel, reflected on Pike's "reminding us again how this academic work could be harmonized perfectly with the spiritual emphasis which all of us share[,] which is the real motivation of our whole life." It was not unusual for SIL linguist-translators to feel that the academic aspect of their work was without spiritual significance. Pike, with his holistic understanding of faith and science, modeled an integrative approach that melded scientific work with the spiritual task of Bible translation. "Ken gave us," Bendor-Samuel went on to explain, "a perfect example of how the two things can go hand in hand [at] the same time and . . . this was a real inspiration and stimulus to our branch. Many of our folk appreciate this, I believe, as never before how our service to the Lord can be both technical and at the same time in the deepest way a spiritual service."[22] Although there always remained the tendency among some SIL members to dichotomize faith and science—valorizing the former over the latter—Pike's unstinting efforts to curb this kind of thinking left a deep impression on the organizational mind, and SIL endeavored to give equal emphasis to spiritual work, scholarship, and humanitarian service.

On a one-to-one basis, Pike mentored and encouraged countless young academics. It is impossible to know exactly how many SIL scholars owe their career trajectory to Pike's prodding and paving the way. A not unusual case is that of SIL's Karl Franklin. "I was meeting with him weekly and towards the end of the time he said, 'Franklin,' he was always

20. Kaye, "Interview with Kenneth Pike," 294.
21. Al Pence, quoted in Pike, "Pike-Talk at Ixmilquipan," 11.
22. John Bendor-Samuel, quoted in Pike, "Pike talk at Ixmilquipan," 14–15.

calling me that, I don't think he knew my first name. He said, 'Franklin, have you ever thought of going to graduate school?' And I said, 'Dr. Pike, I don't think I could get into graduate school with my undergraduate grades.' You know what his response was? 'Where would you like to go?'" Pike wrote Charles Hockett at Cornell University, a leading linguist and president of the Linguistic Society of America that year. "And the next thing I knew," Franklin recalled, "I was accepted into Cornell."[23] Pike was not to be disappointed in the young man. Franklin completed an MA in Linguistics and Anthropology at Cornell in 1965, and earned a PhD in Linguistics at the Australian National University, Canberra, Australia, in 1969. He then went on to produce significant scholarship, serve as the director of SIL's Papua New Guinea branch, and hold the position of Vice President for Academic Affairs in SIL from 1996 to 2001. Over several decades, Pike stimulated and encouraged an entire generation of SIL members to pursue graduate and postgraduate studies at universities around the world. He also recruited a number of scholars who already possessed doctoral degrees, such as Harland Kerr (University of Sydney), Paul Griffith (University of California-Berkeley), Robert Brown (University of Maryland-College Park), and Larry Yost (University of Maryland-College Park). The number of advanced degrees earned by SIL members continued to rise into the new millennium. Although other factors are certainly responsible for this growth, the legacy of Pike's influence was surely a considerable factor behind the increasing number of advanced degree holders in SIL.

Top student or not, finding one's self at the center of Pike's undivided attention could be a rather uncomfortable experience. SIL linguist Doris Bartholomew, in the 1960s, was called upon by Pike to explain "matrix theory," an aspect of tagmemics. While she basked in the glow of his attention, it came with a good dose of apprehension too. Fifty years later Bartholomew recollected the event. "And one summer I happened to be the focus of his attention, and you don't want to be the focus of Ken Pike, too intense!"[24] Future SIL executive director John Watters was no stranger to Pike's penchant for putting young academics on the spot. As one of about two hundred students, Watters imagined that he was safely anonymous on the sixth row of the lecture hall. But as Pike ended his lecture, he suddenly singled him out. "Pike turns to me and says 'Watters! Give us a

23. Franklin, interview.
24. Bartholomew, interview.

summary of what I just said today!,' I thought, 'I guess I'd better stand up internally to the challenge.' And fortunately I'd been paying attention and taking notes."[25] Students whose attention did waver during the brutally hot summers at Norman in the days before air-conditioning were rudely awakened by flying erasers hurled by their impassioned professor.[26] Even his children knew well their father's potency of mind. "We used to say," his daughter Judy reminisced, "it is a fearsome thing to be the sole occupant of father's attention."[27] In part, all this hyper-concentrated intensity was due to a quirk of his personality. The machinery of his analytical mind hummed and churned, but this left little room for everyday affairs. "I love the chitter-chatter of technical stuff—but," he admitted, "am afraid I will die from social chatter if I ever need any."[28] Few who fell under his gaze forgot it, but just as many were grateful for his pushing them along the scholarly path. Likewise, many ordinary working linguists were indebted to Pike for helping them solve seemingly intractable linguistic puzzles that blocked their way to a translated New Testament. Pike was a mule—a missionary and a scholar—and regardless of the mode in which he was operating it was carried out with force and focus.

Pike was as vigorous at play as he was in the classroom, perhaps more so. Volleyball was a passion he pursued during SIL summer sessions at Norman, Oklahoma. Afternoons would find him rallying students and faculty for volleyball games as a way to let off some steam and encourage camaraderie. He is remembered more for his gusto than being a talented player. It was "a game," one student later wrote, "which for Ken was somehow a warm-up for Armageddon."[29] Much the same could be said of his feistiness when playing water polo with the "Flounders." Matt Mann, swimming coach at the University of Michigan, Ann Arbor, initiated thrice weekly intramural water polo sessions in 1926 for faculty, graduate students, and local townsmen of all ages. These sessions continued for over fifty years. By any measure, "The Flounders" played a rough and tumble game tempered only by sportsmanship. Pike characterized it as "more like football-in-the-water than official water polo."[30] Lengthy

25. Watters, interview.
26. Watters, interview.
27. Judith Schram, interview.
28. Eunice Pike, *Ken Pike: Scholar and Christian*, 174.
29. Branks, "On Ken Pike's Death."
30. Pike, "Water-Broken," xx.

dunkings of the opposition were considered fair play. Tongue-in-cheek it was quipped that the informal rules prevented one to "hold a married man under water for more than five minutes."[31] Sheridan Baker, a professor of English literature, declared that Pike was "skinny . . . as a paper knife . . . but he was also remarkably tenacious and aggressive, and could hold out underwater and come back for more longer than anyone I can think of."[32] Opponents recalled being bruised by Pike's bony elbows as he fought his way out of an underwater stranglehold. "He handles his classes in the same roughneck way that he practices his favorite sport," a former Flounder recalled. "To know what that means, all I had to do was talk to some of the numerous bruised athletes limping around campus. The chances were pretty high that they would tell me they got their wounds playing waterpolo [sic] with Professor Pike—and not necessarily on the opposing team."[33] He suffered his share of blows too. The sixty-four-year-old Pike was sidelined by a ruptured ear drum inflicted during a polo session, but was back in the water two weeks later.[34] Pike's daughter Barbara penned a poem reminiscing about her father's water polo days, and the visible effects of the rough play:

> Pops came home with a black eye.
> His lip was swollen giving
> His mouth a battered look.
> A slight smirk reminiscent
> Of a tattered, scrawny alley cat,
> Made me wonder
> What the other guy looked like.
> I didn't have to ask, because
> I knew.[35]

He was not only an avid water poloist for many years, but he was also seen as an exemplar of the Flounders ethic, a combination of spirited play and sportsmanship. At work or play Pike was intense and vigorous, giving his fullest measure.

---

31. Watkins, "Water Polo," 81.
32. Baker, "Flounders Club," xv.
33. Fillmore to Evelyn (Griset) Pike, 2.
34. Pike to Bob and Mady, February 20, 1977, PSC.
35. Ibach, "Stones of Remembrance for Papa," 1.

Whither Tagmemics and the Continuing Battle for Scholarship

Even as Pike strained every nerve to make SIL both a Bible translation mission and an academic powerhouse, he continued to develop and expand his tagmemic theory of linguistics.[36] Indeed, tagmemics was seamlessly woven into Pike's teaching, consulting, workshops, and academic publications. Some of SIL's top linguists, including his wife Evelyn, added their insights to tagmemics and produced textbooks and other materials to make the theory more accessible to the average SIL linguist-translator. By the late 1980s, however, tagmemics was fading from the scene in SIL. The very theory into which he poured so much of his energy was giving way to a competing theory, one that he had criticized rather sharply, Noam Chomsky's generative-transformational grammar.[37]

Tagmemics was one of a small number of linguistic theories to emerge in the 1950s and 1960s, but to one degree or another all of them were relegated to the second rank by the appearance of Noam Chomsky's generative-transformational grammar. Chomsky promised to deliver a purely mechanistic generative grammar. He also aimed to uncover the universal properties that lay behind all languages. Pike himself had once hoped to produce a mechanistic theory, one that could account for "the total productive possibilities within [a] language" by way of a "mechanical discovery procedure." It was a dream that soon faded as the complexities involved multiplied. In part, it was Pike's insistence that meaning should not be divorced from structural analysis that compounded the complexity of tagmemics.[38] It was also his determination to avoid setting theory and logic above person that muddied the waters for tagmemics. In a word, the theistic underpinnings of tagmemics undercut any moves in the direction of purely mechanical analysis. Conversely, Chomsky specifically eschewed meaning, a move which streamlined his approach and lent to it the possibility of a mathematical-like representation. Put another way, Chomsky was looking to reveal the linguistic structure of the mind, Pike was looking for the structure of human experience created by God.

---

36. Pike's development of tagmemic theory is discussed at length in chapter 6.

37. For detailed background on Chomsky's generative-transformational grammar and Pike's tagmemics refer to chapter 6.

38. Pike, "Toward the Development of Tagmemic Postulates," 94–97.

By the early 1960s, Chomsky's generative-transformational grammar in various permutations was at the forefront of structural linguistics, and some of the discipline's best minds were gathering around the grand master at the Massachusetts Institute of Technology. Although Chomsky's theory, or variations thereof, dominated structural linguistics in the US from the early 1960s, tagmemics continued to hold its own into the 1980s. In North America, tagmemics was alive and well at the University of Michigan at Ann Arbor, Bowling Green State University in Ohio, Georgetown University, and the University of Oklahoma at Norman. Notably, with its more humanistic quality, tagmemics enjoyed a fine reputation in Europe, where Chomsky's more mechanistic theory did not initially garner the same level of interest. One of the most remarkable books on tagmemics to appear—due at least in part to SIL's openness to serving Roman Catholics—came from a Jesuit professor at Georgetown University, Walter A. Cook, SJ, who published *Introduction to Tagmemic Analysis* in 1969.[39] *Language in Relation to a Unified Theory of the Structure of Human Behavior*, Pike's tagmemic magnum opus, was reprinted in 1971. It was in 1977 that *Grammatical Analysis*, a textbook co-written by the Pike's was published, and it proved a popular text for teaching grammar at the University of Michigan.[40] Tagmemic articles, dissertations, monographs, language descriptions, and books numbered nearly five hundred by the mid-1970s, a point at which the theory was reaching its peak of development.[41] Pike's *Linguistic Concepts: An Introduction to Tagmemics*, one of his most readable books on the theory, appeared in 1982. Although various aspects of tagmemic theory would continue to appear in areas as diverse as discourse theory, cognitive linguistics, literature, and anthropology, the theory was, despite apparent success, enjoying its last days in the limelight in the mid-to-late 1980s. Within SIL some veteran linguists continued with the theory, but it slowly disappeared from SIL schools and Chomsky's generative-transformational grammar became the dominant theory in the organization's classrooms in the 1990s. By the turn of the century, tagmemic scholarship and teaching had virtually vanished both within and without SIL, although elements of the theory were absorbed into newly emerging theories such as cognitive linguistics. Tagmemics was not a failed theory; it simply

39. Cook, *Introduction to Tagmemic Analysis*.
40. Pike and Pike, *Grammatical Analysis*; Pike to Becker, March 29, 1979, PSC; Becker to Pike, April 20, 1979, PSC.
41. Waterhouse, *History and Development of Tagmemics*, 59–140.

suffered the same fate as other approaches to structural linguistics as generative-transformational grammar led the field.

Pike naturally favored tagmemics over all other theories, and was especially critical of Chomsky's mechanistic approach. In 1955, before Chomsky had become well known and was still at Harvard, Pike confronted the younger linguist at a conference. "I argued for meaning in linguistics plus form," he wrote his sister Eunice. "Chomsky from Harvard argued for phonemics without meaning. I thought his stuff sloppy, incoherent, and inconsistent. On three points I tried to force him to change—and at the moment he would budge, but not modify his basic position apparently, even though these things were relevant."[42] (Since Pike gave no details, it is impossible to know if his critiques had any merit.) Although Pike remained critical of generative-transformational grammar, mostly because of its mechanist presuppositions, he nevertheless urged his students at Michigan and in SIL to examine and learn what they could from competing theories such as Chomsky's, and even going so far as to invite non-tagmemic theorists to lecture in his classes and seminars, including Chomsky himself. Pike also encouraged SIL doctoral candidates to pursue studies at places such as Cornell University, the University of Pennsylvania, and Indiana University where they would learn other theoretical approaches.[43] These scholars returned to SIL where they conducted research and taught from a number of theoretical perspectives. In fact, this ecumenical approach to linguistic theories became official policy in 1967, when the corporate conference mandated it as standard practice.[44] The conference motion is worth quoting since it clearly demonstrates SIL's deep commitment to broad-based research. "Resolved: That the SIL Corporation reaffirm its long-standing de facto policy of encouraging research into and use of a variety of theoretical viewpoints and approaches, insofar as they interest our scholars, or contribute to immediate practical usefulness in research programs."[45] Pike was primarily responsible for this motion, and it reflected his abiding conviction that SIL's top scholars should explore the frontiers of knowledge. Indeed, Pike had, on more than one occasion, argued against a merely practical motivation for dissertation topics and research in SIL. In 1958, he broached

42. Pike to Eunice Pike, April 18, 1955, PSC.

43. Pike, "Reminiscences," 46; Pike and Pike, "Live Issues in Descriptive Linguistics," i, 2.

44. Pike to Pittman, et al., December 26, 1967, 3, PSC.

45. SIL Corporate Conference, minutes, May 1967, 15.

this topic with Ben Elson, who was then the SIL Mexico branch director. "I take it as a very high priority judgment," Pike wrote, "that the individual should in principle be allowed to do a dissertation in line with his personal interest. This would apply within certain limits even if the topic did not seem to be of the highest immediate practical application for the work. The reason for this is that whenever a research program is geared to practical ends it inevitably suffers long-range defeat—even from a practical point of view—because the most effective human discoveries are not made in strait jackets."[46] Coming from within the evangelical movement that prized activism over erudition, this attitude is remarkable. And the 1967 motion clearly signaled that SIL aimed to keep the life of the mind alive and was not afraid to make a heavy investment in scholarship. It also demonstrated that neither Pike nor the organization wished to build a tagmemic fiefdom in SIL.

The sheer complexity and philosophical cast of tagmemics was another factor in its ultimate fate. As the theory developed, especially the Pikean formulation, it became increasingly labyrinthine. The attempt to handle multiple levels of analysis and meaning at the same time demanded expansion of the methodology beyond what many of SIL's ordinary working linguists could feasibly control. As SIL linguist John Watters put it, "You have to be a theoretician to want to do that [tagmemics] the rest of your life." It was "easy," he added, "to get so lost in the structures, and Pike was overwhelming after a while."[47] The philosophical aspect of tagmemics was also cause for confusion at times.[48] As more and more SIL linguists studied generative-transformational grammar, it became evident that it was a superior heuristic tool in the hands of the average SIL linguist-translator. Pike himself noted the methodological or procedural utility of the generative-transformational approach. "You see," he told some of his colleagues at the University of Michigan, "one of the things which amuses me, but I haven't dared say in Chomsky's presence because I don't want an enemy, I really don't, but it seems to me that Chomsky's biggest contribution is heuristics, which he despised. It's is very funny . . . but—see, he has been useful to a lot of us. And his mode of argumentation is a heuristic."[49] What the typical translator in

---

46. Pike to Elson, October 28, 1958, 2, PSC.

47. Watters, interview.

48. Poythress to Pike.

49. Pike, faculty seminar, September 20, 1976, 41–42; see also: Pike, faculty seminar, February 21, 1977, 14.

the field required was a serviceable heuristic device that most easily facilitated language analysis, and one without the burden of capturing every conceivable grammatical and hierarchical relationship, while at the same time sustaining reference to meaning. The generative-transformational approach was, if more limited in scope, nonetheless more technically efficient than tagmemics. Thus, whereas Pike and a small cadre of linguistic scholars in SIL maintained an avid interest in linguistic theory, a majority of linguist-translators simply wanted to analyze the language in the most efficient manner possible so that they could move on to Bible translation. Hence, it was concluded that Chomsky's theory and its heuristic methodology best served their needs.

It is obvious from all this that there was some tension in SIL between the pledge to pursue scholarship at the highest theoretical level and the countervailing pressure to construe linguistics as a mere technical tool. The general orientation of SIL toward applied linguistics, as opposed to theoretical linguistics, also served to undermine the viability of tagmemics within the organization. Engagement with other approaches to linguistics in SIL opened up opportunities for other theories to challenge tagmemics. And, when the heuristic potential of generative-transformational grammar became evident, pragmatic concerns had the upper hand.

But there was yet another salient factor at work in all this. As the Chomskyan revolution played out it reconfigured the entire structural linguistic landscape, and this had repercussions for SIL. When Cameron Townsend linked SIL to the discipline of structural linguistics in the 1930s, research on Amerindian or other non-Indo-European languages was all the rage. Understanding of humanity was thought to be a process of examining human diversity. Hence, SIL, from the 1930s to the early 1960s, found itself on the cutting edge of the linguistic sciences as its linguist-translators produced numerous structural descriptions of indigenous languages. Chomsky turned this paradigm on its head. He insisted that the structure of the human mind could be explored through the study of a single language, in his case English. What he sought was the discovery of linguistic universals, ostensibly present in every language. By way of abstract representation, the basic patterns and process of all human languages could presumably be illuminated. As the paradigm shifted, linguistic fieldwork and language descriptions fell out of vogue. The move from the study of diverse languages to the search for linguistic universals effectively displaced the SIL linguistic program from the center to the periphery of the discipline of linguistics in North America.

The effect of this paradigm shift in linguistics was consequential for SIL, where applied linguistics remained at the forefront. Since the organization's research on indigenous languages was no longer in vogue, it became increasingly difficult for SIL linguist-translators to get their articles published. Looking back on these events from the vantage point of 1982, Pike lamented that "our production cut way down. Before that we were publishing in one journal an article every issue, sometimes two, sometimes three, and once the whole issue. After that our production got *way* down relative to our numbers."[50] SIL linguists would continue making contributions to various theories, including tagmemics, generative-transformational grammar, and stratificational grammar among others. But with Chomsky's theory dominant, SIL's applied linguistic focus was no longer at the center of a discipline now heavily focused on purely theoretical matters.

Defending Scholarship

Pike was always ready to mount a spirited defense of academic rigor and scholarly productivity, and he remained sensitive to undercurrents of missionary activism and anti-intellectualism that occasionally threatened scholarship in SIL. In 1967, the Papua New Guinea branch of SIL noted that the Bible translation projects of linguist-translators involved in lengthy doctoral degrees were seeing long delays. Worse yet, some members left SIL to teach in academia shortly after taking their advanced degrees. The branch's executive committee, in late 1967, took action to check what it saw as a double threat by officially prioritizing Bible translation over scholarship. The committee also barred both first term linguist-translators and those not demonstrating outstanding academic ability from entering advanced study programs. Only members who gave every indication of remaining in SIL long-term and who would almost certainly progress rapidly in their studies were to be considered for doctoral programs. These actions clearly upset SIL's president. "*One* of our goals," Pike reminded the executive committee, "is the translation. From the earliest history of our work we have also included scientific contribution

---

50. Pike, "Philosophy and Tagmemics," 17 (emphasis in the original).

and cultural contribution."[51] Pike was not going to allow scholarship to be subordinated to Bible translation on his watch.

In retrospect, Pike would discover that he had over-reacted by taking some of the committee's notes out of context, but he had good reason to worry in any case. Ben Elson, recently installed as SIL's first executive director, was brooding over the same trend. "I have been feeling uneasy for several years," Elson wrote Pike in early 1968, "and increasingly uneasy since last [corporate] Conference because I began to sense a kind of anti-academic attitude on the part of some of the delegates."[52] Opinion on the importance of scholarship within the organization was shifting. As WBT-SIL expanded, the number of members in non-linguistic support roles and administration increased. There was a tendency among this group to view scholarship as less important than Bible translation. Moreover, Wycliffe—the explicitly religious and missionary side of the dual organization—was becoming more influential in the 1960s as it developed a wider presence in the United States, where it engaged in fundraising and recruiting. Some members who identified with or worked strictly within the Wycliffe side of the dual-organization downplayed academics as a priority. A case in point was none other than Wycliffe president George Cowan, who wrote in 1966 that "I would . . . hope that we would never lose the emphasis in our work that completing a translation and giving the Word of God to a tribe is our calling, should have priority of time and effort as much as possible, and that sacrifices should be made at other points in the work where necessary in order to achieve it."[53] Cowan was not against scholarship, but he certainly saw it as a lesser priority than the missionary goal of Bible translation. Pike, of course, did not agree. He wanted "our people to act like scholars, talk like scholars, and look like scholars—not act, walk, look like preachers."[54]

Pike too, as he had from his earliest days in SIL, continued as a standardbearer for the role of women in academics. Arguing in the *Journal of the American Scientific Affiliation* in 1979, Pike countered those who took Pauline restrictions on women's roles as universal within the Christian faith by contending that the Apostle's teaching was culturally conditional. To emphasize his point, Pike allowed that in Paul's day it

---

51. Pike to Pence, February 16, 1968, PSC (emphasis in the original).
52. Elson to Pike, February 28, 1968, PSC.
53. Cowan to Pittman.
54. Pike to Pittman, March 12, 1962, 6, PSC.

might have been "best for the women to be quiet, and to wait to ask their husbands about matters at home. But," he emphasized, "such a situation has little culturally in common, or in rational demands on its subculture, with the Wycliffe [SIL] situation with its large number of trained women—[who are] often more erudite than the particular men present for a particular discussion or lecture." He had more to say on this topic. "Since, furthermore, brains are genetically evenly distributed, across the the sexes, as far as I know, and since many of our most competent men . . . have been elected to administrative office (by women, through majority vote), the major proportion of remaining academic brilliance is left with the women."[55] As long as Pike had anything to do with it, women scholars in SIL were going to enjoy absolute equality with their male counterparts.

Strains of missionary activism and anti-intellectualism remained threats to Pike's vision of what SIL should be. He had done much to build SIL into a truly academic institution, but there was always an undertow of anti-intellectualism and activist pragmatism that threatened to undermine these gains. Pike was unceasing in his efforts to make SIL a credible scientific institute, and his success on this front was undeniable. A major contribution to this effort was his small volume of essays published in 1962, entitled *With Heart and Mind: A Personal Synthesis of Scholarship and Devotion*.[56] As its title suggests, he sought to emphasize both missionary activism and the life of the mind. Pike lamented that "the evangelical wing of the Christian church has viewed scholarship with suspicion. Reeling under attacks internally from higher criticism and externally from science, it has sometimes withdrawn into a defensive cyst formation in order to weather the storm." To counter this trend, he urged evangelicals to undertake active designs for "making positive contributions to the world's knowledge."[57] He then reminded his readers that scholarship had long been integral to Christian thinking in America until the disaster of fundamentalism struck. For an example, he specifically pointed to the Puritans. "If we could succeed in re-establishing the old Puritan academic devotional witness on a broad front," Pike conjectured, "a changed intellectual climate for graduate schools as a whole would perhaps result. Secularism would cease being the only academic

---

55. Pike, "Christianity and Culture," 144–45.
56. Pike, *With Heart and Mind*, viii.
57. Pike, *With Heart and Mind*, 26.

option visible to many students of our universities."[58] This was not only a tall order but probably an impossible one, yet it reveals the depth of Pike's feeling on the subject.

Pike's voice was heard and, despite countercurrents, the weight of opinion remained behind his position. At the 1971 corporate conference, the delegates voted to "reaffirm our historical commitment to producing and publishing technical linguistic papers and monographs as an essential and substantial part of our task."[59] This did not mean that the problem simply vanished. He was forced to continue fighting anti-academic sentiments. At the 1975 corporate conference, for example, he charged that "any branch—and I think there are dozens of them this way . . . any branch which does linguistics only under special pressure, has a drop of poison in its bloodstream which will someday kill us. We can't survive it as an academic organization."[60] When he visited the Bolivia branch of SIL three years later, in 1978, he sensed that the "biggest problem" in the branch was the old divide between linguistics and translation. Linguistic analysis was still seen by too many translators as a task to get out of the way so that the "real" work of translation could begin in earnest.[61] This tendency to downplay academics and scholarship is clear evidence of an ongoing anti-intellectual strain within the evangelical movement. Even in SIL, where academics was stressed at every turn, this inclination to valorize the religious task of translation over linguistics persisted, and Pike was forced to push back against it. Yet, with that said, SIL remained a place where one could serve the cause of missions with both the heart and mind to the fullest possible extent.

A Labor of Love

Pike's Christian faith and personal humility served him well as Noam Chomsky's theory overshadowed tagmemics. In the summer of 1976, speaking to students at SIL's University of Washington linguistics course in Seattle, he said that "I was not as vulnerable to personal psychological collapse as many of my generation when TG [generative-transformational grammar] moved in and changed the outlook for most of the world."

58. Pike, *With Heart and Mind*, 27.
59. WBT-SIL Conference, S–7.
60. Pike, "SIL President's Report," 7.
61. Pike, "Translation Theory is Linguistics."

Why? He went on to explain: "My task was to take care of you first of all, rather than my ego first of all—don't forget, it is normal to take care of your ego, and it is normal to want to be dominant first of all. That's what Jesus said when He spoke about Gentiles wanting to dominate, etc. But that's not supposed to be ours—so your goals make a huge difference, in terms of survival. If what you're after is to do a job rather than make a name for yourself, it doesn't matter so much if someone pricks your balloon."[62] Service and dedication to students, to SIL linguist-translators, and to the WBT-SIL organization were more important to Pike than his theoretical or scholarly ambitions. He was not engaged in a war for academic turf or fame, rather he was dedicated to helping his colleagues analyze languages, produce scholarship, and translate the Bible. Above all else, Pike was obedient to what he saw as his calling.

If he seemed to have survived the decline of tagmemics with grace and humility, he nonetheless paid a price for his unwavering dedication to SIL. During the 1960s and 1970s, Ken Pike maintained a grueling pace as the president of SIL, serving on the board of directors of WBT-SIL, teaching at the University of Michigan and summers at SIL Norman, making multiple foreign tours, and conducting lengthy linguistic workshops. He gave the impression, at least to those who did not know him well, that all of this came easy. For the most part, it was only his wife Evelyn and sister Eunice who knew the full extent of Pike's suffering as he pushed himself to the breaking point. He was a deeply introspective man, and therefore given to lacerating himself for perceived failures, as his journals and private letters painfully reveal. The intensity of his mind was cause for much psychological stress.

In the heat of the moment, though, he could unwittingly lash out and would later suffer terrible remorse. This was especially true in the combative arena of academics, where the gloves sometimes came off. One SIL member recalled that he and other SIL faculty were "aghast" when Pike publicly castigated a fellow SIL linguist for a perceived weakness of logic in the man's lecture.[63] Pike knew that he was capable of bludgeoning those with whom he disagreed. He once recalled "trading blows" with George Trager in the 1950s over sharply differing theoretical perspectives. "And I decided," he later told some colleagues, "that wasn't a

---

62. Pike, "On Technical Writing," 14.
63. Franklin, interview.

good way of living. I didn't want to live that way."⁶⁴ Personal mastery is, of course, an uphill battle. In the early 1960s, he lost patience with Dick Pittman, who was less willing to demand exacting academic standards of SIL linguists than was Pike.⁶⁵ From a 1963 linguistic workshop in the Philippines, he wrote Evelyn that "I've had a terrifying battle again—my old struggle with bitterness towards people. Got word Dick would be coming from Viet Nam in April and all the flare up of old problems poured in.... May the Lord do something to change me.... After 25 years, this still is terrifying as I imagine fighting [and] scratching."⁶⁶ Former SIL President Frank Robbins recollected that he once observed Pike, who in an absent-minded moment, offhandedly dismissed a student requesting permission to hang up some posters around the campus. "He didn't do it meanly or anything, but as the guy was leaving he said, 'I was harsh on him wasn't I?' He teared up and couldn't talk, that was the end of the conversation. That really moved me."⁶⁷ Pike eventually achieved a good measure of control over his impulsiveness and social ineptitude. And, in fact, one must be careful not to read too much into his self-critical recriminations, since there are more extant testimonies to his kindness than his abrasiveness. In an early 1970s letter, Larry Kiddle, a fellow faculty member at the University of Michigan, wrote Pike saying, "your behavior as a linguist has always reflected your religious belief. I have heard your serene, self-disciplined presentation and defense of your point of view when your opponents resorted to degrading tactics and arguments. I admired you then as I admire you now."⁶⁸ Polemics in the discipline of linguistics were often rough and tumble affairs, and Pike with his intense nature was not immune to pugilism, but his Christian faith certainly softened his nature over time.

Pike also worked hard to cultivate humility. During the summers at Norman, he took his turn in the sweltering kitchen washing pots and pans alongside students and other faculty.⁶⁹ In the early 1970s, the Christian author J. C. Pollack considered writing a biography of Pike. Although the biography never materialized, it is worth quoting from Pike's response to

64. Pike, faculty seminar, October 18, 1976, 41.
65. Pike to Pittman, January 19, 1963, 2–3, copy of longer letter, PSC.
66. Pike to Evelyn (Griset) Pike, April 2, 1963, supplement B, PSC.
67. Robbins, interview.
68. Kiddle to Pike, August 20, 1971, 1–2, PSC.
69. Rupp, interview.

the writer. "It is very clear—painfully so—to me that I am a sinner; and a halo would not fit restfully upon my head. Insofar as I am concerned, I would want you to tell the truth, as you saw the truth."[70] He also displayed a healthy degree of intellectual humility. Among his notes is a prayer he penned in 1970. "Lord: I promise to try hard not to complain if someone else gets credit for results, provided (1) I can 'work' and get 'something done,' and (2) the credit in a deep sense goes to YOU—Psalm 115."[71] It is not too surprising, then, that when he discovered a festschrift was in the works he quashed the idea. Although Pike was "deeply honored and highly pleased" that friends and colleagues wished to honor him, he felt that articles appearing in such a volume would be "lost." It would be better, he thought, for such materials to appear in academic journals. "To do something which in my opinion is damaging to the discipline, but which at the same time is in my honor, puts me in a shame which I am not able to shake."[72] Pike was willing to trade on his status as a world-class scholar to serve SIL, but he was always reticent to accept personal accolades. If he was not always as gentle as he might have wished, to his credit he rarely let pride get the upper hand.

If he worried over stepping on the feelings of others and pined for humility, he suffered even more from some kind of ill-defined nervousness or the "jitters," as he called it. These episodes were, as they had been all his life, especially pronounced when he was under the pressure of extended social interaction or in situations that involved controversy or debate. Corporate conferences, lengthy workshops, and intense government and university relations work were all sources of unrelieved stress that produced extreme nervous tension. The severity of these attacks varied, but at their worst produced oral canker sores, stomach upsets, and blisters on his feet.[73] He sometimes wore sandals, even in winter, to combat the problem. He leaned heavily upon Evelyn for emotional support, and when forced to travel alone he suffered more than usual. A four-month round-the-world trip in 1963, one that took him from India to the Philippines and then to the West Coast for SIL meetings without Evelyn at his side, was just the kind of lonely and stress-producing journey that could lay him low. "Darling," he wrote Evelyn

70. Pike to Pollack, June 19, 1973, 1, PSC.

71. Pike, note, October 23, 1970, attached to Pike to Elson, December 16, 1970, PSC.

72. Pike to Rensch, January 24, 1978, PSC.

73. Pike to Evelyn (Griset) Pike, June 27, 1965, PSC.

from Calcutta, "Again tired, stomach queasy, spirits weary. Got annoyed today [and] it showed."[74] Pike's letters to her are frequently laced with such laments over stress, low energy, and the "jitters." Without Evelyn at his side, the heaviness could be almost unbearable. "I about died wishing you were here today," he wrote her from Manila, "or I there, all day long, just us two alone."[75] Heavy workloads without sufficient rest were also a source of anxiety, and sometimes even Evelyn's presence could not ease his burden. "The pressures here are intense," he wrote his sister Eunice from Ann Arbor during an exceptionally demanding semester. "I am not coping very well this fall."[76] In the late 1950s, he had resorted to taking tranquilizers prescribed by his doctor to relieve "tension."[77] For the next two decades, although repeatedly attempting to manage without them, he often resorted to tranquilizers when under pressure. During one particularly difficult European trip he was taking up to three Librium (chlordiazepoxide) daily.[78] Fortunately, it seems that he never became addicted nor experienced any major depressive episodes that might have produced suicidal tendencies. Pike suffered, and suffered often, as he carried out his heavy load of responsibilities in SIL, but he displayed fortitude in the face of his struggles.

We have already seen that the younger Ken Pike was beset by a lack of self-confidence. Despite his many outstanding accomplishments, he continued to be dogged by feelings of inadequacy throughout his life. One gets the sense that this was due at least in part to the habit of pushing himself when he could just as easily have taken a less demanding path. Two events that occurred in the 1960s illustrate this point. Linguists generally had to demonstrate proficiency in German during their doctoral studies, but Pike was allowed to substitute his fluency in Mixtec. He was distressed by this lack of competence in German, especially when in Europe. In 1964, he was scheduled to appear at the Fifth International Congress of Phonetic Sciences in Münster. Reading his paper in English would have been perfectly acceptable. Instead he began learning German, even going so far as to audit a reading course in German. The lightning speed with which he solved complex linguistic problems seemed to fail

74. Pike to Evelyn (Griset) Pike, February 13, 1963, supplement B, PSC.
75. Pike to Evelyn (Griset) Pike, May 8, 1963, supplement B, PSC.
76. Pike to Eunice Pike, October 28, 1969, PSC.
77. Pike to Evelyn (Griset) Pike, September 11, 1959, PSC.
78. Pike to Evelyn (Griset) Pike, May 10, 1976, PSC.

him when trying to memorize vocabulary or master spoken language. At the railroad station in Germany, he butchered the language severely enough that a clerk asked him to switch to English. Pike did manage to deliver three lectures in German, but often bungled the syntax. He found the entire process of struggling with a foreign language debilitating and humiliating. After all, was he not a linguist?[79] He wrote a poem, "Crushed," to express his feelings, which in part reads,

> Through culture strain
> Where words like spears
> Pierce rebel ear
> Where screams with pain
> Both dumb and blind.[80]

For the 1968-1969 academic year, Pike was awarded a fellowship to study at the Center for Advanced Behavioral Sciences located next to Stanford University. Rather than focus on an aspect of tagmemics, he instead chose to study mathematics and its relationship to linguistics.[81] Again, as with German, it was a slog and he never made the hoped for progress. He poured out his frustrations to Ivan Lowe, who had earned a PhD in physics from Cambridge before joining SIL. "I am ten percent of where I wanted to be, I bumped my head on my ceiling of speed."[82] It was a frank admission of failure. He was able to salvage enough of the experience to publish an article in *Language*, and it led him to push others, such as Lowe, to study the application of mathematics to linguistics. At the peak of his academic career, Pike was willing to risk failure when he could have taken the path of least resistance. The old fight against pride was certainly at work here, especially with the drive to prove himself in German. But when it came to mathematics, his aim was to aid his SIL colleagues by searching for potentially helpful approaches to linguistic analysis. Mostly defeated on both fronts, he nonetheless put on a brave face while encouraging others to risk failure.

---

79. Eunice Pike, *Ken Pike: Scholar and Christian*, 212–17.
80. Pike, "Crushed."
81. Pike to "gang," December 4, 1968, 2, PSC.
82. Pike to Lowe, April 29, 1969, PSC.

Pike and Townsend

Cameron Townsend remained a source of stress for Pike in these years. Their differing personalities and perspectives produced a relationship filled with tension, and it was one that at times threatened to fly to pieces. A continual source of strain was the general director's unrelenting demands for Pike to shoulder greater executive responsibility. In 1960, he pushed Pike to lead SIL's advance into Sub-Saharan Africa. He also hoped that Pike would at last relent and accept the position of deputy general director.[83] Pike prayed, wavered, but ultimately declined. He reminded Townsend of the need for an emphasis on scholarship in SIL, and warned that saddling him with additional administrative burdens would threaten his research and publishing agenda, and it would severely limit his ability to help others with the same. Pike also sensed that he could not handle the pressure. "I do not trust myself," he wrote Townsend, "with more responsibility. I doubt that I am in a position to handle it with humility, gentleness, and evenness of temperament."[84] This was very likely a wise decision, since he was already under incredible strain. Had he assumed responsibility for establishing SIL in Africa, it is a near certainty that it would have led to psychological breakdown, not to mention the deleterious effects on his scholarly output.

Another factor played a role in his decision not to take the deputy general director position, his turbulent relationship with Townsend. "Nor do I trust myself, he wrote Townsend, "to work intimately with you. God has helped me to learn to serve happily and vigorously at just a bit of psychological distance. It is by no means certain that I could do so closer."[85] It was simply impossible for Pike to work at close quarters with Townsend for any length of time without experiencing mental exhaustion. We get a sense of just how bruising these encounters could be from something Pike related to one of Townsend's biographers. "There is no one known to me in our organization," he told author James Hefley in the early 1970s, "who has worked closely with Uncle Cam without getting terribly clobbered. In some senses he's one of the most ruthless men I've ever known. . . . He is kindly to Latin Americans. He's ruthless to his colleagues."[86] Townsend's soft touch with government officials and

---

83. Townsend to Bendor-Samuel, November 8, 1960, PSC.
84. Pike to Townsend, November 22, 1960, 1, PSC.
85. Pike to Townsend, November 22, 1960, 1, PSC.
86. Pike, "Hefley Interview," tape two, 14.

Catholics, for example, was nowhere in sight when he directed his ire at insiders. Over the decades, Pike probably absorbed as many blows from Townsend, both real and imagined, as any top leader in WBT-SIL, and he was therefore not about to place himself in the line of fire by assuming the deputy general director role.

These two men of vastly different temperaments naturally butted heads. Ironically, despite frequent clashes, admiration and respect flowed both ways. Pike was willing to suffer the sometimes mercurial Townsend because he believed that the founder was a man called by God. There is no doubt that Townsend was consumed by a single-minded vision, and the WBT-SIL experiment was the embodiment of that vision. "Uncle Cam," Pike told Hefley, "more than any man I've ever known or expect to see has bent everything to this one point." But it was also a drive that could be carried too far in his opinion. "I feel," Pike emphasized, "that his personal life is bent beyond the point of decency."[87] A classic example of this was Townsend's effort to turn the Pike's wedding ceremony into a public relations event in Mexico.[88] For Townsend, nothing was so sacred that it could not be hitched to the WBT-SIL publicity wagon. Despite Pike's reservations and misgivings, he remained loyal to Townsend and generally backed his overall approach to developing the organization. In a word, he believed in the founder's vision. In 1973, Pike opined of Hefley's Townsend biography that "it is one of the greatest stories ever."[89]

Nevertheless, Pike still had to be nimble around Townsend. In the late 1970s, he told his sister Eunice that "I found that if I got close to him too long I would kind of collapse and lose the very independence of judgment which was part of my contribution to the program. It was a long-term question as to just how to stay close enough to his ideas to be able to get the stimulus and leadership which were very important, and on the other hand not get so close that it killed my own initiative."[90] Choosing to remain at arm's length from Townsend was Pike's solution. There was plenty to do in keeping the academic and scholarly machinery running, and this was work that could be carried out independently from the general director.

---

87. Pike, "Hefley Interview," tape two, 13.
88. This event is covered in ch. 3.
89. Pike to Hefley, February 13, 1973, 2, PSC.
90. Pike, "Questions with Eunice," diary, 1977, 7.

Family Man

By all accounts Ken Pike was a fine husband and father.[91] He and Evelyn were well matched, which made for an excellent marriage. Although Ken was very protective of women, this never kept Evelyn from being her own person. While serving alongside Ken, she carved out a professional career in SIL that complimented her husband's. A gifted teacher, she was able to take Ken's often abstruse ideas and writings and render them in a more straightforward fashion for use in the classroom and in textbooks. She also had a flair for crafting exams, and wrote many for her husband's classes. Their 1977 textbook, *Grammatical Analysis*, is probably the best example of how the Pike's collaborated to produce a better product than either could have done individually. It was not always easy, and in this case produced more rows than any other of their joint ventures. Ken was at first indignant when Evelyn failed to understand something he had written or when she criticized his sometimes awkward style. However, when a professional editor echoed many of Evelyn's criticisms, he was forced to acknowledge his mate's wisdom. In "a most annoying way," Pike wrote of the professional editor's comments, "she kept putting her finger on places which my wife had put her finger on, but I had just brushed it off. After that I tried to listen to my wife—it was still hard, but I tried harder."[92] The ever-sociable and socially-adept Evelyn was also ideally suited to helping her somewhat socially-inept husband. Finding the ordinariness of small talk monotonous, Ken nearly always directed conversations toward the theoretical or technical. When such redirection of topic was in poor taste or verged on becoming wearisome, with grace and ease Evelyn deftly interjected to keep the conversation earth bound. Providence certainly smiled on Ken Pike when Evelyn accepted his marriage proposal, and the couple enjoyed a lifetime of service together.

For all his erudition and scholarly stature, Pike nonetheless remained a kid at heart. His son Steve fondly recalls his father "belly busting down hills" on a bobsled during Michigan winters.[93] In Peru, Pike set aside the seriousness of linguistic workshops to race around in a canoe with his son or a daughter. Daughter Barbara tells of her father

---

91. Much of what follows in this section is based on Judith Schram, interview; Stephen Pike, interview; Ibach, interview; Terry Schram, interview; and, Evelyn (Griset) Pike, interview.

92. Pike, "On Technical Writing," 1–2.

93. Stephen Pike, interview.

and brother playfully exploding tin cans with cherry bombs and shooting off Roman candles. Evelyn was also known to have joined in on the fireworks, lighting off firecrackers with laughter and delight.[94] The family traveled frequently by automobile around the country. These excursions became celebrated events. Pike piled suitcases on the floor of the car in front of the backseat, and then layered cardboard on top of the suitcases to make a platform for the kids to sit on. A cringe-worthy setup by today's safety-minded standards perhaps, it nonetheless made for a wonderful perch upon which the children could huddle just behind their parents and join in convivial conversation. But, best of all, were their father's hugely imaginative stories that included the figure of Charlie the Giant, who could magically shrink small enough to ride an electron inside an atom or explore the molecular structure of steel. Another was of Shaggy Dog and his adventures. These stories were long and involved, and could last all the way from California to Michigan. So memorable were these lengthy drives with the elaborate stories and family camaraderie that when son Steve was asked what he wanted for Christmas, he suggested a road trip. It was, after all, a time during which the children could count on the undivided attention of their parents. Ken, and also Evelyn to a lesser extent, traveled extensively and the family was often separated for extended periods of time. Ken and Evelyn put forth an extraordinary effort to make the most of the family's time together. Indeed, the fact that the family survived the demands and hardships of their father's vocation and mother's own professional commitments is a testament to Ken and Evelyn's determination to ensure their children knew they were loved. Of course, the children's fortitude had something to do with the family's carrying the burden well too.

Ken Pike was an explorer, and he imbued his children with a curiosity to explore the world around them, whether it was music, nature, sports, or just plain intellectual curiosity. It would seem that there was an almost endless stream of adventures into places such as a university chemistry lab or a factory tour of one sort or another. Whether it was the world of ideas or the world around them, Pike never lost the opportunity to learn or teach.

Pike, the consummate intellectual, brought a literary sensibility to the family. He could be found of an evening reading Shakespeare, Milton's *Paradise Lost*, or the novels of C. S. Lewis to the family while the

---

94. Ibach, "Papa Ken and the *Canadian River*."

children amused themselves at quiet play. Thus, it is no surprise that he turned to writing poetry. It became a way for him to express his inner feelings and thoughts. After the children left home, his letters to them often featured his own brand of unique poetry, which was later gathered into a five-volume edition published by SIL in 1997. One reviewer described his poems as "Blunt. Staccato. Jarring. Plosive." Pike, she wrote, "does not waste words."[95] A poem expressive of Pike's fusion of heart and mind certainly demonstrates this penchant for brevity:

> Heart with mind
> Marry them together
> Lest both be
> Fruitless—
> Forever.[96]

He often wrote of pain and stress in life too, and the necessity of both. His "Pain Teaches Choice" speaks to the former:

> *Pain, when sent from God, teaches us. Without the need to make choices, in the face of possible pain, we do not grow to maximum strength.*

> No sun, yet quiet heart
> Has rested soul in gloomy sky.
>   Better far, we know,
>   Than raging pain in sunny light.
> Paradoxes light the fires
> With thoughts of night in realms of light
>   With tensions gone our drive is cooled
>   Away from battle, growth, or gain.
> So we face the drain of foe or pain
> And meet the night of daytime ache.
>   God loves enough to force a choice
>   Of paths unlit by darkened clouds.[97]

"Violin under Stress" is an excellent example on the stress of life from this genre of Pike poetry:

---

95. Harvey, "*Seasons of Life* Reviewed," 55.
96. Pike, "Heart with Mind."
97. Pike, "Pain Teaches Choice."

> *The focus, here, looks at the violin—needed for the stress to make music. Tension for us is the price of serving others. We've seen it in Jesus; we see it in Paul. II Corinthians 12:7.*
>
> Now, there's music.
> Without you,
> Who hears tears?
> Autonomous string can't sing.
>
> Play on!
> Let pain remain.
> Continue the refrain,
> Play on![98]

It has been said that the God in Milton's *Paradise Lost* is a rather distant and dull figure beside the more colorful Satan. Of course, human nature is drawn toward the errant and aberrant; one only need pick up the daily paper or peruse the shelves of a bookstore or go to the cinema to prove the point. However, we save our admiration and accolades for the upright, the one who fights the good fight, the who lives an ethical and commendable life in the face of trial and temptation. To examine the life of Ken Pike is to discover a man of moral rectitude, who through suffering and personal sacrifice sought to serve others. And we find a man unusually successful in that pursuit. Often socially isolated because of his superior intellect, Ken Pike nonetheless matured into a man who reached out to help others regardless of their station or the caliber of their mind. And he also strained every nerve to be an excellent father and husband.

Pike survived the dark valleys through his profound faith in God. His son-in-law, Terry Schram, remarked that Pike was "really aware of himself as living for God." Schram went on to add that he "would do things painful to himself because it was the right thing to do."[99] In a 1967 interview, Ken Pike reflected upon his sense of obedience in ministry, even if it meant suffering. "And men, broken in body, broken in pride, broken in spirit but willing to trust and willing to follow in order that the little ones, the scattered ones, the crumbs might hear the word of God . . . and therefore they would listen and a few of those would hear. It has been a great privilege for 32 years to see God's hand at work. That's just

---

98. Pike, "Violin under Stress."
99. Terry Schram, interview.

a part of it."[100] Anyone who knew Pike even passingly well would agree that, when it came to commitment to God, his faith was unequivocal. He never claimed to have all the theological answers, but he possessed an unshakable belief that God was to be served with all of one's heart, soul, and mind. Here it is best to let Pike speak for himself. In his devotional book *Stir, Change, Create*, he wrote: "The curious paradox: The scholar of Ecclesiastes sought to avoid pain, but ended up in mental anguish. Paul chose service, accepted pain, and through weakness became strong in God. Death is swallowed up in new life. Deep service costs pain. Whereas for nothing one gets nothing."[101] Obedience to his calling and a willingness to suffer were hallmarks of Pike's life as a missionary and scholar. So too was his honesty about failures, even when it was perhaps humiliating. From Calcutta in 1972, he wrote his friends and supporters of his struggle with the conditions he found there. "I am not yet immune to culture shock, nor, I find, are my colleagues who have been here several years. The constant tug of compassion for beggars, [and the] explosive annoyance at their bumping, pushing, following, incessant heckling, strains the strings of the soul."[102] Despite failings, setbacks, struggles, and feelings of inadequacy, Pike never doubted his calling to serve God. And this was something he strove to pass onto his WBT-SIL colleagues. Faith and service were frequently the topic of chapel talks, and some still recall him leading the hymn "It Will Be Worth it All" with heartfelt emotion.[103] Pike was imbued with an enduring sense that he owed his life to God, and he never abandoned his commitment to serve obediently down to his dying day.

100. Pike, "Peru 1943," 3.
101. Pike, *Stir, Change, Create*, 59.
102. Pike to supporters, March 4, 1972, 1, PSC.
103. Judith Schram, interview; Joice Franklin, interview.

8

Philosophy and Peace in an Era of Conflict

AT SIXTY-EIGHT YEARS OF age, Ken Pike was retired from his University of Michigan professorate and from his position as the president of SIL, but he was far from idle. He remained active as SIL's most eminent linguist and elder statesman. He also continued to enjoy the status of an internationally-known scholar and intellectual. In 1980, Ken and Evelyn Pike took up residence in Dallas, Texas. It was here in the early 1970s that SIL established its headquarters. The International Linguistics Center (ILC) provided SIL with a campus independent from Wycliffe, which retained its base of operations in Huntington Beach, California.[1] SIL launched a linguistic school on the ILC campus, and entered into a cooperative academic program with the nearby University of Texas at Arlington (UTA). The joint SIL-UTA program, which began with the fall semester of 1972, provided for the sharing of faculty between the two schools and the opportunity for students to pursue graduate studies in linguistics. By 1996, over 800 Master of Arts degrees had been awarded.[2] Pike joined the UTA faculty in 1980, and taught philosophy of language courses.[3] Thus, down to the time that his health began to decline in the early 1990s, he continued to be very much a part of the life and work of SIL. Pike's move to Texas was also the occasion for exploring new intellectual frontiers.

1. Wycliffe-USA is now located in Orlando, Florida.
2. Pike to Witt, October 17, 1996, PSC.
3. Perkins to Pike, April 28, 1980, PSC.

The confluence of several factors precipitated Pike's move into philosophy. The first, and probably the strongest, was his insistence on the integration of meaning into linguistic analysis; that is, he never accepted purely detached abstract analysis. Pike was always reminding his readers and auditors that the individual person was above logic. Language in context, human thought, and social interaction were all at the center of his approach to linguistics, and thus he was inexorably pulled into thinking about the totality of the human experience. "Person," he wrote to SIL members in 1987, "has to give the presuppositions by which we do our linguistics. It has to start with person, it cannot start with logic; it cannot start with facts. It starts with inner personal reaction to life, to God, to reality, to the world. And then some of these things that are in us, we can't put into logical propositions. They are by feelings."[4] It is doubtful that any other American linguist went this far in allowing meaning and sensation into theoretical linguistics. But, as already argued, Pike was something of a Christian humanist, and it was therefore all but inevitable that he would range well beyond the normal disciplinary confines.[5]

The cultural and revolutionary ferment of the late 1960s and 1970s and the collapse of overarching metanarratives under the onslaught of postmodernism also combined to push Pike into a more reflective or philosophical mode. He was an eyewitness to the tumult of student protests and demonstrations of this era. His response was neither that of a conservative reactionary nor that of a fellow traveler. He saw the student unrest as stemming not so much from revolutionary desire for change as from a "thirst for meaning."[6] The moral relativity embodied and espoused in much of secular academia over the previous generation or two had, he believed, undermined classical humanism and stifled the moral imagination. What was left in the wake of this process was a more materialistic and scientific view of life. Thus, students lacked the moral resources to address the social and economic injustices they saw around the world, not to mention the perceived injustices perpetrated upon them by unresponsive institutional and governmental bureaucracies. Judging that students were deprived of a larger sense of meaning, he concluded that they were predictably lashing out in fear and anger. To wit, in 1967, Pike wrote that he "believed the current generation was demanding a

---

4. Pike, *Pikes Perspectives*, 161–62.
5. Ch. 6.
6. Pike, *Stir, Change, Create*, 78.

kind of moral security which they had—unfortunately—not been given by our generation."[7] In his view, a larger share of the blame rested not upon the students but upon academia and Pike's own generation.

The upheavals of the late 1960s did not eventuate in a renewal of old moral certainties or shared metanarratives in American society. And, in much of secular academia, all that flies under the banner of postmodernism suffused the humanities as the twentieth century drew to a close. Increasingly, the loss of belief in truth and traditional values in the wider culture precipitated the culture wars and led to social fragmentation. Rather than preach jeremiads, Pike instead looked to the consolation of philosophy, albeit with an underlying Christian epistemology and ontology. He sought to construct a plausibility structure that would permit non-Christians to regain confidence in human reason and recover the possibility of apprehending some ultimate truths—with hopes that this step would perhaps then lead them to belief in God. At the same time, he aimed to help Christian students survive and even thrive in secular academia without losing their faith.

To accomplish his goal, Pike grounded his philosophy in person and language. "We cannot *start* with logic," he wrote in *Talk, Thought, and Thing*, a small eighty-five page book summarizing his philosophical ideas, "unless we *first* have 'ourselves.' A child *is* before it is *grown*. A child trusts its mother—a person must trust unproven convictions about life before using them to argue about other things. Here we come full circle—from person, to language-in-society, to knowledge, to arguments for validity, and back to person so arguing."[8] "And I want," he emphasized, "my postulates to begin with the ontological, moral, and aesthetic validity of the person."[9] For Pike, then, it was a philosophy grounded in "person as interacting through language with other persons, along with interaction with things and events in that environment."[10] It was an altogether sensible place to begin, for as philosophers since Wittgenstein increasingly understood, language and social interaction are fundamental to human experience; and, without language there was in human terms nothingness, not meaninglessness, but a total psychological and social vacuum.

---

7. Pike, *Stir, Change, Create*, 87.
8. Pike, *Talk, Thought, and Thing*, viii (emphasis in the original).
9. Pike, *Talk, Thought, and Thing*, 59.
10. Pike, *Talk, Thought, and Thing*, vii–ix.

Throughout his academic career, Pike had taken pains to keep his Christian belief at some distance from his scholarly writings. As we have seen, his theism certainly formed the epistemological base of his theory of language, but he only rarely acknowledged this fact in secular settings. As he moved into philosophy, he became even more committed to observing—at least on the surface—the post-enlightenment separation of science and religion, and therefore crafted a philosophy that would not easily offend the sensibilities of the non-Christian. He explained his position in some detail to Harvard philosopher Willard Quine, with whom he had struck up a friendship. "My current purpose," he wrote Quine in 1983, "is to talk—when I am discussing philosophy—about metaphysics and epistemology, and to avoid carefully, if I can, ethics and theology. I am, as you probably know, very much interested in Christian issues. But I very much fear that if I should attempt to talk about them in this other context that I would do more harm than good. It could arouse antagonism from people whom I could not help that way, when there is a chance that I might help them if I stick closer to my own discipline."[11] He wanted to fashion an integrated philosophy, he told theologian Bernard Ramm (with whom he had much in common intellectually), that on the surface appeared as secular and mechanistic but, at the same time, "leaves the door open to theism."[12] Back of it all, however, was his Christian ontology: human beings were created by God in God's image. But this was implicit rather than explicit. Hence, *Talk, Thought, and Thing* did not give the appearance of something produced by an evangelical Christian, although he explained in passing that he believed in a "theistic accounting for the universe."[13] Of course, it must be emphasized that he was not constructing an overtly Christian apologetic. *Talk, Thought, and Thing* was an attempt to buttress faith in reason on the one hand while parrying postmodern relativism on the other.

The thrust of Pike's philosophical argument was that theory construction and scientific reasoning were expressions of what it means to be a human being. Therefore, theory construction and scientific reasoning were not simply abstract mechanical processes devoid of emotional or spiritual content.[14] By starting with person and human

11. Pike to Quine, September 7, 1983, PSC.
12. Pike to Ramm, January 5, 1983, PSC.
13. Pike, *Talk, Thought, and Thing*, 69.
14. Pike, *Talk, Thought, and Thing*, 74–75.

social interaction, Pike attempted to construct a philosophy that one could "live in" and "think by."[15] This was an effort to undercut postmodern skepticism. He believed that if a skeptic could be brought this far, then perhaps he or she could go on to at least consider the plausibility of something higher: a creator and maker of truth. For the Christian reader, he had modeled a method of philosophical inquiry that conformed to the post-enlightenment science-religion dichotomy. A Christian student or scholar could, he argued, think with a Christian mind while speaking and writing in the voice of secular academia. It was not necessary, as he saw it, to thrust God or the Bible into every conversation or piece of academic writing.

It is impossible to know how much influence *Talk, Thought, and Thing* had on readers. As of 2020 it had been quoted or referenced in no fewer than eighty-seven different scholarly books or articles.[16] That said, it was certainly not Pike's most engaging work. It has an almost medieval scholastic feel to it. By and large, the book was more a model of how to think like a Christian while writing in the vocabulary of science than anything else. However, that *Talk, Thought, and Thing* was quoted and referenced by scholars suggests that it did accomplish what Pike had set out to do: to put his theistic-based philosophy before secular scholars in a non-threatening fashion.

The widening and deepening of Pike's intellectual life made an impact on the Summer Institute of Linguistics and its members, and by extension on the peoples and communities it served. As SIL's leading linguist and intellectual he continued to exert considerable influence on the organization. As we have observed in previous chapters, whenever pragmatic or anti-academic strains of thought threatened to undercut SIL's scholarly approach, Pike would contend for the historical status quo that he had helped to sustain since the late 1930s. While not underestimating the influence of Cameron Townsend, Dick Pittman, George Cowan, and Ben Elson, among others, on the nature and work of SIL, it remains that without Pike's steady hand on the tiller the organization would likely have turned out to be far less scholarly. Likewise, WBT-SIL could well have ended up staying closer to the fundamentalist camp than the moderate-to-progressive wing of evangelicalism. Hence, Pike was an intensifying stimulus for linguistic research and a moderating influence religiously. He

15. Pike, *Talk, Thought, and Thing*, 10.
16. I am indebted to Gary Simons, SIL's chief research officer, for this data.

brought a sense of intellectual breadth to SIL, something not often found in mid-twentieth-century North American evangelical organizations.

Pike was also forceful in maintaining that linguistic research and community development were essential to SIL. Whereas Townsend averred that "scientific work is not a spiritual ministry" and that literacy or other such projects should be "dropped into the lap of the national government" when Bible translation was completed, Pike insisted from his more holistic humanitarian perspective that these projects were integral parts of SIL's threefold mission of Bible translation, linguistic research, and community development.[17] Pike wrote in June 1987 that "the will of God was for man to be creative in the image of God, creating through his world view, organizing his environment, his ecology and all the rest of it too, through linguistics and part of our will from God, as I believe it to be and has been from 1935 when I moved into it, is linguistics for linguistics' sake. NOT just for Bible translation. Because we were created to be that."[18] If he tended to keep his science and religion apart in his scholarship—at least in an explicit fashion—as a leader in SIL he unstintingly emphasized integration. Science was not unspiritual when it was done for the glory of God and the good of humanity. Pike's impact upon the organization was indelible, and it was a key factor in SIL manifesting both a durable and broader humanistic vision than any other mission or organization within the evangelical movement of the time.

Despite its atypical nature, WBT-SIL had navigated successfully the rupture between the fundamentalists and neo-evangelicals in the 1950s and 1960s. As the internecine struggles within North American evangelicalism subsided, WBT-SIL found itself in harmonious company with the majoritarian wing of the evangelical movement that was itself beginning to shift in the direction of WBT-SIL's longstanding ethos. However, a new set of critics lurked on the horizon, this time coming from the secular world, anthropologists to be specific. By the mid-1970s, WBT-SIL was under a barrage of sustained and severe attacks that threatened its hard-won academic reputation and its operations in more than a few countries, especially in Latin America.

17. Townsend, report to board of directors, 1; Townsend to Cowan, November 10, 1977, TA 33648.
18. Pike, *Pike's Perspectives*, 165.

Attacks from the Left

In the late 1960s, the discipline of anthropology was seized by the revolutionary fervor that was spreading around the world, visible in events such as the 1968 Paris riots, the Vietnam War protests, and the decolonization of Africa. Redressing the wrongs of the past visited upon less-developed nations and minority peoples by the West became a crusade within the discipline of anthropology. SIL was bound to attract the attention of anthropologists and the Left in general. By the late 1960s, SIL was an international organization cooperating with governments around the world to bridge indigenous peoples into national life through language development, education, and community development. In other words, SIL was not only highly visible but probably the largest and most significant private organization in the world intimately involved in indigenous communities. Its sources of financing also attracted unwanted attention. While a majority of the organization's funding flowed through its individual members, who developed their own sources of income, SIL was increasingly garnering funds from entities such as United States Agency for International Development and from wealthy capitalists. At a time when the protests by the political Left were most potent, WBT-SIL was suddenly under scrutiny from anthropologists who were becoming increasingly vocal about western imperialism and the destruction of minority cultures.

WBT-SIL leaders were aware of the increasing revolutionary and anti-western sentiment, but there was no sense that a crisis was afoot. All that changed when American anthropologist Laurie Hart published an article in 1973 entitled "Story of the Wycliffe Translators: Pacifying the Last Frontiers." It was a scathing indictment published in the North American Congress on Latin America's (NACLA) journal *Latin America & Empire Report*. She argued that SIL's strategy was designed to leave indigenous peoples in a "decultured" condition so they could be reprogrammed as subjects of the state. Moreover, she construed the effects of evangelical religion, with its "millennial expectation" and "submission," as dampening the revolutionary impulses of minority groups and thus making them less likely to engage in class struggle. The "WBT worldwide 'evangelical advance,'" Hart argued, was nothing less than "a religious manifestation of U.S. cultural and economic imperialism."[19]

---

19. Hart, "Story of the Wycliffe Translators," 17.

The anti-SIL crusade reached the University of Michigan at Ann Arbor when twenty-three-year-old anthropology major David Stoll read Hart's article and connected the dots to Professor Pike. Stoll's article, "Onward Christian Soldiers," appeared in the March 26, 1974, edition of the *Michigan Daily*, a University of Michigan campus newspaper. Much of the piece was a rehash of Hart's article, and Stoll repeated the ethnocide charge. Moreover, he considered it "perverted" that the university, through its employment of Professor Kenneth Pike, was complicit in the destruction of indigenous cultures.[20] Pike's response was printed in the same issue of the *Michigan Daily*. "I am very grateful," he wrote, "that the students of this country, including those of this university, for taking leadership in insisting that there should be a moral component in international, university, and personal affairs." What he could not agree with was the idea that indigenous peoples were best served by either leaving them alone or agitating against the state. Pike believed they were in dire need of help to survive the incursions into their domains by governments and corporations, both foreign and domestic. "I would prefer," Pike concluded, "to take the risk of trying to be helpful, while praying that God will make more good come from my good intentions and positive efforts than damage from my cultural insensitivities and ignorance."[21] In the aftermath of Stoll's *Michigan Daily* denouncement, Pike invited the young man to observe SIL's work at first hand in Latin America, in hopes that it would alter his perception of SIL.[22] Stoll accepted the offer and, in 1976, spent several weeks with SIL anthropologist James Yost in Ecuador. He also later visited SIL's operation in Peru. Pike's overture unwittingly launched Stoll's academic career as one of WBT-SIL's major critics.

SIL was in a precarious situation. As the critics saw it, the organization was a staunch supporter of powerful rightwing imperial interests. And, it was argued, by cooperating with repressive regimes, SIL was aiding and abetting the enemies of the people it professed to serve. Above all else, critics charged that by inculcating Christian pacifism and national patriotism, SIL was making compliant and deracinated citizens out of minority peoples, which amounted to nothing less than ethnocide. On top of all this were the accusations that the organization was fronting for the US Central Intelligence Agency, an unsubstantiated claim that

20. Stoll, "Onward Christian Soldiers," 1.
21. Pike, "Professor Pike Replies."
22. Hibbard to Robbins, May 7, 1982, TA 938931.

was repeated so often it became a cliché which could be tossed around in lieu of anything else to say. The animus toward WBT-SIL spread like a fire among anthropologists.[23]

By the mid-1970s there was a sense within WBT-SIL that it was under siege. Clarence Church, director of the Wycliffe US division, in 1976 reacted to WBT-SIL's woes with the words "we are living in a most confusing time, not only in the history of our country and the world, but also for us as an organization."[24] Church had good reason to worry. SIL had just departed from Vietnam and Nepal, it faced eminent ejection from Peru, and its contract with the Colombian government was threatened. At meetings of the American Anthropological Association, SIL scholars found themselves recipients of withering criticism. They also experienced much the same kind of vitriol at meetings of the International Congress of Americanists. The blows kept coming and SIL's antagonist looked forward to SIL's demise.

That was not to be. SIL's foes underestimated the object of their scorn. A case in point is an ethics investigation of SIL undertaken by the American Anthropological Association (AAA). After reading the anti-SIL articles authored by Laurie Hart and David Stoll, Catherine A. Callaghan, an associate professor of linguistics at Ohio State University, recommended in 1975 that the AAA ethics committee investigate the organization. No specific charges were leveled by the AAA against SIL, but the object of the investigation was to ascertain whether or not the wide-ranging accusations made by Hart and Stoll had any merit.[25]

It fell to Pike, as president of SIL at the time, to compose a response. In his thirteen-page rebuttal, he first argued that SIL's language development and literacy efforts bolstered the cultural confidence of indigenous peoples. "Many of these persons," Pike wrote, "have found their psychological strength greatly increased after becoming literate. The dignity of the new literate under pressure from old literates around him is greatly strengthened." To back up this claim, he submitted SIL's 1972 bibliography, in which there were no fewer than 2,361 literacy items listed representing some 372 languages. He pointed out that with increasing frequency it was newly literate indigenous individuals themselves who were producing these literacy materials under SIL's guidance. "It should

23. A more comprehensive account of the criticism of SIL in the 1970s and 1980s can be found in Aldridge, *For the Gospel's Sake*, 194–222.

24. Church to Cowan, March 22, 1976, TA 33470.

25. Callaghan to Spradley.

be especially noted," Pike wrote, "that many of the more recent materials listed in the bibliography were written by persons who recently were totally preliterate. There has been extensive emphasis upon developing vernacular authors, writing in their own languages, on topics chosen by themselves, and of interest to their own communities."[26] SIL was clearly providing sorely needed literacy and language development help to impoverished indigenous communities worldwide, which otherwise would have been bereft of such help.

But what about Christian religion? Pike pulled no punches in defending SIL's "metaphysics." He argued that "the psychological welfare of any society, as a whole, requires a moral component. We are therefore quite unwilling to treat individuals whom we study as if they were merely non-moral objects, or purely physical-social ones." And he was clear as to what moral system SIL offered. "We wish to leave with them Biblical documents, which we consider to be the best documents of humanity, and which still have a heavy impact on many of us as individuals." This was a bold statement, bolder yet when considering that in the mid-1970s the hostility toward missionaries in secular anthropological circles was at a fevered pitch. But it was the truth, and Pike was in the habit of telling the truth. He even went on to explain that it was their Christian faith which primarily motivated SIL members. To accomplish its goals, he stated, "SIL has to recruit members whose motive is to serve God and to serve man simultaneously." As if all this was not clear enough, he explained that "we have explicitly and publicly made the choice to base our convictions about reality upon the Bible, interpreted in a way commonly known as 'evangelical.'"[27] Critics could anathematize SIL's evangelical religion and the propagation thereof, but they would be hard pressed to sustain the argument that the organization was hiding its religious motives behind the scientific veneer of SIL.

As for shielding indigenous peoples from outside influences, something for which many anthropologists were arguing, Pike pushed back in no uncertain terms. "We explicitly reject the view that any minority culture ought to be artificially kept in some kind of social museum for the benefit of anthropological observers; persons of minority groups should have every right that we claim for ourselves to develop as persons within a larger sociological context." He was as much as accusing anthropologists

26. Pike to Beals, 3.
27. Pike to Beals, 6–9.

of their own brand of cultural imperialism, if not racism. As Pike saw it, SIL actually had great respect for indigenous peoples and their ability to make informed choices. He summarized SIL's strategy of serving indigenous communities from within the context of state modernization by framing the discussion in terms of "cultural pluralism." He declared, "we believe that the separate cultural entities in the modern world need to be provided an opportunity for self-realization within the larger society to lead to national coherence-in-diversity within which each group ultimately supports the other."[28] Perhaps it was an overly optimistic strategy, but the organizational philosophy of culture change orientated SIL toward constructive action.

In the last place Pike laid bare the questionable practices of North American Congress on Latin America (NACLA), the publisher of the Hart article. By including extracts from the *NACLA Research and Methodology Guide* with his AAA rebuttal, Pike provided unequivocal evidence that the organization practiced subversive tactics. Quoting at length from the booklet illustrated that NACLA instructed its operatives clandestinely to infiltrate institutions and organizations that it opposed and hoped to defame.[29] It was damning evidence that there was a darker side to NACLA.

Pike's exposition of the SIL strategy laid all the cards on the table before the most prestigious and respected scholarly anthropological association in America. The reviewing subcommittee of the AAA's committee on ethics issued its findings in November 1975. The reviewers stated that "further investigation of the matter . . . is unlikely to be fruitful." In part, they noted that the vague wording of the AAA's statement of ethics made for difficult application to the specific charges against SIL. If, however, they had discovered sufficient grounds to sustain the accusations, it is doubtful that the reviewers would have let this stand as an obstacle. More significantly, the reviewers had good things to say. They complimented SIL for the timely "remedial measures" it took when some of its members inadvertently introduced a non-native disease into an indigenous community. "The organization [SIL] is almost unique among anthropological organizations in its concern with disease prevention and medical treatment."[30] Perhaps the most startling aspect of this affair was the

---

28. Pike to Beals, 4–6.
29. Pike to Beals, 10–12.
30. Recommendations subcommittee for Case 75-2, 1.

committee's unwillingness to condemn Pike's statements on the merits of propagating Christianity. Considering the anti-religious temperament of the times, it would be expected that this point would almost certainly have drawn fire. That was not the case at all. "These are not," the report stated, "the sorts of issues that an investigation is likely to resolve." While not exactly an endorsement of SIL's religious aims, this amounted to an implicit consent. The subcommittee's report was unanimously accepted by the full AAA ethics committee and, at the Eighty-Fifth AAA meeting of May 1976, the association's executive board unanimously placed its seal of approval on the report.[31] The AAA not only exonerated SIL, but it also acknowledged that the institute was a legitimate anthropological organization and that its religious nature was not sufficient reason for indictment.

Of course the AAA's acquittal of SIL did not end the criticism. In 1982, David Stoll published *Fishers of Men or Founders of Empire?: The Wycliffe Bible Translators in Latin America*. As Ken Pike had suggested, Stoll undertook a study of SIL's work at close range. He left few stones unturned. This 344-page volume is detailed and wide ranging, covering SIL's operations in Brazil, Columbia, Ecuador, Mexico, Peru, and several other locales. The book examined SIL's varied relationships with, and its willingness to serve, corporations, national governments, and military regimes of various stripes. It also covered the connections between SIL and the US Government, such as the organization's receiving sizable aid from the United States Agency for International Development. The fact that SIL was such a large presence in indigenous communities made it an obvious target for Stoll's criticism.

What Stoll questioned was SIL's strategy and aims. Whereas Pike and SIL assumed that indigenous peoples' entry into the modern world was best carried out under the aegis of the state, Stoll was convinced that this was rather a case of SIL working hand-in-glove with free-market capitalists, neo-colonialists, and American imperialists. He believed that indigenous peoples were best served by protecting them *from* multi-national-corporations, the state, and the negative effects of US foreign policy. Stoll also focused on the nature of the dual-organization, arguing that it was mostly a ruse, and thus simply a part of WBT-SIL's larger strategy to smuggle evangelical Christianity into otherwise inaccessible indigenous communities. "Even if," Stoll wrote, "some form of contact

---

31. Lehman to Pike.

with the world market was inevitable, WBT-SIL's hidden church-planting agenda, with its sweeping disrespect for religious tradition and subservient attitude toward bad government, was not."[32] SIL was, in other words, on the wrong side of the fence.

Fishers of Men or Founders of Empire? is arguably the most frequently quoted book about the organization. Although it generally paints WBT-SIL in poor light, it is nonetheless constructed with ample facts and is often well documented. Indeed, Stoll proved himself a gifted investigative journalist, and the book provides nuanced insights into the organization's mindset and methodology. There is a tendency, however, for the book to veer off into innuendo or into strained interpretations of events. Thus, while *Fishers of Men* is, at many points, a well-informed evaluation of the WBT-SIL strategy, it is nonetheless marred by the young Stoll's eagerness to cast a pall over SIL. In any case, when all was said and done, David Stoll and Ken Pike remained at odds over how best to serve and support indigenous communities.

In 1981, the year before Stoll's *Fishers of Men* was published, *Is God an American?* appeared. Flawed by poor scholarship and more than a few *ad hominem* attacks, this was a collection of anti-SIL essays by North American and European anthropologists.[33] Investigative journalists Gerald Colby and Charlotte Dennett, in 1995, published a nine-hundred-page tome that alleged a conspiratorial relationship between Nelson Rockefeller and Cameron Townsend to exploit Latin America's natural resources.[34] Despite its extraordinary length and exceedingly complex plot, the authors failed to furnish any evidence that the two men ever met.[35] Time and again SIL's critics stooped to muckraking rather than presenting an objective critique of SIL. Sometimes these allegations even turned comical. Rumors that SIL had constructed a secret missile base and operated a uranium mine at the bottom of Lake Lomalinda in Colombia were some of the more fanciful. Military scuba divers failed, after

---

32. Stoll, *Fishers of Men*, 17.
33. Hvalkof and Aaby, *Is God an American?*
34. Colby, *Thy Will Be Done*.
35. There is evidence suggesting that Townsend and Rockefeller might have met. According to James Wroughton, a retired SIL government relations officer, the two men crossed paths at the 1945 Peace Conference in Chapultepec, Mexico. Seven years later, in 1952, Townsend sent Wroughton to call on Rockefeller at his hotel in Lima, but the oil magnate had no time for SIL (Wroughton to Rockefeller, 28 June 1952, TA 8404; Wroughton, interview).

five days of underwater searching, to discover the fabular mine.[36] Hence, while the various charges and critical works made for a lot of fireworks, their lack of factuality and objectivity rendered them period pieces from a time when the discipline of anthropology and the Left in general were awash with revolutionary ferment. When the dust settled, SIL was still standing and still mostly doing business as usual.

SIL owed much of its durability to Ken Pike. His resolute determination that SIL would be a truly academic institution, his insistence that SIL's humanitarian service was integral to its nature, and his broad philosophical approach—his Christian humanism—which he impressed upon the organizational mind, all helped to create and sustain a strategy that met the needs of indigenous communities in ways that affirmed their cultures, their languages, and their place in the world. Cameron Townsend, of course, was the visionary and the one who invented new ways for evangelicals to engage the world. Without his ambition and ideas none of this would ever have happened. But he was a pragmatist and tended to view the non-translation aspects of the WBT-SIL strategy as a means unto an end. Pike, with his holistic philosophy, his insistence upon the irrevocable relationship between form and meaning, and his concept of person above logic, fused means with ends and thus overrode the evangelical tendency to prioritize evangelization at the expense of all else.

Of course, it must be admitted that some of the criticism leveled at WBT-SIL had merit. Both Hart and Stoll raised legitimate questions and made pertinent observations. Hart introduced the issue of the separation between church and state, and in doing so illuminated a potentially troublesome aspect of SIL's government contracts. "Certainly Protestant groups would be outraged," Hart wrote, "if Roman Catholics formed an agency and contracted with the U.S. Government to provide all basic education for American Indians."[37] It was a relevant question, but it went unanswered.

Stoll touched on another uncomfortable reality. "While the Summer Institute was organized as an intrigue," he wrote in *Fishers of Men*, "it is clearly an evangelical intrigue with its own jealously guarded objectives. The deeper problem is the group's naivete, its capacity for looking the other way and serving dictatorships, if that will serve the

---

36. Branks and Branks, "I Was a Stranger," 2, 171, 238–39; Lansdale, "Summer Institute of Linguistics," 6.
37. Hart, "Story of the Wycliffe Translators," 4.

Great Commission."[38] Whether SIL was unequally yoked with the state could be debated endlessly, and the organization's critics spilled much ink on this very subject. Depending upon one's own perspective on this topic, Pike's argument that the SIL strategy merely followed the pattern laid down by the biblical prophet Daniel, who served the Babylonian Empire while yet remaining true to God, might or might not prove very convincing. From day one, Townsend insisted on serving rather than opposing governments. Hence, the prophet Daniel was taken as a model for SIL. One could accomplish more from inside the system than railing against it from the outside. SIL was not a traditional evangelizing mission, and therefore the New Testament apostolic model for ministry was not well-fitted to the organization's strategy. "God has not called us to be 'Paul's' in this institution," Pike told SIL students in June 1987. "If you're going to be a Paul, you need to join a regular mission. . . . As I see it, in this institution, Daniel is our role model." If Daniel could faithfully serve the Babylonian Empire, why should SIL not serve governments and cooperate with academic institutions? For Pike it was not just an acceptable policy but actually a God-given strategy.

One of the most significant repercussions of the attacks on SIL was the termination of its school at the University of Oklahoma at Norman. The cooperative linguistics program, which had been in place since 1942, ended in 1987 when the university disassociated itself from SIL. The Linguistics Committee convened to reconsider the cooperative program concluded, in an eleven to one vote, that the SIL courses did not "represent the main currents of contemporary linguistic theory as reflected in recent journal literature and course textbooks," and furthermore that the courses were "not sufficiently grounded in the principles and models of language developed for applied linguistics."[39] The first of the allegations, that SIL courses did not represent the contemporary linguistic mainstream, was perhaps reasonable in light of the fact that generative-transformational grammar was the reigning theory, and in view of the fact that Pike's tagmemics was fading from the scene. The second contention, that SIL courses were "not sufficiently grounded in the principles and models of language developed for applied linguistics" would be difficult to sustain. After all, SIL was a leading institution of applied linguistics, as has been amply demonstrated. What went missing in the SIL curriculum,

---

38. Stoll, *Fisher of Men*, 86.
39. Linguistics Committee to Madeland, 1.

according to the Linguistic Committee, were up-to-date courses in psycholinguistics and sociolinguistics.[40] But this was to take the narrow view of the matter. The University of Oklahoma at Norman did not request a widening of courses or a shift of emphasis in the program. The Linguistic Committee peremptorily ended the program without negotiating its future with SIL. Moreover, in SIL's favor, was the fact that the University of Texas at Arlington was, at that very moment, building up its cooperative linguistics program with SIL. Something else was afoot. Pike, who had his finger on the pulse of university sentiment, saw it as a result of the left wing attacks on SIL.[41] It is difficult to know for certain that this was the case, but the evidence strongly suggests that Pike was correct in his view of the matter. It was a setback for SIL, but far from fatal since SIL continued to enjoy other North American cooperative ventures, not only at the University of Texas at Arlington, but also at the University of North Dakota and the University of Oregon, not to mention its many international university associations.

Winds of change were blowing elsewhere, too. As David Stoll matured as a scholar, his research became more objective and sophisticated, and his interest widened to encompass the growth of Protestantism in Latin America. In *Is Latin America Turning Protestant?* (1990) he marshaled ample evidence for collusion between American rightwing political activists and American evangelicals in Latin American affairs. But, in this volume, he gave equal weight to indigenous agency. Evangelicalism, which includes the subgenre of Pentecostalism, was not simply imposed on poor hapless Latin American peasants. They had good reasons of their own for accepting evangelical religion rather than alternatives, such as liberation theology, which had the approbation of the Left. Liberation theology, with its Marxist overtones that sought structural change through revolution and class struggle has, Stoll noted, "tended to be suicidal in many places."[42] Moreover, Latin American peasants were rarely inclined to confrontation, preferring instead more subtle and indirect forms of resistance. "In contrast to liberation theology," Stoll therefore concluded, "evangelicals offered to improve one's life through simple personal decision, to surrender to Christ. That sounded easier than overturning the

---

40. Linguistics Committee to Madeland, 2.
41. Pike to SIL tagmemicists, January 23, 1988, PSC.
42. Stoll, *Is Latin America*, 313.

social order."[43] There was also the fact that evangelical religion, especially Pentecostalism, ostensibly offered protection against evil spirits. This was something that liberation theology or Marxism was powerless to confront. The SIL strategy therefore proved most compatible within the realities of the existing socio-political milieu and the felt needs of indigenous peoples.

Stoll still harbored some hope that structural reforms could be effected to liberate the Latin American poor. Indeed, he thought that SIL's work might even contribute to this end. To make his point, Stoll cited the fact that Peru's indigenous rights leadership, in many cases, hailed from SIL's bilingual education program. These leaders, he speculated, might take a radical turn. "Like liberation theology in more obvious ways," Stoll wrote, "the new organizations and institutions that result from evangelicalism could place new pressures on elites and conceivably redefine the political culture."[44] Stoll likewise acknowledged that although SIL could introduce the Bible, win converts, and teach people to read, ultimately the organization did not exercise control over what the indigenous peoples might do with their new found religion and the empowerment that resulted from becoming literate. Indigenous agency was far more powerful than many of the critics supposed.

When the organization came under fire from anthropologists and other critics, it withstood the assault because it was much more than a faith mission hiding behind a pseudo-scientific facade. SIL was not only the genuine article from the standpoint of linguistic expertise and humanitarian service, but proved its nonsectarian credentials by serving governments and communities and institutions without respect of political persuasion or religious affiliation. Pike had done much to ensure that SIL would survive yet another tumultuous period in its history, during which it was criticized by those who often did not fully understand, or refused to understand, that which they attacked. Moreover, Pike's reputation suffered no apparent injury from the controversies of the 1970s and 1980s. His career at the University of Michigan was stellar in all respects, and the University of Texas at Arlington welcomed him when SIL established its cooperative program there.[45] Perhaps the most significant indicator of Pike's stature in academia came when he

---

43. Stoll, *Is Latin America*, 314.
44. Stoll, *Is Latin America*, 330.
45. Perkins to Pike; Eunice Pike to Pikes, August 27, 1985, PSC.

was elected to the National Academy of Sciences in 1985, and to the anthropology section no less.[46] By and large, SIL came out of the 1970s unscathed, and Ken Pike's reputation probably stood higher than it ever had at any time in his long career.

In Pursuit of Peace

In 1984, Pike penned a letter to University of Texas at Arlington linguist Virgil Poulter, in which he recommended his colleague Robert Longacre for a faculty award in the humanities. This short letter is worth quoting at some length, since it vividly displays Pike's philosophical commitments applied to the human condition. "In these days of war threat, nuclear holocaust, and microcomputer revolution our nation faces a threat often unidentified: that we will assume that the 'real' way to peace, prosperity, and power (national, economic, political, personal) is via bombs, machines, and growing technology. History should teach us that this is a frightening hyperbole. Bombs are lit by people. Machines work only with men in artificial saddle." This was written in 1984. Ronald Reagan was in the White House and the neoconservative movement, with which much of conservative evangelicalism was in close alignment, was pressing for a decidedly hawkish foreign policy. If he was out of step with a majority in the evangelical subculture of his day, he was also in a minority as an American, a people strongly oriented toward technocratic problem-solving. Peace, prosperity, and pursuit of the common good, Pike insisted, could only be had through mutual respect and understanding, both of which depend on the proper and careful use of language. And, as well, relationships could only be fostered if they were grounded in the wisdom that lady philosophy could provide. "Words," he therefore went on to argue, "explode before cannons do. If we do not control utterances, guns will kill.... Fighting words grow from ideas, expressed in words, sentences, and the conversations of diplomats, constitutions, [and] philosophical affirmations. It is philosophy that turns the key to building or destroying new worlds.... How, then," he asked, "are we to make our contribution to the long-term world, if we fail to support the humanities equally with physical research?"[47] Neither science and technology, nor materialist and economic conceptions alone, could bring about human flourishing.

46. Pike to Family, July 25, 1985, 2, PSC.
47. Pike to Poulter, February 1, 1984, 42, PSC.

Pike's unstinting efforts to promote human understanding and peaceful relations did not go unnoticed. In 1982, Hungarian émigré Adam Makkai, a professor of English and linguistics at the University of Illinois at Chicago, spearheaded the nomination of Pike for the Nobel Peace Prize—the first linguist ever nominated. At the time of the nomination, Makkai was also the executive director of the Linguistic Association of Canada and the United States, of which Pike was president in 1978. Illinois Republican Congressman Robert McClary initiated the nomination, but the official nomination was made by Democrat Senator Alan J. Dixon, also of Illinois. Letters from around the globe supporting the nomination fill a 283-page volume compiled in honor of Pike's seventieth birthday. Among these are letters from Yale Professor of Linguistics Rulon S. Wells, University of California at Irvine Professor Emeritus of History Gerald White, Professor Emeritus Franz Szemler of Loyola University in Chicago, and Orthodox Jewish Professor of Hebrew Saul Levin of the State University of New York at Binghamton. Pike was never selected to receive the prize, but he was renominated for it every year down to 1997.[48]

Pike was more than a missionary or a scholar. He was an internationally-known intellectual, perhaps the only twentieth-century American evangelical to enjoy this distinction. His influence on SIL goes without saying. Cameron Townsend had refashioned what it meant to be a faith missionary and an evangelical. Without hesitation Pike yoked his missionary career to Townsend's vision, and then set out to make the founder's promises of a real contribution to science a reality. He modeled for other SIL colleagues what it might look like for an evangelical Christian to engage deeply as a scholar and intellectual in the secular world. Pike also buttressed the humanitarian aspect of SIL, making certain that it was more than a pragmatic function in support of Bible translation. If it was Cameron Townsend, the classical American entrepreneur, who radically reshaped the evangelical missionary enterprise, it was Ken Pike who possessed the intellectual breadth and depth to realize the true possibilities of SIL's place in the world.

---

48. Makkai, "To Honor Kenneth Lee Pike"; Pike, *Pikes Perspectives*, 129–30.

Epilogue
A Life in Retrospect

WELL INTO HIS LATER years Ken Pike remained remarkably fit, and he continued to swim three days a week and play water polo.[1] It was only in his early eighties that he began to experience short-term memory loss and was forced to turn down conference invitations. He was also increasingly unable to retain the details of what he read. For a man who had long enjoyed capacious powers of recall and command of scholarly material, this proved devastating and embarrassing.[2] In early 1997, he was diagnosed with congestive heart failure but continued to take walks and swim.[3] On July 1, 1998, after sixty-three years of service, Pike retired as an active member of WBT-SIL.[4] Following a brief illness, Ken Pike passed away at eighty-eight years of age on December 31, 2000. He was survived by his wife Evelyn, who died at the age of 101 on June 3, 2016.

Pike was a key player in SIL from the time it began to take shape in the 1930s, and he contributed much to making it the world's foremost institution of applied linguistics and Bible translation. It was Cameron Townsend who proclaimed that SIL would make the "scientists sit up and take notice." More than anyone else, it was Ken Pike who made sure this was more than an idle boast.[5] But there would never be another Ken Pike. He alone of all SIL scholars developed a major linguistic theory, one that took its place among the dominant theories of the day. His was a landmark achievement that was not to be repeated.

1. Headland to Barnard, January 15, 1996, 2, PSC.
2. Judith (Pike) Schram, interview.
3. Pikes to Andersens, September 22, 1998, 2, PSC.
4. Burnham to Pikes, December 8, 1998, PSC.
5. Hibbard, "Quotable Uncle Cam," 2:3.

To his credit, Pike encouraged his top students to master and carry out research from theoretical perspectives other than his own tagmemic theory. Rather than build a tagmemic citadel, he instead helped to foster a scholarly community in SIL where competing theories flourished. For Pike, it was more about the search for truth and pushing the frontiers of human knowledge than self-aggrandizement. He endorsed scholarship at every opportunity, yet he never envisioned SIL becoming an academic ivory tower. Under Pike's leadership, service to indigenous communities remained one of SIL's hallmarks. Hence, theory and practical application were woven together in SIL. In large part, Pike's integrated approach to scholarship and practical service derived from his faith, which called for love of one's neighbor. His Christian devotion and scientific commitment were both followed with dogged perseverance.

His temperament made for a dynamic personality, but behind the passionate enthusiasm he often suffered as he pushed himself to the limits of endurance time and again. Obedience, to his calling and to God, was deeply ingrained. "There is no escape from mental anxiety and tension," Pike wrote in 1967. "There are tools with which to try to meet it," he acknowledged, "but no real way to keep from 'dying.' We must die to ourselves, die to our wishes, die to our hopes, die to the point at which we are willing to accept tension. Once we have found that we are powerless, and unable to do a job which is our responsibility, we are more likely to call on God to do it. He is able."[6] Throughout his life, Pike was unswerving in his commitment to God.

Ken Pike was an evangelical and an intellectual. The fact that he was doctrinally orthodox in his Christian belief was no impediment to high thinking. Indeed, it would seem that the very nature of his belief produced intellectual courage. Exceedingly secure in his faith and belief in God, he was a fearless explorer of ideas. One approach to characterizing the Pikean mind is to employ historian Richard Hofstadter's distinction between "intelligence" and "intellect." "Intelligence," Hofstadter wrote, "works within the framework of limited but clearly stated goals, and may be quick to shear away questions of thought that do not seem to help in reaching them." Conversely, "Intellect is the . . . contemplative side of the mind." Putting it another way, Hofstadter elaborated that "Intelligence will seize the immediate meaning in a situation and evaluate it. Intellect evaluates evaluations and looks for the meanings of situations as a

---

6. Pike, *Stir, Change, Create*, 64.

whole."⁷ Pike, who was of a decidedly speculative and comprehensive cast of mind, clearly exhibited what Hofstadter refers to as "intellect." Arguably, then, Pike was an exception to historian Mark Noll's conjecture "that, at least in the United States, it is simply impossible to be, with integrity, both evangelical and intellectual."⁸

Hence, Pike was an outstanding exception to the failure of intellect in the North American evangelical subculture. As we saw in chapter 2, when he joined SIL in 1935, Pike was marked by the fundamentalist mentality. He could be militant and even somewhat anti-intellectual. However, he quickly adapted to Cameron Townsend's strategy of "service to all" in Mexico, which moderated his religious sensibilities. Eventually his SIL experience and sojourn at the University of Michigan in pursuit of a doctorate eliminated any latent fundamentalist qualities. His move out of a fundamentalist mindset put Pike in the vanguard of the neo-evangelical movement, which sought to restore evangelicalism's lost intellectual heritage. Although Pike never self-identified as a neo-evangelical, he certainly deserves to be classed with progressive evangelical figures such as Bernard Ramm, Edward J. Carnell, George Eldon Ladd, and Paul Jewett, among others.

Pike's life is a demonstration that it was possible for an evangelical Christian to flourish in secular academia and the wider world without diminishing one's faith. It was not necessary to brandish one's religion; it was only necessary to live faithfully and demonstrate one's religious commitments through serving others. He was able to transcend the separatist reflexes of conservative evangelicalism to engage fully with the world around him. He seemed to embody the teaching of Christ that "the kingdom of God is within you."⁹ It was not so much organizations, social conventions, or personal associations that mattered; rather it was the orientation of one's heart, soul, and mind that were of chief importance.

Ken Pike was, therefore, much more than just a Bible translator and linguist. It has been argued within these pages that he was nothing less than an evangelical Christian humanist. This is not to say that he was uninterested in evangelism; it is simply to say that there was much more to the Pikean mind than what typified many evangelicals, even scholarly evangelicals. As former SIL president John Watters aptly remarked, Pike

---

7. Hofstadter, *Anti-Intellectualism in American Life*, 25.
8. Noll, *Scandal*, ix.
9. Luke 17:21 AV.

was "open to the variety of human nature and the variety of people and the way God acts in the world, and that has allowed for the richness that SIL has experienced."[10] Townsend broke with convention and Pike took advantage of the breach created by the founder. While Bible translation remained the primary motivating force behind the organization, under their leadership, SIL transcended the usual boundaries of a faith mission to become an organization committed to human flourishing through language development and education.

Pike's legacy of devotion to others lives on in SIL's altruistic service to indigenous communities, academia, and governments. SIL today is comprised of an international staff numbering nearly 5,000, and has trained over 20,000 students in various aspects of linguistics, literacy, and other cross-cultural work through a network of training programs that now involves 26 institutions in 18 countries. Today SIL works alongside speakers of more than 1,600 languages in 100 countries, and more than two million people have learned to read and write as a direct result of SIL's literacy efforts. SIL's Language and Culture Archives houses over 60,000 works of various kinds, including scholarly publications, Bible translations, and vernacular literacy materials in addition to SIL's flagship publication, the Ethnologue—an online database of the world's more than 7,000 living languages. SIL also continues to play a key role in the global Bible translation movement. Not only does SIL directly facilitate Bible translation on a large scale, it also carries out foundational research on the world's languages and cultures. It does this primarily through applied work in developing alphabets, dictionaries, local literatures, and programs of literacy instruction. When Townsend founded SIL to be a research organization, he saw it as an important strategy for getting beyond the gaps in knowledge that were hindering ministry.[11] Ken Pike took up the challenge of filling these gaps not only in ministry but also in the world's knowledge of languages.

It seems fitting to close this narrative with one of Pike's poems, one that conveys in his own unique fashion the way in which he would perhaps have summarized his life.

---

10. Watters, interview.
11. I am indebted to SIL's Gary Simons for much of this paragraph.

The End

Regarding Daniel 12:9–13, and "the end of the days."

In tears, then joy!
Life in contrast
Sets the pace
Of learning
Good, through bad . . .

Both now and "then"
Hold to trust,
In God, in time
To light our stars,
Forever there.[12]

---

12. Pike, "End."

Bibliography

Abercrombie, David, et al., eds. *Towards a History of Phonetics*. Edinburgh: Edinburgh University Press, 1981.
Alatis, James E., ed. *Georgetown University Round Table on Languages and Linguistics 1992*. Washington: Georgetown University Press, 1993.
Aldridge, Boone. *For the Gospel's Sake: The Rise of the Wycliffe Bible Translators and the Summer Institute of Linguistics*. Grand Rapids: Eerdmans, 2018.
Ammerman, Nancy Tatom. *Bible Believers: Fundamentalists in the Modern World*. New Brunswick, NJ: Rutgers University Press, 1987.
"Announcement of the Fourth Annual Session of the Summer Institute of Linguistics." Brochure, July 19 to October 8, 1937. Document no. 2241, William Cameron Townsend Archives, JAARS Center, Waxhaw, NC.
Award of Professor Emeritus of Linguistics to Kenneth L. Pike, University of Michigan, December 1979, photocopy. Honors and awards series, Pike Special Collection, SIL Language and Culture Archives, Dallas, TX.
Baker, Sheridan. "The Flounders Club." In *The Flounders: Fifty Years*, edited by Clark Hopkins, xii–xvix. Ann Arbor, MI: n.p., 1976.
Balyeat, F. A. Letter to Kenneth L. Pike, July 26, 1947. Corporation history series, Pike Special Collection, SIL International Language and Culture Archives, Dallas, TX.
Bartholomew, Doris. Interview by author, May 23, 2017, Catalina, AZ.
Bays, Daniel H., and Grant Wacker, eds. *The Foreign Missionary Enterprise at Home: Explorations in North American Cultural History*. Tuscaloosa: University of Alabama Press, 2003.
Beaver, R. Pierce, ed. *American Missions in Bicentennial Perspective*. South Pasadena, CA: William Carey, 1977.
Bebbington, David W. *Evangelicalism in Modern Britain: A History from the 1730s to the 1980s*. New York: Routledge, 1989.
Becker, A. L. "Foreword." In *Language and Life: Essays in Memory of Kenneth L. Pike*, edited by Mary Ruth Wise, et al., xiii–xiv. Arlington: The University of Texas at Arlington and SIL International, 2003.
"Biographical Information on W. Cameron Townsend, Founder of Wycliffe Bible Translators." Document no. 42948, William Cameron Townsend Archives, JAARS Center, Waxhaw, NC.
Black, Matthew, and William Smalley, eds. *On Language, Culture, and Religion: In Honor of Eugene A. Nida*. The Hague: Mouton, 1974.
Bloomfield, Leonard. *Language*. New York: Henry Holt, 1933.

Boone, Kathleen C. *The Bible Tells Them So: The Discourse of Protestant Fundamentalism*. Albany: State University of New York Press, 1989.

Branks, Tom. "On Ken Pike's Death." Unpublished manuscript, n.d., copy in author's possession.

Branks, Tom, and Judy Branks, eds. "I Was a Stranger: Tales from Colombia SIL." Booklet, copy in author's possession.

Brend, Ruth M., ed. *Advances in Tagmemics*. London: North-Holland, 1974.

Brend, Ruth M., and Kenneth L. Pike, eds. *The Summer Institute of Linguistics: Its Works and Contributions*. The Hague: Mouton, 1977.

———. *Trends in Linguistics: Tagmemics, Theoretical Discussion*, vol. 1. The Hague: Mouton, 1976.

———. *Trends in Linguistics: Tagmemics, Theoretical Discussion*, vol. 2. The Hague: Mouton, 1976.

Brereton, Virginia Lieson. "The Bible Schools and Conservative Evangelical Higher Education." In *Making Higher Education Christian*, edited by Joel A. Carpenter and Kenneth W. Shipps, 110–36. Grand Rapids: Eerdmans, 1987.

Buss, Dietrich G., and Arthur F. Glasser. *Giving Wings to the Gospel: The Remarkable Story of Mission Aviation Fellowship*. Grand Rapids: Baker, 1995.

Bynon, Theodora, and F. R. Palmer. *Studies in the History of Linguistics*. New York: Cambridge University Press, 1986.

Callaghan, Catherine A. Letter to James Spradley, American Anthropological Association, committee on ethics, Macalester College, April 17, 1975. Corporation history series, Pike Special Collection, SIL International Language and Culture Archives, Dallas, TX.

Cammack, Helen. Letter to Eric M. North, January 13, 1944. Correspondence series, Pike Special Collection, SIL International Language and Culture Archives, Dallas, TX.

"Camp Wycliffe Chronicle." Vol. 1, no. 2, (June 1936) 1–3. Document no. 44972, William Cameron Townsend Archives, JAARS Center, Waxhaw, NC.

Carnell, Edward John. *Christian Commitment: An Apologetic*. New York: The Macmillan Company, 1957.

Carpenter, Joel A. "Propagating the Faith Once Delivered." In *Earthen Vessels: American Foreign Missions, 1880–1980*, edited by Joel A. Carpenter and Wilbert R. Shenk, 92–132. Grand Rapids: Eerdmans, 1990.

———. *Revive Us Again: The Reawakening of American Fundamentalism*. New York: Oxford University Press, 1997.

Carpenter, Joel A., and Wilbert R. Shenk, eds. *Earthen Vessels: American Foreign Missions, 1880–1980*. Grand Rapids: Eerdmans, 1990.

Carpenter, Joel A., and Kenneth W. Shipps, eds. *Making Higher Education Christian*. Grand Rapids: Eerdmans, 1987.

Carroll, John B., ed. *Language, Thought, and Reality: Selected Writings of Benjamin Lee Whorf*. Cambridge: Massachusetts Institute of Technology Press, 1956.

Case, Kenneth G. Letter to Eric M. North, American Bible Society, January 14, 1944. Correspondence series, Pike Special Collection, SIL International Language and Culture Archives, Dallas, TX.

Chapman, Siobhan and Christopher Routledge, eds. *Key Thinkers in Linguistics and the Philosophy of Language*. Oxford: Oxford University Press, 2005.

"Chicago Sending Plane to Ecuador." *Chicago Daily News*, December 17, 1955. Document no. 44099, William Cameron Townsend Archives, JAARS Center, Waxhaw, NC.

Chomsky, Noam. *Syntactic Structures*. 'S-Gravenhage: Mouton, 1957.

Colby, Gerald, with Charlotte Dennett. *Thy Will Be Done: The Conquest of the Amazon; Nelson Rockefeller and Evangelism in the Age of Oil*. New York: Harper Perennial, 1995.

Coke, Milton M., Jr. "An Ethnohistory of Bible Translation Among the Maya." PhD diss., The School of World Mission and Institute for Church Growth, Fuller Theological Seminary, 1978.

"Consent to First Meeting of the Directors of the Summer Institute of Linguistics." September 15, 1942, Wycliffe Bible Translators and SIL International Corporate Archives, Dallas, TX.

Cook, Walter A. *Introduction to Tagmemic Analysis*. Washington, DC: Georgetown University Press, 1969.

Cowan, George M. Letter to Member Missions of the IFMA, December 1, 1959. Document no. 17389, William Cameron Townsend Archives, JAARS Center, Waxhaw, NC.

———. Letter to Richard S. Pittman, July 23, 1966. SIL University of North Dakota folder, Pittman Special Collection, SIL Language and Culture Archives, Dallas, TX.

Cross, George L. Letter to Kenneth L. Pike, October 1, 1949. Record group 3, Presidential Papers, George L. Cross, box 66, folder Linguistic Institute, Western History Collection, University of Oklahoma Archives.

Crystal, David. *A Dictionary of Linguistics and Phonetics*. 4th ed. Cambridge, MA: Blackwell, 1997.

D'Elia, John. *A Place at the Table: George Eldon Ladd and the Rehabilitation of Evangelical Scholarship*. New York: Oxford University Press, 2008.

Dochuk, Darren. *From Bible Belt to Sunbelt: Plain-Folk Religion, Grassroots Politics, and the Rise of Evangelical Conservatism*. New York: W. W. Norton, 2012.

Dorrien, Gary. *The Remaking of Evangelical Theology*. Louisville: Westminster John Knox, 1998.

Falk, Julia S. "The LSA Linguistic Institutes." Paper presented at the Ninetieth Anniversary of the Linguistic Society of America: A Commemorative Symposium, La Jolla, California, January 4, 2014, 1–13.

Fiedler, Klaus. *The Story of Faith Missions: From Hudson Taylor to Present Day Africa*. Irvine, CA: Regnum, 1994.

Fillmore, Charles J. Letter to Evelyn (Griset) Pike, "Introductory Remarks." October 21, 1987. Correspondence series, Pike Special Collection, SIL International Language and Culture Archives, Dallas, TX.

"The Five Principles." *In Other Words* 8 (1982) 18.

Franklin, Joice. Interview by author, January 9, 2017, Waco, TX.

Franklin, Karl. Interview by author, January 9, 2017, Waco, TX.

Frizen, Edwin L., Jr. *75 Years of the IFMA, 1917–1992: The Nondenominational Missions Movement*. Wheaton, IL: Interdenominational Foreign Mission Association, 1992.

Garrard-Burnett, Virginia. *Protestantism in Guatemala: Living in the New Jerusalem*. Austin: University of Texas Press, 1998.

"Gift of Plane to Peru." *Peruvian Times*, September 28, 1956, 10, photocopy. Document no. 45694, William Cameron Townsend Archives, JAARS Center, Waxhaw, NC.

Goodenough, Ward H. "Anthropology in the 20th Century and Beyond." *American Anthropologist* 104 (2002) 423–40.

Gudschinsky, Sarah C. "Literacy." In *The Summer Institute of Linguistics: Its Works and Contributions*, edited by Ruth M. Brend and Kenneth L. Pike, 39–42. The Hague: Mouton, 1977.

Harris, Harriet A. *Fundamentalism and Evangelicals*. New York: Oxford University Press, 1998.

Harris, Randy Allen. *The Linguistic Wars*. New York: Oxford University Press, 1993.

Hart, D. G. *Defending the Faith: J. Gresham Machen and the Crisis of Conservative Protestantism in Modern America*. Phillipsburg, PA: P&R, 2003.

Hart, Laurie. "Story of the Wycliffe Translators: Pacifying the Last Frontiers." *Latin America and Empire Report* 7 (1973) 16–31.

Hartch, Todd. *Missionaries of the State: The Summer Institute of Linguistics, State Formation, and Indigenous Mexico, 1935–1985*. Tuscaloosa: The University of Alabama Press, 2006.

Harvey, Jana R. "*Seasons of Life* Reviewed." In *Language and Life: Essays in Memory of Kenneth L. Pike*, edited by Mary Ruth Wise, et al., 55–56. Arlington: The University of Texas at Arlington and SIL International, 2003.

Hassler, Gerda, ed. *History of Linguistics 2008: Selected Papers from the 11th International Conference on the History of the Language Sciences*. Philadelphia: John Benjamins, 2011.

Headland, Thomas N. "Introduction: A Dialogue Between Kenneth L. Pike and Marvin Harris on Emics and Etics." In *Emics and Etics, The Insider/Outsider Debate*, edited by Thomas N. Headland, et al., 13–27. Newberry Park, CA: Sage, 1990.

———. "A Tribute to the Life of Kenneth L. Pike: A Perspective from One of His Students." In *Language and Life: Essays in Memory of Kenneth L. Pike*, edited by Mary Ruth Wise, et al., 11–20. Arlington: The University of Texas at Arlington and SIL International, 2003.

Headland, Thomas N., et al., eds. *Emics and Etics: The Insider/Outsider Debate*. Newbury Park, CA: Sage, 1990.

Heimbach, Sharon, ed. *On Pain, Beyond Suffering: Kenneth L. Pike Poetry*, vol. 1. Dallas: Summer Institute of Linguistics, 1997.

———. *On the Philosophy of Life, A Kaleidoscope: Kenneth L. Pike Poetry*, vol. 2. Dallas: Summer Institute of Linguistics, 1997.

———. *On Scholarship and the Work, Service and Success: Kenneth L. Pike Poetry*, vol. 4. Dallas: Summer Institute of Linguistics, 1997.

Hibbard, Calvin, ed. "Quotable Uncle Cam." Vol. 1 (2009). William Cameron Townsend Archives, JAARS Center, Waxhaw, NC.

———. "Quotable Uncle Cam." Vol. 2 (2009). William Cameron Townsend Archives, JAARS Center, Waxhaw, NC.

Hill, Archibald A. "History of the Linguistic Institute." Bulletin reprint, Linguistic Society of America (n.d), 16–22. Dallas International University Library, Dallas, TX.

Hill, Patricia R. *The World Their Household: The American Woman's Foreign Mission Movement and Cultural Transformation, 1870–1920*. Ann Arbor, MI: University of Michigan Press, 1985.

Hockett, Charles F., ed. *A Leonard Bloomfield Anthology*. Bloomington: Indiana University Press, 1970.
Hofstadter, Richard. *Anti-Intellectualism in American Life*. New York: Alfred A. Knopf, 1970.
Hopkins, Clark, ed. *The Flounders: Fifty Years*. Ann Arbor, MI: n.p., 1976.
Hutchison, William R. *Errand to the World: American Protestant Thought and Foreign Missions*. Chicago: University of Chicago Press, 1993.
Huttar, George L. "Scales of Basicness in Semantic Domains and Their Application to Creolization." In *Language and Life: Essays in Memory of Kenneth L. Pike*, edited by Mary Ruth Wise, et al., 119–37. Arlington: The University of Texas at Arlington and SIL International, 2003.
Hvalkof, Søren, and Peter Aaby, eds. *Is God an American? An Anthropological Perspective on the Missionary Work of the Summer Institute of Linguistics*. London: Survival International, 1981.
Hymes, Dell. "Introduction: Traditions and Paradigms." In *Studies in the History of Linguistics: Traditions and Paradigms*, edited by Dell Hymes, 1–40. Bloomington: Indiana University Press, 1974.
Hymes, Dell, ed. *Studies in the History of Linguistics: Traditions and Paradigms*. Bloomington: Indiana University Press, 1974.
Hymes, Dell, and John Fought. *American Structuralism*. New York: Mouton, 1981.
Ibach, Barbara (Pike). "Papa Ken and the *Canadian River*." Unpublished poem, July 4, 2018, copy in author's possession.
———. "Stones of Remembrance for Papa." Unpublished poems, 1997, copy in author's possession.
———. Telephone interview by author, July 27, 2018.
Kaplan, Steven, ed. *Indigenous Responses to Western Christianity*. New York: New York University Press, 1995.
Kaye, Alan S. "An Interview with Kenneth Pike." *Current Anthropology* 35 (1994) 291–98.
Koerner, E. F. K., and R. E. Asher, eds. *A Concise History of the Languages Sciences: From the Sumerians to the Cognitivists*. New York: Pergamon, 1995.
Krauze, Enrique. *Mexico: Biography of Power, A History of Modern Mexico, 1810–1996*. New York: HarperCollins, 1977.
Kuklick, Henrika, ed. *A New History of Anthropology*. Malden, MA: Blackwell, 2008.
Lansdale, Sidney I. "Summer Institute of Linguistics Hangs On in Colombia." *Latinamerica Press*, September 2, 1976, photocopy. Document no. 43861, William Cameron Townsend Archives, JAARS Center, Waxhaw, NC.
Larson, Mildred L., and Patricia M. Davis, eds. *Bilingual Education: An Experience in Peruvian Amazonia*. Washington, DC: Center for Applied Linguistics, 1981.
Larson, Mildred L., et al., eds. "Overview." In *Bilingual Education: An Experience in Peruvian Amazonia*, edited by Mildred L. Larson and Patricia M. Davis, 37–48. Washington, DC: Center for Applied Linguistics, 1981.
Larsen, Timothy, ed. *Biographical Dictionary of Evangelicals*. Downers Grove, IL: InterVarsity, 2003.
Leeds-Hurwitz, Wendy. "The Committee on Research in Native American Languages." *Proceedings of the American Philosophical Society* 129 (1985) 129–60.

Lehman, Edward J. Letter to Kenneth L. Pike, September 20, 1976. Corporation history series, Pike Special Collection, SIL International Language and Culture Archives, Dallas, TX.

Lewis, Donald M., ed. *Christianity Reborn: The Global Expansion of Evangelicalism in the Twentieth Century*. Grand Rapids: Eerdmans, 2004.

Linguistics Committee, Department of Modern Languages, Literatures, and Linguistics, The University of Oklahoma. Letter to Helga S. Madeland, Interim Chair, Department of Modern Languages, Literature, and Linguistics, September 29, 1987. Corporation history series, Pike Special Collection, SIL International Language and Culture Archives, Dallas, TX.

Livingstone, David N., et al., eds. *Evangelicals and Science in Historical Perspective*. New York: Oxford University Press, 1999.

Long, Kathryn T. *God in the Rain Forest: A Tale of Martyrdom & Redemption in Amazonian Ecuador*. New York: Oxford University Press, 2019.

Lyman, Larry. Interview by author, May 22, 2017, Catalina, AZ.

Makkai, Adam, compiler. "To Honor Kenneth Lee Pike on the Occasion of His 70th Birthday: Papers of His Nomination for the Nobel Peace Prize for the Year 1982." (June 1982). Honors and awards series, Pike Special Collection, SIL International Language and Culture Archives, Dallas, TX.

Mandelbaum, David G., ed. *Selected Writings of Edward Sapir*. Berkeley: University of California Press, 1949.

Marak, Andrae M. "The Failed Assimilation of the Tarahumara in Postrevolutionary Mexico." *Journal of the Southwest* 45 (2003) 411–35.

Marsden, George M. "The Collapse of American Evangelical Academia." In *Faith and Rationality: Reason and Belief in God*, edited by Alvin Plantinga and Nicholas Wolterstorff, 219–64. Notre Dame: University of Notre Dame Press, 1983.

———. *Fundamentalism and American Culture: The Shaping of Twentieth-Century Evangelicalism, 1870–1925*. New York: Oxford University Press, 1980.

———. *Reforming Fundamentalism: Fuller Seminary and the New Evangelicalism*. Grand Rapids: Eerdmans, 1987.

May, Bernard (Bernie). Interview by author, September 18, 2009, Waxhaw, NC.

May, Richard B. *Private Thoughts of a Village Remembered, 1930–1980*. Photocopy, Pike Special Collection, SIL International Language and Culture Archives, Dallas, TX. N.d.: Vanity Press, n.d.

McCutcheon, Russell T. "Kenneth L. Pike, Etic and Emic Standpoints for the Description of Behavior." In *The Insider/Outsider Problem in the Study of Religion: A Reader*, edited by Russell T. McCutcheon, 28–36. New York: Cassel, 1999.

McCutcheon, Russell T., ed. *The Insider/Outsider Problem in the Study of Religion: A Reader*. New York: Cassell, 1999.

McKim, Donald K., ed. *How Karl Barth Changed My Mind*. Grand Rapids: Eerdmans, 1986.

McMahon, Ambrose. "Minutes of the Summer Institute of Linguistics." July 26, 1947. Document no. 42563, William Cameron Townsend Archives, JAARS Center, Waxhaw, NC.

McQuown, Norman A. Review of *Selected Writings: To Commemorate the 60th Birthday of Kenneth Lee Pike*, Janua Linguarum, Series Major 55, edited by Ruth M. Brend. The Hague: Mouton, 1972. *American Anthropologist* 76 (1974) 931–32.

Meyer, Michael C., and William L. Sherman. *The Course of Mexican History*. 3rd ed. New York: Oxford University Press, 1987.
Migliazzo, Arlin C. " 'She Must Be a Proper Exception:' Females, Fuller Seminary, and the Limits of Gender Equity Among Southern California Evangelicals, 1947–1952." *Fides and Historia* 45 (2013) 1–19.
"Minutes of the Summer Institute of Linguistics." July 26, 1947. Document no. 42563, William Cameron Townsend Archives, JAARS Center, Waxhaw, NC.
"Ministry of Public Education Textbook Authorization for Bilingual Jungle Schools." Supreme Resolution No. 275, July 2, 1957. Document no. 40835, William Cameron Townsend Archives, JAARS Center, Waxhaw, NC.
Moberg, David O. *The Great Reversal: Reconciling Evangelism and Social Concern*. Eugene, OR: Wipf & Stock, 2011.
Montgomery, Almerene. Letter to Kenneth L. Pike, August 13, 1941. Correspondence series, Pike Special Collection, SIL International Language and Culture Archives, Dallas, TX.
Moore, Hyatt. "Editorial: PhD's and Fools." *In Other Words* 8 (1982) 3.
Myers, Minne E. Letter to Eric M. North, American Bible Society, January 13, 1944. Correspondence series, Pike Special Collection, SIL International Language and Culture Archives, Dallas, TX.
Nelson, Rudolph. *The Making and Unmaking of an Evangelical Mind: The Case of Edward Carnell*. New York: Cambridge University Press, 1987.
Newmeyer, Frederick J. *Linguistic Theory in America*. 2nd ed. New York: Academic, 1986.
Nida, Eugene A. Letter to WBT-SIL Board of Directors, September 9, 1953. Document no. 9256, William Cameron Townsend Archives, JAARS Center, Waxhaw, NC.
———. "Minutes of the Summer Institute of Linguistics." July 26, 1947. Document no. 42563, William Cameron Townsend Archives, JAARS Center, Waxhaw, NC.
Noll, Mark A. *Between Faith and Criticism: Evangelicals, Scholarship, and the Bible in America*. San Francisco: Harper and Row, 1986.
———. *The New Shape of World Christianity: How American Experience Reflects Global Faith*. Downers Grove, IL: IVP Academic, 2009.
———. *The Scandal of the Evangelical Mind*. Grand Rapids: Eerdmans, 1994.
———. *Turning Points: Decisive Moments in the History of Christianity*. Grand Rapids: Baker Academic, 1997.
North, Eric M. "Eugene A. Nida: An Appreciation." In *On Language, Culture, and Religion: In Honor of Eugene A. Nida*, edited by Matthew Black and William Smalley, vii–xx. The Hague: Mouton, 1974.
Noss, Philip A., ed. *A History of Bible Translation*. Rome: Edizioni Di Storia E Letteratura [American Bible Society], 2007.
Orlinsky, Harry M., and Robert G. Bratcher. *A History of Bible Translation and the North American Contribution*. Atlanta: Scholars, 1991.
Pike, Eunice V. *Ken Pike: Scholar and Christian*. Dallas: Summer Institute of Linguistics, 1981.
Pike, Evelyn (Griset). Interview by author, July 19, 2006, Dallas, TX.
Pike, Kenneth L. "An Autobiographical Note on My Experience with Tone Languages." October–November 1980. Lecture series, B, Pike Special Collection, SIL International Language and Culture Archives, Dallas, TX.

——. "An Autobiographical Note on Phonetics." In *Towards a History of Phonetics*, edited by David Abercrombie et al., 181–85. Edinburgh: Edinburgh University Press, 1981.

——. "Chief Turning Points." September 1973, diary. Personal history series, Pike Special Collection, SIL International Language and Culture Archives, Dallas, TX.

——. "Christianity and Culture III: Biblical Absolutes and Certain Cultural Relativisms." *Journal of the American Scientific Affiliation* 31 (1979) 139–45.

——. "Crushed." In *On Scholarship and the Work, Service and Success: Kenneth L. Pike Poetry*, edited by Sharon Heimbach, 4:82. Dallas: SIL International, 1997.

——. "Diary of Brazil Trip." April 13–29, 1956. Corporation history series, Pike Special Collection, SIL International Language and Culture Archives Dallas, TX.

——. "Draft Lecture." 1965. Lecture series, A, Pike Special Collection, Dallas, TX.

——. "The End." In *On the Philosophy of Life: A Kaleidoscope*, edited by Sharon Heimbach, 2:102. Dallas: SIL International, 1997.

——. Faculty Seminar, September 20, 1976. Lecture series, B, 1976 M1, Pike Special Collection, SIL International Language and Culture Archives, Dallas, TX.

——. Faculty Seminar, October 18, 1976. Lecture series, B, 1976 M3, Pike Special Collection, SIL International Language and Culture Archives, Dallas, TX.

——. Faculty Seminar, October 25, 1976. Lecture series, B, 1976 M4, Pike Special Collection, SIL International Language and Culture Archives, Dallas, TX.

——. Faculty Seminar, November 29, 1976. Lecture series, B, 1976 M6, Pike Special Collection, SIL International Language and Culture Archives, Dallas, TX.

——. Faculty Seminar, February 21, 1977. Lecture series, B, 1976 M7, Pike Special Collection, SIL International Language and Culture Archives, Dallas, TX.

——. "Family Report of Presentation Ceremony." September 6, 1956. Correspondence series, Pike Special Collection, SIL International Language and Culture Archives, Dallas, TX.

——. "General Report." February 21, 1944. Document no. 3875, William Cameron Townsend Archives, JAARS Center, Waxhaw, NC.

——. "Grammatical Prerequisites to Phonemic Analysis." *Word* 3 (1947) 155–72.

——. "Heart with Mind." In *On the Philosophy of Life, A Kaleidoscope: Kenneth L. Pike Poetry*, edited by Sharon Heimbach, 2:31. Dallas: Summer Institute of Linguistics, 1997.

——. "Hefley Interview." C. 1970. Tape one, in June–December 1971 correspondence series, Pike Special Collection, SIL International Language and Culture Archives, Dallas, TX.

——. "Hefley Interview." C. 1970. Tape two, in June–December 1971 correspondence series, Pike Special Collection, SIL International Language and Culture Archives, Dallas, TX.

——. "Here We Stand: Creative Observers of Language." *Approaches du Langue*. Actes du colloque interdisciplinaire tenu á Paris, Sorbonne, December 8, 1978, Serie Études, 9–45.

——. "How Do You Know When You've Thought?." January 1962. Research topics series, Pike Special Collection, SIL International Language and Culture Archives, Dallas, TX.

——. "IFMA Issue." Work Papers I–VI, September 1959. Mexico Branch Archives, SIL International, Catalina, AZ.

———. Interview by Ron Gluck, February 24, 1987. Personal history series, Pike Special Collection, SIL International Language and Culture Archives, Dallas, TX.

———. "A Journey With God—From Bible Translation to Linguistics to Philosophy to Poetry—For Him." November 6, 1996. Correspondence series, Pike Special Collection, SIL International Language and Culture Archives, Dallas, TX.

———. *Language in Relation to a Unified Theory of the Structure of Human Behavior.* 2nd rev. ed. The Hague: Mouton, 1967.

———. Letter to Alan R. Beals, Chairman of Recommendation Subcommittee on Ethics, American Anthropological Association, May 21, 1973. Corporation history series, Pike Special Collection, SIL International Language and Culture Archives, Dallas, TX.

———. Letter to Charles C. Fries, University of Michigan, February 2, 1937. Pike Special Collection, SIL International Language and Culture Archives, Dallas, TX.

———. Letter to Department of Philology, Yale University, December 28, 1936. Correspondence series, Pike Special Collection, SIL International Language and Culture Archives, Dallas, TX.

———. Letter to Leonard Bloomfield, University of Chicago, September 2, 1938. Correspondence series, Pike Special Collection, SIL International Language and Culture Archives, Dallas, TX.

———. Letter to Miles L. Hanley, Visiting Lecturer at Harvard University, December 28, 1936. Correspondence series, Pike Special Collection, SIL International Language and Culture Archives, Dallas, TX.

———. Letter to Miles L. Hanley, Visiting Lecturer at Harvard University, April 19, 1937. Correspondence series, Pike Special Collection, SIL International Language and Culture Archives, Dallas, TX.

———. Letter to Otis Leal, "Topic: Inspiration." August 15, 1966. Document no. 24502, William Cameron Townsend Archives, JAARS Center, Waxhaw, NC.

———. Letter to "Ta ni taa!" [supporters]. C. late 1930s. Correspondence series, undated, Pike Special Collection, SIL International Language and Culture Archives, Dallas, TX.

———. *Linguistic Concepts: An Introduction to Tagmemics.* Lincoln: University of Nebraska Press, 1982.

———. "Minutes of the Summer Institute of Linguistics." July 26, 1947. Document no. 42563, William Cameron Townsend Archives, JAARS Center, Waxhaw, NC.

———. "My Blue Refrigerator." In *On Scholarship and the Work, Service and Success: Kenneth L. Pike Poetry,* edited by Sharon Heimbach, 4:150. Dallas: SIL International, 1997.

———. "On Technical Writing." July 12, 1976. Lecture series, A, Pike Special Collection, SIL International Language and Culture Archives, Dallas, TX.

———. "Our Own Tongue Wherein We Were Born: The Work of the Summer Institute of Linguistics and of the Wycliffe Bible Translators." *Bible Translator* 10 (1959) 3–16.

———. "Pain Teaches Choice." In *On Pain, Beyond Suffering: Kenneth L. Pike Poetry,* edited by Sharon Heimbach, 1:38. Dallas: Summer Institute of Linguistics, 1997.

———. "Peru 1943." Recording transcript. Corporation history series, Pike Special Collection, SIL International Language and Culture Archives, Dallas, TX.

———. "Philosophy and Tagmemics." July 12, 1982. Lecture series A, 1982 D, Pike Special Collection, SIL International Language and Culture Archives, Dallas, TX.

———. "Phonemics Lecture." June 12, 1951. Lecture series, A, Pike Special Collection, SIL International Language and Culture Archives, Dallas, TX.

———. *Phonetics: A Critical Analysis of Phonetic Theory and a Technic for the Practical Description of Sounds*. Ann Arbor, MI: University of Michigan, 1943 [2011].

———. "Pike-Talk at Ixmilquipan." May 28, 1967. Lecture series, B, Pike Special Collection, SIL International Language and Culture Archives, Dallas, TX.

———. "The Problem of Unwritten Languages in Education." Paper presented at the Meeting of Experts on the Use of Vernacular Languages, UNESCO, Paris, France, 1951, 1–27.

———. "Professor Pike Replies." *Michigan Daily*, March 26, 1974, photocopy. Document no. 44737, William Cameron Townsend Archives, JAARS Center, Waxhaw, NC.

———. "Questions Concerning the Possible Work in Philosophy." September 16, 1982. Research topics series, Pike Special Collection, SIL International Language and Culture Archives, Dallas, TX.

———. "A Reconstruction of Phonetic Theory." PhD diss., University of Michigan, 1941.

———. "Reminiscences by Pike on Early American Anthropological Linguistics." In *Language and Life: Essays in Memory of Kenneth L. Pike*, edited by Mary Ruth Wise, et al., 31–54. Arlington: The University of Texas at Arlington and SIL International, 2003.

———. "Report Concerning SIL." September 7, 1951. Corporation history series, Pike Special Collection, SIL International Language and Culture Archives, Dallas, TX.

———. "Report of the General Director's Appointee on Linguistic Matters." SIL board of directors, minutes, appendix I, September 12–18, 1949, Wycliffe Bible Translators and SIL International Corporate Archives, Dallas, TX.

———. "Report to General Director, Board, and Branch Directors on the First Phase of Ecuador Trip." May 5–14, 1956. Corporation history series, Pike Special Collection, SIL International Language and Culture Archives, Dallas, TX.

———. "Report of the President of the Summer Institute of Linguistics, 1957 Biennial Conference." Corporation history series, Pike Special Collection, SIL International Language and Culture Archives, Dallas, TX.

———. "Report on Studies in the Linguistic Workshop at Yarina Cocha." October 26, 1955 to March 31, 1956. Lecture series, B, 1955 (Peru), Pike Special Collection, SIL International Language and Culture Archives, Dallas, TX.

———. "SIL President's Report to the 1975 Biennial Conference." Corporation history series, Pike Special Collection, SIL International Language and Culture Archives, Dallas, TX.

———. "Statistics on Camp Wycliffe." C. July 1947. Corporation history series, Pike Special Collection, SIL International Language and Culture Archives, Dallas, TX.

———. *Stir, Change, Create: Poems and Essays in a Contemporary Mood for Concerned Students*. Grand Rapids: Eerdmans, 1967.

———. *Talk, Thought, and Thing: The Emic Road Toward Conscious Knowledge*. Dallas: The Summer Institute of Linguistics, 1993.

———. "A Theory of Meaning." June 29, 1960. Lecture series, A, Pike Special Collection, SIL International Language and Culture Archives, Dallas, TX.

———. "Toward the Development of Tagmemic Postulates." In *Trends in Linguistics: Tagmemics, Theoretical Discussion*, edited by Ruth M. Brend and Kenneth L. Pike, 2:91–127. The Hague: Mouton, 1976.

———. "Transformations Versus Tagmemics: Differences in Approach." May 1961 lecture series, B, Pike Special Collection, SIL International Language and Culture Archives, Dallas, TX.

———. "Translation Theory is Linguistics." February 12, 1978. Lecture series, B, Pike Special Collection, SIL International Language and Culture Archives, Dallas, TX.

———. "Valedictory Address." *Putnam Patriot*, June 21, 1928, photocopy. Personal history series, Pike Special Collection, SIL International Language and Culture Archives, Dallas, TX.

———. "The Value of General Principles." June 13, 1978. Lecture series, A, Pike Special Collection, SIL International Language and Culture Archives, Dallas, TX.

———. "Violin under Stress." In *On Pain, Beyond Suffering: Kenneth L. Pike Poetry*, edited by Sharon Heimbach, 1:75. Dallas: Summer Institute of Linguistics, 1997.

———. "'Water-Broken' to the Flounder Family." In *The Flounders: Fifty Years*, edited by Clark Hopkins, xx–xxii. Ann Arbor, MI: n.p., 1976.

———. "Why I Believe in God." *His* 18 (1957) 3–7. SIL International Language and Culture Archives, Dallas, TX.

———. *With Heart and Mind: A Personal Synthesis of Scholarship and Devotion*, 2nd ed. Duncanville, TX: Adult Learning Systems, Inc., [1962] 1996.

———. "Women in Wycliffe." A Summary of Comments Made by Kenneth L. Pike to the Annual Meeting of the Mexico Branch, September 18, 1992. Lecture series, Pike Special Collection, SIL International Language and Culture Archives, Dallas, TX.

Pike, Kenneth L., and Marvin Harris. *Etics and Emics: The Insider/Outsider Debate*. Newbury Park, CA: Sage, 1990.

Pike, Kenneth L., and Evelyn G. Pike. *Grammatical Analysis*. Dallas: Summer Institute of Linguistics and University of Texas at Arlington, 1977.

———. "Live Issues in Descriptive Linguistics." Santa Ana, CA: Summer Institute of Linguistics, 1966. SIL International Language and Culture Archives, Dallas Texas.

Pike, Kenneth L., with Hugh Steven. *Pikes Perspectives: An Anthology of Thought, Insight, and Moral Purpose*. Langley, BC: Credo, 1989.

Pike, Stephen. Telephone interview by author, July 11, 2018.

Pinnock, Clark. "The Inerrancy Debate Among Evangelicals." *Theology, News and Notes*, special issue (1970) 11–12. Quoted in Gary Dorrien, *The Remaking of Evangelical Theology* 134n121. Louisville: Westminster John Knox, 1998.

Pittman, Richard S. Letter to Kenneth L. Pike, November 4, 1957. Folder SIL West Coast, Pittman Special Collection, SIL Language and Culture Archives, Dallas, TX.

Plantinga, Alvin, and Nicholas Wolterstorff, eds. *Faith and Rationality: Reason and Belief in God*. Notre Dame: University of Notre Dame Press, 1983.

Poythress, Vern S. *In the Beginning Was the Word: Language: A God-Centered Approach*. Wheaton, IL: Crossway, 2009.

———. Letter to Kenneth L. Pike, February 17, 1979. Correspondence series, Pike Special Collection, SIL International Language and Culture Archives, Dallas, TX.

———. *Philosophy, Science, and the Sovereignty of God*. n.p.: Presbyterian and Reformed, 1976.

———. *Symphonic Theology: The Validity of Multiple Perspectives in Theology.* Phillipsburg, NJ: P&R, 2001.

Radney, J. Randolf. "Confluence, Convergence, and Contextualization in Philosophy and Linguistics: The Methodologies of Ricoeur and Pike." PhD diss., The University of Texas at Arlington, 1999.

Ramm, Bernard. *After Fundamentalism: The Future of Evangelical Theology.* New York: Harper & Row, 1983.

———. "Helps from Karl Barth." In *How Karl Barth Changed My Mind*, edited by Donald K. McKim, 121–25. Grand Rapids: Eerdmans.

Recommendations subcommittee for Case 75–2. Letter to Committee on Ethics of the American Anthropological Association, November 19, 1975. Corporation history series, Pike Special Collection, SIL International Language and Culture Archives, SIL International Language and Culture Archives, Dallas, TX.

Riding, Alan. *Distant Neighbors: A Portrait of the Mexicans.* New York: Vintage, 1986.

Riley, William B. "Protocols and Communism." Pamphlet, 1934, 17. Quoted in George M. Marsden, *Fundamentalism and American Culture: The Shaping of Twentieth-Century Evangelicalism, 1870–1925*, 210n14. New York: Oxford University Press, 1980.

Robbins, Frank. Interview by author, September 9, 2009, Dallas, TX.

Robert, Dana L. *American Women in Mission: A Social History of their Thought and Practice.* Macon, GA: Mercer University Press, 1996.

Robins, R. H. *A Short History of Linguistics.* 2nd ed. New York: Longman, 1979.

Rosell, Garth M. *The Surprising Work of God: Harold John Ockenga, Billy Graham, and the Rebirth of Evangelicalism.* Grand Rapids: Baker Academic, 2008.

Rupp, Jim. Interview by author, May 23, 2017, Catalina, AZ.

Sampson, Geoffrey. *Schools of Linguistics.* Stanford: Stanford University Press, 1980.

Sanneh, Lamin. *Translating the Message: The Missionary Impact on Culture.* Maryknoll, NY: Orbis, 1989.

Sapir, Edward. *Language: An Introduction to the Study of Speech.* New York: Harcourt, Brace, 1921.

Sapir, Edward. Letter to Kenneth L. Pike, May 1, 1937. Correspondence series, Pike Special Collection, SIL International Language and Culture Archives, Dallas, TX.

Sargent, Mary. Letter to William Cameron Townsend, c. mid-1956. Document no. 13126, William Cameron Townsend Archives, JAARS Center, Waxhaw, NC.

Schram, Judith (Pike). Interview by author, May 22, 2017, Catalina, AZ.

Schram, Terry. Interview by author, May 22, 2017, Catalina, AZ.

Sheldon, Steve. Email to author, February 23, 2018.

Shelley, Bruce. "The Rise of Evangelical Youth Movements." *Fides and Historia* 18 (1986) 47–63.

Shenk, Wilbert R. *Changing Frontiers of Mission.* Maryknoll, NY: Orbis, 2003.

SIL Articles of Incorporation. August 12, 1942. Wycliffe Bible Translators and Summer Institute of Linguistics Corporate Archives, Dallas, TX.

SIL Board of Directors. Minutes, September 9, 1947. Wycliffe Bible Translators and Summer Institute of Linguistics Corporate Archives, Dallas, TX.

SIL Corporate Conference. Minutes, May 1967. Wycliffe Bible Translators and Summer Institute of Linguistics Corporate Archives, Dallas, TX.

Simons, Gary F. "The Call to Academic Community." In *Language and Life: Essays in Memory of Kenneth L. Pike*, edited by Mary Ruth Wise, et al., 83–96. Arlington: The University of Texas at Arlington and SIL International, 2003.

Smalley, William A. *Translation as Mission: Bible Translation in the Modern Missionary Movement*. Macon, GA: Mercer University Press, 1991.

Smith, Timothy L. *Revivalism and Social Reform*. New York: Abingdon, 1957.

Soesilo, Daud. "Bible Translation in Asia-Pacific and the Americas." In *A History of Bible Translation*, edited by Philip A. Noss, 163–81. Rome: Edizioni Di Storia E Letteratura [American Bible Society], 2007.

Speed, William G. Letter to Eric M. North. American Bible Society, January 10, 1944. Correspondence series, Pike Special Collection, SIL International Language and Culture Archives, Dallas, TX.

Steven, Hugh. *Manuel*. Old Tappen, NJ: Fleming H. Revell, 1970.

———. *Manuel: The Continuing Story*. Langley, BC: Credo, 1987.

Stine, Philip. *Let the Words be Written: The Lasting Influence of Eugene A. Nida*. Atlanta: Society of Biblical Literature, 2004.

Stoll, David. *Is Latin America Turning Protestant? The Politics of Evangelical Growth*. Berkeley: University of California Press, 1990.

———. "Onward Christian Soldiers." *Michigan Daily*, March 26, 1974, photocopy. Document no. 44737, William Cameron Townsend Archives, JAARS Center, Waxhaw, NC.

Svelmoe, William Lawrence. *A New Vision for Missions: William Cameron Townsend, the Wycliffe Bible Translators, and the Culture of Early Evangelical Faith Missions, 1896–1945*. Tuscaloosa: University of Alabama Press, 2008.

Thomas, Margaret. "Gender and the Language Scholarship of the Summer Institute of Linguistics in the Context of Mid Twentieth Century American Linguistics." In *History of Linguistics 2008: Selected Papers from the 11th International Conference on the History of the Language Sciences*, edited by Gerda Hassler, 389–97. Philadelphia: John Benjamins, 2011.

Thuesen, Peter J. *In Discordance with the Scriptures: American Protestant Battles over Translating the Bible*. New York: Oxford University Press, 1999.

Townsend, William Cameron. "An Airplane Crusade to the Unevangelized Jungle-Lands of Latin America." August 1930. Document no. 41806, William Cameron Townsend Archives, JAARS Center, Waxhaw, NC.

———. "Answer to Critics." November 29, 1939. Document no. 2436, William Cameron Townsend Archives, JAARS Center, Waxhaw, NC.

———. "Camp Wycliffe Activities." September 1936. Document no. 902024, William Cameron Townsend Archives, JAARS Center, Waxhaw, NC.

———. "Is Religion Doomed in the Land of Cuauhtemoc?" 1935. Document no. 42599, William Cameron Townsend Archives, JAARS Center, Waxhaw, NC.

———. Letter to Eric M. North, General Secretary, American Bible Society, September 15, 1937. Document no. 2094, William Cameron Townsend Archives, JAARS Center, Waxhaw, NC.

———. Letter to José Soto, Offical Mayor, Secretaría de Gobernación, October 6, 1933. Document no. 2077, William Cameron Townsend Archives, JAARS Center, Waxhaw, NC. (translation by Svelmoe, *A New Vision for Missions*, 241–42).

———. "Mexico's Gift Airplane 'Amauta Moises Saenz' Continues to Serve Peru's Amazonian People." 196. Document no. 42690, William Cameron Townsend Archives, JAARS Center, Waxhaw, NC.

———. "The Psychophonemic Method of Teaching to Read." *América Indígena* 16 (1956) 123–32.

———. "Record of Mexican Trip." December 21, 1933 to February 12, 1934. Document no. 1892, William Cameron Townsend Archives, JAARS Center, Waxhaw, NC.

———. Report to Board of Directors, April 1976. Document no. 32598, William Cameron Townsend Archives, JAARS Center, Waxhaw, NC.

———. "Suggestions for the Construction of a Psycho-Phonetic Primer." Document no. 42189, William Cameron Townsend Archives, JAARS Center, Waxhaw, NC.

———. "What is Our Task?" May 1976. Document no. 50135, William Cameron Townsend Archives, JAARS Center, Waxhaw, NC.

Townsend, Cameron, et al. *The Wycliffe Sapphire*. Huntington Beach, CA: Wycliffe Bible Translators, 1991.

Townsend, Elvira. "Message at Gravette, Arkansas." August 16, 1936. Document no. 42583, William Cameron Townsend Archives, JAARS Center, Waxhaw, NC.

Tucker, Ruth A. "Women in Missions: Reaching Sisters in 'Heathen Darkness.'" In *Earthen Vessels: American Evangelicals and Foreign Missions, 1880–1980*, edited by Joel A. Carpenter and Wilbert R. Shenk, 251–80. Grand Rapids: Eerdmans, 1990.

"United Nations Seeking Linguists." *Translation*, 1952. Document no. 47017, William Cameron Townsend Archives, JAARS Center, Waxhaw, NC.

Wallis, Ethel Emily. *It Takes Two to Untangle Tongues: The Story of Evelyn Griset Pike*. Huntington Beach, CA: Wycliffe Bible Translators, 1985.

———. *Lengthened Cords: How Dawson Trotman—Founder of the Navigators—Also Helped Extend the World-Wide Outreach of the Wycliffe Bible Translators*. Glendale, CA: Wycliffe Bible Translators, 1958.

Waterhouse, Viola G. *The History and Development of Tagmemics*. The Hague: Mouton, 1974.

Watkins, Doug, "Water Polo: Only the Fittest Survive." In *The Flounders: Fifty Years*, edited by Clark Hopkins, 81–82. Ann Arbor, MI: n.p., 1976.

Watters, John. Interview by author, February 14, 2017, Dallas, TX.

WBT Articles of Incorporation. August 1942. Document no. 41523, William Cameron Townsend Archives, JAARS Center, Waxhaw, NC .

WBT Board of Directors. Minutes, April 12, 1948. Wycliffe Bible Translators and Summer Institute of Linguistics Corporate Archives, Dallas, TX.

———. Minutes, May 21, 1948. Wycliffe Bible Translators and Summer Institute of Linguistics Corporate Archives, Dallas, TX.

WBT-SIL Conference. Minute extracts, May 24 to June 2, 1971. Wycliffe Bible Translators and Summer Institute of Linguistics Corporate Archives, Dallas, TX.

Weathers, Kenneth T. "Some Intimate Observations Relating to the Short-Lived Inter-American Service Brigade." Unpublished paper, 1997, copy in author's possession.

Weyl, Nathaniel, and Sylvia Weyl. *The Reconquest of Mexico: The Years of Lázaro Cárdenas*. New York: Oxford University Press, 1939.

Whorf, Benjamin L. "Science and Linguistics." *Technology Review* 42 (1940) 229–31, 247–48. Reprinted in *Language, Thought, and Reality: Selected Writings of Benjamin Lee Whorf*, edited by John B. Carroll, 207–19. Cambridge: Massachusetts Institute of Technology Press, 1956.

Wilt, Paul. "Biographical Data and Historical Data Regarding Elbert McCreery." December 2003. Document no. 43051, William Cameron Townsend Archives, JAARS Center, Waxhaw, NC.
Wise, Mary Ruth, et al., eds. *Language and Life: Essays in Memory of Kenneth L. Pike*. Arlington: The University of Texas at Arlington and SIL International, 2003.
Woodward, Julia V. Letter to Eric M. North. American Bible Society, January 20, 1944. Correspondence series, Pike Special Collection, SIL International Language and Culture Archives, Dallas, TX.
Worthen, Molly. *Apostles of Reason: The Crisis of Authority in American Evangelicalism*. New York: Oxford University Press, 2014.
Wroughton, James. Telephone interview by author, March 6, 2009.

Index

activism, as evangelicalism characteristic, xvii, 45, 55, 128, 138, 172, 174, 176
"Air Crusade to the Wild Tribes," 89
alcohol, 62
Alexander, Ruth Mary, 74
American Anthropological Association (AAA), 198–201
American Anthropologist, 81
American Bible Society (ABS), 74–75, 76, 85, 88, 97, 110, 130
Amerindian languages, 10, 144
anthropology, 196
anti-SIL crusade, 196–207
Arenas, Manuel, 73–74
Aschmann, Herman, 73
Ashdown, Helen, 74
Association of Baptists for World Evangelism (ABWE), 123
Australia, 93, 98

Baker, Sheridan, 167
Barth, Karl, 136
Bartholomew, Doris, 166
Bebbington, David W., xvii
Becker, A. L., 133
Beeson, Sheldon, 128
behavior, language and, 147–48, 151
Bendor-Samuel, John, 165
Berkemeyer, Fernando, 129
The Bible: An American Translation, 84
Bible translation, 53, 68–75. *See also* specific languages; specific translators

biblical inerrancy, debates regarding, 99
biblical inspiration, 140
biblicalism, as evangelicalism characteristic, xvii
bilingual education, literacy and, 100–101
Bloch, Bernard, 38, 39, 100, 141
Bloesch, Donald, 136
Bloomfield, Leonard, 10, 35–36, 38, 43, 87, 140–42
Blount, Turner, 114–15
Boas, Franz, 10
Boice, James Montgomery, 164
Boice, Linda Ann, 164
Bolivia, 76, 177
Bowling Green State University, 170
Brazil, 106–7
Brown, Robert, 166
Brunstetter, Della, 80
Burns, Don, 117, 118

California, 84
Callaghan, Catherine A., 198
Calles, Plutarco Elías, 16
Campa language, 102
Camp Wycliffe
    features of, 5, 55
    linguistic approach and, 48–55
    Nida at, 50–55
    Pike at, 14–16, 25, 28–29, 41, 50–55
    population of, 79
    requirements of, 82
    women at, 55–60

Cárdenas, Lázaro, 8–9, 16, 60, 62
Carnell, Edward J., 135–36, 139
Catholics/Catholicism, 16, 77, 85–88, 98, 106–12, 113, 118, 121, 123–24
Center for Advanced Behavioral Sciences, 182
Central American Mission (CAM), 5, 6, 7
Chalcatongo, Mexico, 19
China, 4
China Inland Mission (CIM), 4, 11–13
Chomsky, Noam, 105, 145–46, 155–59, 169–74
Christ, ministry of, 120–21
Christian academia, women within, 103
Christian and Missionary Alliance, 116
Christian Commitment (Carnell), 135
Church, Clarence, 198
Church of the Open Door of Los Angeles, 113
Cicero Bible Church, 115
Civilian Conservation Corps, 14
Cocama, 102
Colby, Gerald, 202
Cole, Rolland, 93
Committee on Research in Native American Languages, 10
comparative method of linguistics, 140
conversionism, as evangelicalism characteristic, xvii
Cook, Walter A., 170
Copenhagen, Denmark, 105
Cowan, George, 175
crucicentrism, as evangelicalism characteristic, xvii
Cueto, Alberto Colunga, 110
cultural pluralism, 200
Cummings, Thomas E. F., 20
Cuthbert, M., 108

Daley, Richard J., 119
Daniel (prophet), 204
Dargue, Herbert A., 89
Dayuma, 117
Dennett, Charlotte, 202
Dixon, Alan J., 208
Dyk, Ann, 74

Ecuador, 76, 115–21
Edgerton, Franklin, 38
Edwards Brothers, 75
Elliot, Jim, 116
Elson, Benjamin "Ben," 112, 172, 175
emic viewpoint, 149–50, 151, 159
"End" (poem), 213
England, 98
etic viewpoint, 149–50, 159
European languages, comparative method of linguistics within, 140
Evangelical Foreign Missions Association (EFMA), 123, 127
evangelicalism, xvii, 123, 195, 205–6
The Evangelical Student, 3–4
evangelical youth movement, 82–83

faith, Pike's theory of, 151–52
faith missions, 47, 56–58, 114
1 John, Pike's translation of, 22
Fishers of Men or Founders of Empire? (Stoll), 201–202
Fisk, Sam, 14
five-tone language, in South America, 102
Fleming, Peter, 116
Flounders Club sports team, 166–67, 168
Foreign Missions Conference of North America, 82
Franklin, Karl, 165–66
Fraser, James O., 61
"Friendship of Orange County" Helio Courier, 118, 128–30
Fries, Charles C., 38, 42, 45, 143
Fuller, Charles, 114
Fuller, Daniel, 105, 136
Fuller Seminary, 103, 137
fundamentalist/fundamentalism

changes within, 47–48
characteristics of, xviii
defined, xvii–xviii
faith missions of, 47
militancy within, 3
Nida and, 84–85
Pike's viewpoint of, 2–3
reforming, 133–37
women in ministry and, 58
The Fundamentals, xvii
Fuster, Eloino Nácar, 110

Garrard-Burnett, Virginia, 6
Garza, Antonio Guellano, 19
Gelinas, Frank, 128, 129
generative-transformational grammar, 145–46, 155–59, 169–74, 204
Georgetown University, 170
German language, 181–82
Glover, Robert Hall, 13
God, language role of, 151–52
Goodner, E. S., 92, 93
Goodspeed, Edgar J., 84
"Goodspeed Bible," 84
Gordon College of Theology and Missions, 2, 3–4
Gospel Missionary Union (GMU), 116, 121–22
Graham, Billy, 119, 123–24, 137
grammar, 145–47, 155–59, 169–74, 204. *See also* linguistics
Grammatical Analysis, 170, 185
Great Reversal, 47
Greene, Elizabeth "Betty," 90
Grimes, Joseph, 103
Griset, "Deedee," 63
Griset, Evelyn. *See* Pike, Evelyn Griset
Guatemala, 6–7
Gudschinsky, Sarah, 100, 103, 107

Hahn, E. Adelaide, 104
Hansen, Florence, 55–56, 58–59
Harris, Zellig, 38, 42
Hart, Laurie, 196, 203
HCJB Radio, 116
Helio Courier, 118, 128–30

higher education, women within, 103
Hockett, Charles, 166
Hofstadter, Richard, 210
House Un-American Activities Committee, 84
Howard, Philip E., Jr., 118
Hubbard, David, 105
humility, 178–80
Huttar, George, 147, 152
Hymes, Dell, 157

Ibach, Barbara Pike, 168, 185–86
Independent Fundamental Churches of America (IFCA), 114–15
indigenous people, social injustice to, 23–24
inerrancy, debates regarding, 99
Instituto Mexicano de Investigaciones Lingüísticas (IMIL), 18
intelligence, 210–11
Inter American Friendship Fleet, 118–19
Inter-American Service Brigade, 9, 60–63
Interdenominational Foreign Mission Association (IFMA), 114, 123–27
Interdisciplinary Colloquium on Language Development in France, 153
International Council of Religious Education, 84
International Goodwill Fleet, 119
International Journal of American Linguistics, 101
International Linguistics Center (ILC), 190
Inter-Varsity Christian Fellowship (IVCF), 82
Introduction to Tagmemic Analysis, 170
Ironside, Henry A., 7
Is God an American? (Hvalkof and Aaby), 202

Is Latin America Turning Protestant?
(Stoll), 205–6

Jesus, ministry of, 120–21
Jewett, Paul, 126
Jones, Bob, Sr., 3
Jungle Aviation and Radio Service
(JAARS), 93

Kaqchikel New Testament, 7
Kaye, Alan S., 160
Kerr, Harland, 166
Kiddle, Larry, 179
Kietzman, Dale, 107
knowledge, common-sense variety
of, 150–51

Ladd, George Eldon, 126, 136
language. *See also* linguistics
  behavior and, 147–48, 151
  as creative image of God,
    151–52
  human factor within, 173
  social aspects of, 157, 158
  speaker role within, 149
Language (Bloomfield), 35–36
Language and Cultural Archives
  (SIL), 212
*Language: An Introduction to the
  Study of Speech* (Sapir), 18
*Language in Relation to a Unified
  Theory of the Structure of
  Human Behavior* (Pike), 148,
  149, 150, 151, 153, 154, 170
Laroza, Enrique, 78
Lathrop, Max, 17, 52, 57
Latin America, evangelicalism
  in, 205–6. *See also specific
  locations*
Laws, Curtis Lee, xvii
Legters, Brainerd, 17, 18, 52, 57
Legters, Elva, 55
Legters, Leonard Livingstone, xvi,
  5–6, 14
Levin, Saul, 208
Lima, Peru, 78
Lindskoog, John, 117, 119–20
Linguistic Circle, 105

*Linguistic Concepts: An Introduction
  to Tagmemics* (Pike), 170
linguistic form, meaning and,
  148–49
linguistic hierarchy, 147
Linguistic Institute, 38–41, 42,
  43–44
linguistics. *See also* grammar;
  language
  morphology in, 29, 141
  overview of, 10–11
  paradigm shift within, 173–74
  phonemics within, 149, 171
  phonetic representation within,
    20, 28, 149
  phonetics within, 141, 143–44
  phonology within, 141
  Pike's knowledge of, 20–21
  polemics in, 179
  structural, 10, 38, 69, 141, 142
  syntax within, 142–43
  theory of, 105
Linguistic Society, 105
Linguistic Society of America, 105
linguistic workshops, 102, 164–65
literacy, 100–101
Llushin, Ecuador, 116
London, England, 105
Longacre, Robert, 51, 80, 103, 207
Lowe, Ivan, 182
Luke, Gospel of, Pike's translation
  of, 22
Luzbetak, Louis, 107–8

Machen, J. Gresham, 2–3
Mak, Cora, 74
Makkai, Adam, 208
Mann, Matt, 166
Marsden, George, xvii–xviii, 123–
  24, 134, 137
Martinez, Eulogio, 17
Mason, J. Alden, 81–82
Mattingly, John G., 114
May, Bernie, 122
Mayan people, 5
Mazatec people, 58–59
McAlister, A. J., 75
McCarrell, William, 115

INDEX

McCarthy, Eugene, 84
McCarthyism, 114
McClary, Robert, 208
McCreery, Elbert, 15, 26
McCully, Ed, 116
McKaughan, Howard, 103
McKinney, Richmond, 17, 20, 23, 52, 57
McQuown, Norman A., 154
meaning, linguistic form and, 148–49
Mellis, Charles, 90–91
mentalism, 141, 142
mentoring, 165–66
Merecias, Angel, 73, 74, 84, 96, 97
Mexican Institute of Linguistic Research, 8
Mexico
  government in, 61–62
  missionary work within, 5–6
  Pike in, 16–21
  revolutionary climate of, 6
  Revolution within, 16
  SIL members in, 10–11
  social injustice within, 23–24
  Townsend in, 5–6, 8–9, 17, 48, 60–63
Missionary Aviation Fellowship (MAF), 89–93
Mitla, Mexico, 102
Mixtec
  Luke, Gospel of, translation within, 22
  Pike's focus on, 17, 23, 42–43
  research of, 146
  tonal features of, 37
  translators of, 69–73
Mixtec New Testament, 74–75, 96
morality, 191–92
morphology, 29, 141
Morris, Alice Vanderbilt, 104
mule, Pike as, 162–168
"My Blue Refrigerator" (poem), 163–64

Nácar y Colunga diglots, 109–10
Nahuatl (Aztec) people, 5
Nalo, story of, 71–72

National Association of Evangelicals (NAE), 123
National Council of Churches (NCC), 84
neo-evangelicalism, xvi, xviii, 123–24, 126–27, 134–35, 137–40, 195, 211
New Tribes Mission, 106
Nida, Eugene
  ABS and, 85, 88, 97, 130
  characteristics of, 130
  contributions of, 52, 97
  as doctoral candidate, 42
  etic-emic paradigm and, 149n52
  fundamentalism viewpoint of, 84–85
  leadership of, 76, 81
  linguistic abilities of, 29
  Linguistic Institute and, 43–44
  physical challenges of, 30
  Pike and, 32, 33
  quote of, 84–85, 130
  resignation of, 88, 110
  Tarahumara tribe and, 33
  as teacher, 49
  transition of, 29–30
  work of, 28, 29, 31, 49–50
Nixon, Richard M., 119, 128
Nobel Peace Prize, 208
Noll, Mark, xv–xvi, 134
non-sectarianism, 107, 111, 121
North, Eric, 76
North American Congress on Latin America (NACLA), 200
Northern Presbyterian Church, 3
Nyman, William, 83, 93, 115

Oaxaca, Mexico, 19
The Obedience of a Christian Man (Tyndale), xix
observer-related components, 149
Orthodox Presbyterian Church, 3
Oslo, Norway, 105

Page, Isaac, 68
"Pain Teaches Choice" (poem), 187
Palmer, O. R., 117
Papua New Guinea, 93, 104, 174

Paris, France, 105
Pentecostalism, 206
perception, 150, 151
Peru
    IFMA controversy in, 123–27
    language discoveries within, 102
    Pike in, 76, 102
    SIL within, 77–78, 89–93, 95–96, 206
Peunte, Teresa de la, 129
philosophy, Pike and, 191–95
phonemics, 149, 171
Phonemics (Pike), 144
phonetic representation, 20, 28, 149
phonetics, 141, 143–44
Phonetics: A Critical Analysis of Phonetic Theory and a Technic for the Practical Description of Sounds (Pike), 44
phonetics manuscript, 39–40
phonology, 141
phrase structure rules, 155
Pike, Ernest R., 1, 2, 24, 132
Pike, Eunice Victoria, 2, 56, 58–59, 62, 107, 129
Pike, Evelyn (Griset)
    characteristics of, 65–66
    emotional support from, 180–81
    family of, 185–89
    home of, 65
    marriage of, 63–67
    in Mexico, 17
    Pike's letter to, 59
    work of, 28
    writings of, 185
Pike, Galen, 24
Pike, Kenneth Lee
    accusation to, 12–13
    athleticism of, 3
    characteristics of, 14–15, 30–31, 32–33, 70–71, 77, 133, 186–87, 211
    "Chief Turning Points" of, 95
    childhood of, 2
    as classical faith missionary, 127–31
    contributions of, 52, 97, 161
    death of, 209
    as doctoral candidate, 41–46
    education of, 2, 3–4, 14
    "End" (poem), 213
    as evangelical, 112
    faith of, 43, 132–33, 137–40, 151–53, 177, 188–89, 193, 210, 211
    family of, 1, 185–89
    financial needs of, 24–25
    With Heart and Mind, 132, 153, 176
    home of, 65
    intellectual challenges of, 34
    Language in Relation to a Unified Theory of the Structure of Human Behavior, 148, 149, 150, 151, 153, 154, 170
    laziness of, 4, 35
    leadership of, 75–79, 81, 85–86, 88, 90, 91–92, 94, 98, 105, 120, 122–23, 124–26, 130–31, 161, 174–75, 176, 178, 198–200, 203, 206–7
    Linguistic Concepts: An Introduction to Tagmemics, 170
    linguistics interest of, 15, 140–144
    marriage of, 63–67
    militancy of, 3
    as missionary, 45
    morality of, 13
    as a mule, 162–68
    "My Blue Refrigerator" (poem), 163–64
    overview of, 209–12
    "Pain Teaches Choice" (poem), 187
    passion of, 162–63, 210
    pastorate of, 13
    personal challenges of, 70–71
    physical challenges of, 19, 27–28, 30, 115, 168, 180–81
    research expedition of, 18–19
    resignation of, 92
    retirement of, 190, 209

scholarship of, 132–33, 140–44, 174–77, 210
self-criticism of, 33–34, 40, 178–79, 181–82
spirituality of, 2, 95
sports and, 166–67, 209
Stir, Change, Create, 189
study focus of, 34–35
Talk, Thought, and Thing, 192, 193–94
as teacher, 25, 41, 45, 104, 162–63
theory of language of, xvi
viewpoint of, 57, 83
"Violin Under Stress" (poem), 187–88
work of, 14, 66, 104, 160–61, 162–68
writings of, 36–37, 39–40, 68, 78, 79, 143–44, 170, 182, 187–88, 213
Pike, May Granniss, 1–2
Pike, Steve, 185, 186
"Pike's Phonetic Manual for Beginners," 28
Pinnock, Clark, 105, 136, 139
Pioneer Mission Agency (PMA), 5, 76
Pittman, Richard "Dick," 80, 91, 94–95
polemics, 179
political Left, attacks from, 196–207
Pollack, J. C., 179–80
postmodernism, 191
Poulter, Virgil, 207
Poythress, Vern, 133
premillennial-dispensationalism, 2
Protestant/Protestantism, 22, 70, 86, 110, 111, 134, 136–37
psycho-phonemic method, 100

Quechuan language, 76, 77
Quine, Willard, 193

Ramírez, Rafael, 8, 18
Ramm, Bernard, 105, 136, 193
Reagan, Ronald, 207

"A Reconstruction of Phonetic Theory" (Pike), 143–44
Reichard, Gladys Amanda, 104
relativism, 150–51
Retts, Bill, 128–29
Revised Standard Version (RSV), 84
revolution, fervor for, 196
Ribeiro, Darcy, 106
Rice, Warner, 104–5
Riley, William Bell, 48
Ritchie, John, 77
Robbins, Frank, 179
Robert, Dana, 56
Rockefeller, Nelson, 202
Roman Catholics/Catholics/Catholicism, 16, 77, 85–88, 98, 106–12, 113, 118, 121, 123–24
Roosevelt, Franklin D., 48

Sáenz, Moisés, 7
Saint, Rachel, 117
San Miguel el Grande, Oaxaca, Mexico, 27, 68–75
Sapir, Edward, 10, 18, 38, 39, 41, 87, 140–41, 142, 145
The Scandal of the Evangelical Mind (Noll), xvi, 47, 134, 211
Scholar and Christian (Pike), 132
scholarship, 174–77, 175–76
School of African and Oriental Studies, 105
Schram, Judy (Pike), 167
Schram, Terry, 188
science, Bible translation *versus,* 53
Scripture Gift Mission, 111
Seattle Pacific College (SPC), 111
secularism, 176–77
Sedat, William, 17
Septuagint, translation of, 77
"service to all" policy, xvi–xvii, 86, 96, 106–12, 113, 211
Shell Mera, Ecuador, 116
SIL-UTA program, 190
Silva y Aceves, Mariano, 8, 18, 36
Smith, Timothy, 47
social gospel movement, 47, 58
social injustice, in Mexico, 23–24

soul winning, 51, 70
sound units, 147–48
South America, five-tone language in, 102
sports, 166–67
Stark, Donald, 73, 74, 97
Stewart, Lyman, xvii
Stir, Change, Create (Pike), 189
Stoll, David, 197, 201–2, 203–4, 205–6
structural linguistics, 10, 38, 69, 141, 142. *See also* generative-transformational grammar
Studia Phonetica, 105
Sturtevant, Edgar Howard, 38, 42
Summer Institute of Linguistics (SIL)
  ABS *versus*, 74–75, 110
  attack to, 196–207
  in Australia, 98
  battle for scholarship at, 169–74
  bilingual education program of, 101
  Billy Graham and, 124
  branches of, 131
  in Brazil, 106–7
  criticism of, 114–15, 117, 119, 196–207
  dissension within, 61–62, 83–84, 85–88, 117, 120–21
  doctorate degrees within, 54, 59–60, 80, 102–3
  in England, 98
  evangelicalism and, 195
  as faith mission, 114, 115–16
  funding for, 196
  generative-transformational grammar within, 158–59
  GMU and, 121–22
  headquarters of, 190
  IFMA and, 123–27
  Language and Cultural Archives, 212
  Linguistic Institute and, 43–44
  linguistics focus of, 53–54
  linguistic workshops in, 102
  in Mexico, 10–11, 65
  as missionary organization, 107
  mission of, 48
  overview of, 5–9
  as parachurch organization, 96
  in Peru, 77–78, 89–93, 95–96
  Pike's influence to, xvi, 97–98, 178, 194–95, 203, 206, 212
  prayer within, 85, 86
  publications of, 99, 101
  purpose of, 53–54, 86–87, 199
  reputation of, 54, 80–81, 98–105, 196
  requirements for, 52
  Roman Catholics at, 107–9
  Seattle Pacific College (SPC) and, 111
  "service to all" policy of, xvi–xvii, 86, 96, 106–12, 113, 211
  social concern of, xvi
  standards of, 99
  strategy of, 112–13
  Townsend's viewpoint of, 99, 113
  University of North Dakota and, 98, 205
  University of Oklahoma at Norman and, 79–89, 98, 100, 107, 204–5
  University of Oregon and, 205
  University of Texas at Arlington and, 190, 205
  University of Washington and, 98, 111–12
  women in, 55–60, 104
  work of, 10
Sunday School Times (magazine), 114, 118, 119
Syntactic Structures, 155–56
syntax, within linguistics, 142–43
Szemler, Franz, 208

tagmemics, 145–55, 158, 169–74, 177–78, 204
Talk, Thought, and Thing (Pike), 192, 193–94
Tarahumara tribe, 33
Taylor, Howard, 4
Taylor, Howard, Mrs., 12
Taylor, Hudson, 4

Tenney, Merrill C., 4
theological liberalism, xvii, 3, 58, 83–87, 109, 111–12, 114, 123, 126, 132, 136–37, 140
theory of language, xvi, 150, 151–54
"There Were Ninety and Nine that Safely Lay" (hymn), 1–2
Thomas, Margaret, 103–4
tone languages, 17–18, 37, 44
Townsend, Elivra, 17, 63, 113–14
Townsend, William Cameron
 ambitions of, 37–38
 background of, 5
 CAM and, 5, 6, 7
 concerns of, 22
 as doctoral candidate, 41
 family of, 9
 faults of, 122
 inerrancy viewpoint of, 99
 Inter American Friendship Fleet and, 118–19, 129–30
 leadership of, 50, 52–53, 65, 76, 95–96, 97, 113–14
 linguistics invention of, 15
 in Mexico, 5–6, 8–9, 17, 48, 60–63
 as missionary, 11
 in Peru, 89
 Pike and, 15, 37, 65, 76, 91–93, 122–23, 124–25, 183–84
 quote of, 37, 49, 59, 60–61, 64, 83, 90, 91, 92–93, 94, 99, 120, 122
 SIL and, 48, 212
 translation work of, 23
 viewpoint of, 6–7, 64–65, 98–99, 109, 113, 116–17
 women in missions viewpoint of, 48
 work of, 5, 195, 208, xvi
Tract Club of the Air, 75
Trager, George, 144, 178
translation. *See also specific languages; specific translators*
 challenges within, 69
 growth of, 22–23
 Pike's work in, 68–75
 process of, 10–11, 69
 science *versus*, 53
 as SIL goal, 174–75
Translation, 114, 117
Truman, Harry S., 119
truth, perception and, 151
Truxton, James, 93
Tucker, Ruth, 56, 57
Twentyman, John and Isabel, 61
Tyndale, William, xix

Under the Chestnut Tree, 148
United Nations Educational, Scientific and Cultural Organization (UNESCO), 100–101, 114–15
United States Agency for International Development, 196, 201
Université René Descartes, 105
University College London, 105
University of Edinburgh, 105
University of Michigan, Ann Arbor, 38, 45, 79–80, 102, 160–61, 170, 197
University of North Dakota, 98, 158–59, 205
University of Oklahoma at Norman, 79–89, 98, 100, 107, 170, 204–5
University of Oregon, 205
University of Texas at Arlington (UTA), 190, 205
University of Washington, 98, 111–12
Uranga, Javier, 18
Urbana Missionary Conference, 82
US Central Intelligence Agency, 197–98

Vachek, Josef, 144
Van der Puy, Abe, 117–18
Versión Popular, 79
"Violin Under Stress" (poem), 187–88
Voegelin, Charles F., 100
volleyball, 166–67

Wallace, Ethel Emily, 64
Wallis, Ethel, 65–66
Walvoord, John F., 126
Waorani (Auca) tribe, 116
water polo, 166–67
Watson, C. Hoyt, 111
Watters, John, 166–67, 172, 211–12
Wells, Rulon S., 208
Westminster Theological Seminary, 2–3, 52
White, Gerald, 208
Whorf, Benjamin Lee, 142
Wise, Mary Ruth, 102–3
With Heart and Mind (Pike), 132, 153, 176
women. *See also specific women*
    doctorate degrees of, 59–60
    in education, 103
    as missionaries, 48, 56–58
    within scholarship, 175–76
    at SIL, 55–60, 104
Wonderly, William, 79–80, 99–100
Woodbridge, Charles J., 126
Worthen, Molly, 135
Wycliffe Bible Translators (WBT), xvi–xix, 5, 11, 23, 33, 49, 75–77, 90–91, 96–97, 107, 110, 112–15, 119, 121, 123–30, 175, 178, 184, 189, 194–98, 201–3
Wyman, Earl, 93

Yost, Helen, 55, 57
Yost, James, 197
Yost, Larry, 166
Youderian, Roger, 116
Youth for Christ, 82

www.ingramcontent.com/pod-product-compliance
Lightning Source LLC
Chambersburg PA
CBHW050847230426
43667CB00012B/2187